A GUIDE TO
THE CANTOS OF
EZRA POUND

William Cookson

A GUIDE TO THE CANTOS OF EZRA POUND

Textbooks contain MINIMUM of what the student
NEEDS to know.
Ezra Pound, in a letter to the author,
27 January 1958

CROOM HELM
LONDON & SYDNEY

First published in Great Britain 1985 by
Croom Helm Ltd, Provident House,
Burrell Row, Beckenham, Kent, BR3 1AT,
Croom Helm Australia Pty Ltd, First Floor,
139 King St, Sydney, NSW 2001, Australia.

British Library Cataloging in Publication Data:

Cookson, William
    A guide to the cantos of Ezra Pound.
    1. Pound, Ezra. Cantos
    I. Title
    811'.52   PS3531.082C28
    ISBN 0-7099-0737-0
    ISBN 0-7099-0738-9 Pbk

Manufactured in the United States of America
First Printing

This book is for Caroline Wright.

It is also dedicated
in loving memory
to Rachel Cookson (1901-1982)

Saluti alla vostra distinta madre
Ezra Pound

Contents

Foreword

For a long time, interested general readers have wanted the kind of help with Ezra Pound's *Cantos* that William Cookson provides here. Indeed, his canto-by-canto, page-by-page guidance will be welcome to all readers, however familiar with the work. The *Cantos* stands very near the heart of modern poetry in English that really counts. It magnetizes attention despite surface difficulties: the passages and phrases in various languages, the allusions to little-known persons and writings and events, the cranky and "controversial" politics, and even the dizzying copiousness and quick shifts of focus that are of the essence of Pound's genius.

These challenging aspects are inseparable from the power and beauty, and the crucial concerns, that give the *Cantos* such vitality. Mr. Cookson's critical pointers and precise annotations open up key connections of meaning and perspective, thereby encouraging us to follow the poetry for its artistic progression and not as a puzzle or obstacle course. Like other serious poets, Pound read widely and with vivid, unfading receptiveness. His head was full of echoing language, voices, and rhythms from many works composed over the centuries. In the *Cantos*, these resonances merge with others from history and from magically reëmbodied mythical sources. They are brought to bear on every deeply human preoccupation: eros and death, war and peace, the social and economic demons that ride herd on us, and the need to discern in life something more than a random series of events. And yet the work is not solemn. Humor, excitement, and pure lyricism accompany its everchanging movement.

It is Mr. Cookson's accomplishment in *A Guide to the Cantos of Ezra Pound* to have elucidated these matters with a full-hearted sympathy indispensable to such a task. He shows clearly what goes on in the successive volumes, providing the necessary orientation, background, and gloss without trying to tell us *everything*. A poet himself and the editor of the distinguished literary magazine *Agenda*, he knows very well that no handbook can substitute for direct experience of the poems. But it is a most unusual handbook nevertheless, the product of a highly sensitized understanding. For anyone who wishes to learn how Pound, our most original and problematical modern American poet, put together his enduringly triumphant structure, reading through the *Cantos* with Cookson's *Guide* to hand is a fine way to begin.

M.L.R.

Acknowledgements

Many people have helped me, either directly or indirectly, in making this book. My primary debt is to Carroll Terrell, editor of *Paideuma*, who generously provided photocopies of the glossaries (for Cantos I-LXXI) of the first half of the *Companion to the Cantos* that he is preparing. Without countless thefts from these, and from documentary material published in *Paideuma* itself, there would be bigger blanks in this *Guide* than there are already. In this connection I should also like to express my gratitude to John Edwards and William Vasse, whose *Annotated Index to the Cantos I-LXXXIV* I have used constantly. A third, and invaluable, source of information about the first eleven cantos has been *The Analyst*, edited by Robert Mayo.

Without the help of Peter Levi and Peter Jay I could not have provided glossaries of the Greek; and for the Chinese, I am similarly indebted to John Cayley and Jamila Ismail. All the graphs of ideograms are by John Cayley and where the glossaries are entirely his, I have signed J.C.

The writers on Pound from whom I have drawn most are: Michael Alexander, Walter Baumann, Donald Davie, Barbara Eastman, Clark Emery, David Gordon, Jamila Ismail, Hugh Kenner, Moelwyn Merchant, Daniel Pearlman, Mary de Rachewiltz, Frederick Sanders, Richard Sieburth, and James Wilhelm.

I am grateful to Basil Bunting, for giving me permission to quote his poem "On the Fly-Leaf of Pound's Cantos."

Michael Alexander, Peter Dale, and Edmund Gray read early drafts of the manuscript and made many valuable suggestions.

Introduction

The aim of this book is a modest one. I have attempted to outline the main themes and structure of the *Cantos*, and to provide sufficient information for new readers to enjoy the poem. "Gloom and solemnity are entirely out of place in even the most rigorous study of an art originally intended to make glad the heart of man" (*A.B.C. of Reading*, page 11). An aspect of the *Cantos* seldom mentioned is their humour and yet this quality is present on nearly every page.

I believe that the growth of a vast critical industry devoted to explaining and interpreting Pound's poetry may have put off some readers of intelligence. Much of this writing, although at times of a brilliance that the present author cannot hope to emulate, is a form of would-be creative work. I think the poetry is less esoteric than the commentaries suggest—it has strata of meaning, but is not often ambiguous. "Ambiguity and inclusiveness are far from the same" (*Selected Prose*, page 97:*83*[1]). The universality of Pound's themes is seldom recognized, but time may make this quality manifest.

Yeats once dismissed the work of a minor poet with the phrase, "He lacks chaos." Too many of Pound's critics have been engaged in vain attempts to squeeze his abundant chaos into various and ingenious systems; but the work is too live for this. "Disciples are more trouble than they are worth when they start anchoring and petrifying their mahatmas. No man's *thought* petrifies.... The basket is, metaphorically, easier to handle than the cat inside the basket." (*Selected Prose*, page 252: *282*.) As Pound wrote in Canto XX: "Wilderness of renewals, confusion/Basis of renewals, subsistence" (92).

This guide is not intended for the Pound scholar. I have, with a few notable exceptions, deliberately avoided drawing upon the sixty or so books on Pound that have appeared in the last thirty years. Instead I have tried to read the poetry with a mind alert to what is actually on the page. Pound's prose provides the best commentary on the *Cantos* and I have quoted liberally from it.

Pound's poetry is part of a living tradition which can be outlined by a list of names: *The Confucian Odes*, Homer, Hesiod, Catullus, Ovid, Li Po, Cavalcanti, Dante, Chaucer, Villon, Shakespeare, Browning. Probably the best introduction to Pound would be to read the long poems which have meant most to him: *The Odyssey*, *The Metamorphoses* (in Latin, or Arthur Golding's Elizabethan translation), *La Divina Commedia*, *Sordello*.

Some words Pound wrote about Dante and Villon also apply to his own poetry:

Dante's vision is real, because he saw it. Villon's verse is real because he lived it; as Bertran de Born, as Arnaut Marvoil, as that mad poseur Vidal, he lived it. For these men life is in the press. No brew of books, no distillation of sources will match the tang of them.

(The Spirit of Romance, page 178.)

The *Cantos*, likewise, has poetic meaning partly because Pound lived and suffered its subject matter directly. This is why it is a book which can be lived with and experienced throughout a lifetime. It does not tire, but reveals new depths—"clear fathoms down"—expressing a beauty of thought which vitalizes, a freshness and rhythmic energy which is probably only to be found to a greater extent in Homer, Dante, Chaucer, and Shakespeare.

"Literature is news that STAYS news" (*A.B.C. of Reading*, page 29). Living poetry must be "associated with discovery. The artist must have discovered something—either of life itself or of the means of expression." (*Literary Essays*, page 56.) I believe that Pound's ideas and subject matter are important in themselves and that is why the poetry is living. *Ut moveat, ut doceat, ut delectet.* "You cannot have literature without curiosity." Whatever mistaken ideas Pound sometimes incorporated in his poetry, he never lost this essential element of curiosity. The sensation a reader gets from the *Cantos* is of "dynamic form," of excitement, of living thought.

"Out of dark, and toward half-light" (CXIII, 786).[2] The reader experiences throughout the poem's 800 or so pages the sense of a journey toward light, but broken and in flashes, "By no means an orderly Dantescan rising" (LXXIV, 443). He travels through states of mind and landscapes, as in *La Divina Commedia*, but without the allegorical paraphernalia.

> periplum, not as land looks on a map
> but as sea bord seen by men sailing
> (LIX, 324).

The imagery and landscapes of the *Cantos* were well described by Pound when he wrote, apropos another poet, "Imagism, or poetry wherein the feelings of painting and sculpture are predominant (certain men move in phantasmagoria: the images of their gods, whole countrysides, stretches of hill land and forest, travel with them)..." (*Selected Prose*, page 394:*424*).

Much twentieth-century poetry bores because it expresses the predictable. There's no point in reading a book if it does not enlarge our experience. "If it...reveals to us something of which we are unconscious, it feeds us with its energy" (*Selected Prose*, page 30). The *Cantos* is a book of this nature. Such books are rare, but they are the reason that literature matters. They deepen the consciousness and enable the potentialities of the mind to be more fully realized. To use a phrase of the English poet, Peter Dale, "they carve out a shape in the unknown." Or, as Pound said, in 1912:

> The function of an art is to free the intellect from the tyranny of the affects, or leaning on terms, neither technical nor metaphysical: the function of an art is to strengthen the perceptive faculties and free them from encumbrance, such encumbrances, for instance, as set moods, set ideas, conventions; from the results of experience which is common but unnecessary, experience induced by the stupidity of the experiencer and not by inevitable laws of nature.
>
> (*Selected Prose*, page 330:*360*.)

In my commentaries and glossaries I have tried to annotate most of the references and allusions which are of major importance to the structure and content of the poem. I provide a translation of the most significant foreign phrases whenever this is not given by Pound himself in adjoining lines. I have had to leave hundreds of references unannotated, particularly in the late cantos where the allusiveness is most dense and multilayered. My omissions are due in part to ignorance, and also because if I'd attempted to explain everything, this book would be at least 2,000 pages long! But the most important reason is that the *Cantos* is a *poem* and not a work of history or scholarship. We can still read Dante and Villon with pleasure even though most of the names they mention may be lost on us.

For those who require more than I have given, a full glossary will soon be available in the two-volume *Companion to the Cantos* which is being prepared by Carroll Terrell at the University of Maine at Orono.

"The essential thing in a poet is that he builds us his world," Pound wrote in 1915. If this guide instigates a few lovers of poetry to explore for themselves the world Pound has made, it will have served its purpose.

---

[1] Throughout this book, I give the differing page numbers of the U.S. edition of *Selected Prose* in italics.
[2] In references to the *Cantos*, the first (roman) number indicates the canto, the second (arabic) number indicates the page. All references are to the revised collected edition (Cantos 1-117) of *The Cantos of Ezra Pound* (New Directions and Faber, 1975).

How to Approach the *Cantos:* A Warning

Some words T. S. Eliot wrote in his preface to another long poem of the twentieth century (David Jones's *In Parenthesis*) apply with equal validity to the *Cantos:* "...if *In Parenthesis* does not excite us before we have understood it, no commentary will reveal to us its secret. And the second step is to get used to the book, to live with it and make it familiar to us. Understanding begins in the sensibility: we must have the experience before we attempt to explore the sources of the book itself."

Pound wrote to John Quinn, soon after the *Cantos* had got under way: "Art is not only long, but bloody, bloody slow." Any new reader must experience the world of the poem as a gradual process. Donald Davie has put this well: "...the *Cantos* are a poem to be lived with, over years. Yet after many years each new reading—if it is a reading of many pages at a time, as it should be—is a new bewilderment. So it should be, for so it was meant to be. After all, some kinds of bewilderment are fruitful. To one such kind we give the name 'awe'—not awe at the poet's accomplishment, his energy, or his erudition, but awe at the energies, some human and some non-human, which interact, climb, spiral, reverse themselves and disperse, in the forming and reforming spectacles which the poet's art presents to us or reminds us of." (*Pound,* page 82.)

The Scottish poet, Hugh MacDiarmid, also gets to the core of what a reader of the poem experiences: "It is true of Pound's *Cantos* as a detective friend of mine said of a criminal investigation: 'Nearly every case begins with a mussy lot of odds and ends we collect. At first you can't tell what's important from what isn't. But you find afterwards that the bits that matter fit in together, and what is junk just drops away. Yes...and as often as not you discover that what at first you took to be junk is actually glittering gold.'"

Finally, Basil Bunting's poem, "On the Fly-Leaf of Pound's Cantos", is short enough to quote entire and worth more than any commentary:

> There are the Alps. What is there to say about them?
> They don't make sense. Fatal glaciers, crags cranks climb,
> jumbled boulder and weed, pasture and boulder, scree,
> *et l'on entend,* maybe, *le refrain joyeux et leger.*
> Who knows what the ice will have scraped on the rock it is smoothing?
>
> There they are, you will have to go a long way round
> if you want to avoid them.
> It takes some getting used to. There are the Alps,
> fools! Sit down and wait for them to crumble.

An Anthology of Statements by Ezra Pound on the *Cantos*

A: I have begun an endless poem, of no known category, Phanopoeia (light- or image-making) or something or other, all about everything.
(1917)   *Letter to James Joyce*

B: Perhaps as the poem goes on I shall be able to make various things clearer. Having the crust to attempt a poem in 100 or 120 cantos long after all mankind has been commanded never again to attempt a poem of any length, I have to stagger as I can.

   The first 11 cantos are preparation of the palette. I *have to* get down all the colours or elements I want for the poem. Some perhaps too enigmatically and abbreviatedly. I hope, heaven help me, to bring them into some sort of design and architecture later.
(1922)   *Selected Letters*, page 180

C: 1. Rather like, or unlike subject and response and counter subject in fugue.
   A. A. Live man goes down into world of Dead
   C. B. The "repeat in history"
   B. C. The "magic moment" or moment of metamorphosis, bust thru from quotidien into "divine or permanent world." Gods, etc.
(1927)   *Selected Letters*, page 210

D: The poem is not a dualism of past against present. Monism is pretty bad, but dualism (Miltonic puritanism, etc.) is just plain lousy.

   The poem should establish an hierarchy of values, not simply: past is good, present is bad, which I certainly do not believe and never have believed.

   If the reader wants three categories he can find them rather better in: permanent, recurrent and merely haphazard or casual.
(1933)   Letter to *New English Weekly*, May 11

E: Most Cantos have in them "binding matter", i.e., lines holding them into the whole poem and these passages don't much help the reader of an isolated fragment.... More likely to confuse than help.
(1933)   *Selected Letters*, page 242

F: Skip anything you don't understand and go on till you pick it up again. All tosh about foreign languages making it difficult. The quotes are all

xvii

either explained at once by repeat or they are definitely *of* the things indicated. If the reader don't know what an elefant is, then the word is obscure.

I admit there are a couple of Greek quotes, one along in 39 that can't be understood without Greek, but *if* I can drive the reader to learning at least that much Greek, she or he will indubitably be filled with durable gratitude. And if not, what harm? I can't conceal the fact that the Greek language existed.
(1934)   *Selected Letters*, page 250–51

G: An epic is a poem including history.
(1935)   *Social Credit: An Impact*

H: There is no mystery about the *Cantos*, they are the tale of the tribe—give Rudyard Kipling credit for his use of the phrase. No one has claimed that the Malatesta cantos[1] are obscure. They are openly volitionist, establishing, I think clearly, the effect of the factive personality, Sigismundo, an entire man. The founding of the Monte dei Paschi as the second episode[2] has its importance. There we find the discovery, or at any rate the establishment, of the true base of credit, to wit the abundance of nature and the responsibility of the whole people.
(1937)   *Guide to Kulchur*, page 194

I: Bartok's Fifth Quartet... is the record of a personal struggle, possible only to a man born in the 1880s.
It has the defects or disadvantages of my Cantos.
(1937)   *Guide to Kulchur*, pages 134–35

J: ...When I get to end, pattern *ought* to be discoverable. Stage set à la Dante is *not* modern truth. It may be O.K. but *not* as modern man's....
I don't expect, in the end, to have introduced ethical novelties or notions, though I hope to light up a few antient bases.
The Protestant world has *lost* the sense of mental and spiritual *rottenness*. Dante has it: "gran sacco che fa merda." The real theologians *knew* it.
Part of the job is *finally* to get all the necessary notes into the text itself. Not only are LI Cantos a part of the poem, but by labelling most of 'em draft, I retain right to include *necessary* explanations in LII-C or in revision.
Binyon has shown that Dante needs *fewer* notes than are usually given the student.
...that *section* of hell[3] precisely has *not* any dignity. Neither had Dante's fahrting devils. Hell is not amusing. Not a joke. And when you get further along you find individuals, not abstracts. Even XIV-XV has individuals in it, but *not* worth recording as such. In fact, Bill Bird rather entertained that I had forgotten which rotters were there. In his edtn. he tried to get the number of..... correct in each case. My "point" being that not even the first but only the last letters of their names had resisted corruption.
Person looking for gibberish is welcome to find it. A Wimmin maun ha her will.

xviii

42–51 are in page proof. . . . I believe they are clearer than the preceding ones.

Doing a note on Hardy (Hardy's *Collected Poems*) for my next prose outbreak. Now *there* is a clarity. There *is* the harvest of having written 20 novels first.

Take a fugue: theme, response, contrasujet. *Not* that I mean to make an exact analogy of structure.

Vide, incidentally, Zukofsky's experiment, possibly suggested by my having stated the Cantos are in a way fugal. There *is* a start, descent to the shades, metamorphoses, parallel (Vidal–Actaeon). All of which is mere matter for little . . . .rs and Harvud instructors *unless* I pull it off as reading matter, singing matter, shouting matter, the tale of the tribe.

If you have *Polite Essays*, you will see note to effect that economics always *has been* in the best large poetry. Bank money wasn't so vital to Odysseus.

(1937)   *Selected Letters*, pages 293–94

K: I believe that when finished, *all* foreign words in the *Cantos*, Gk., etc. will be underlinings, not necessary to the sense, in one way. I mean a complete sense will exist without them; it will be there in the American text, but the Greek, ideograms, etc., will indicate a *duration* from whence or since when. If you find any *briefer* means of getting this repeat or resonance, tell papa, and I will try to employ it.

Narrative not the same as lyric; different techniques for song and story. "would, could," et cetera: Abbreviations save *eye* effort. Also show speed in mind of original character supposed to be uttering or various colourings and degrees of importance or emphasis attributed by the protagonist of the moment.

All typographic disposition, placings of words *on* the page, is intended to facilitate reader's intonation, whether he be reading silently to self or aloud to friends. Given time and technique I might even put down the musical notation of passages or "breaks into song."

There is *no intentional* obscurity. There is condensation to maximum attainable. It is impossible to make the deep as quickly comprehensible as the shallow.

The order of words and sounds *ought* to induce the proper reading; proper tone of voice, etc., but can *not* redeem fools from idiocy, etc. If the goddam violin string is not tense, no amount of bowing will help the player. And *so* forth.

As to the *form* of The Cantos: All I can say or pray is: *wait* till it's there. I mean wait till I get 'em written and then if it don't show, I will start exegesis. I haven't an Aquinas-map; Aquinas *not* valid now.

(1939)   *Selected Letters*, pages 322–23

L: For forty years I have schooled myself, not to write an economic history of the U.S. or any country, but to write an epic poem which begins 'In the Dark Forest', crosses the Purgatory of human error, and ends in the

light, and 'fra i maestri di color che sanno' [Among the masters of those who know].
(1944)   *Selected Prose*, page 137:*167*

M: [A Prison Letter. The censor of the Disciplinary Training Center, Pisa, apparently suspected that the Pisan Cantos contained coded messages. Pound is writing to explain that this is not so.]
   The Cantos contain nothing in the nature of cypher or intended obscurity. The present Cantos do, naturally, contain a number of allusions and "recalls" to matter in the earlier 71 cantos already published, and many of these cannot be made clear to readers unacquainted with the earlier parts of the poem.
   There is also extreme condensation in the quotations, for example "Mine eyes have" (given as mi-hine eyes hev) refers to the Battle Hymn of the Republic as heard from the loud speaker. There is not time or place in the narrative to give the further remarks on seeing the glory of the lord.
   In like manner citations from Homer or Sophokles or Confucius are brief, and serve to remind the ready reader that we were not born yesterday.
   The Chinese ideograms are mainly translated, or commented in the english text. At any rate they contain nothing seditious.
   The form of the poem and main progress is conditioned by its own inner shape, but the life of the D.T.C. passing OUTSIDE the scheme cannot but impinge, or break into the main flow. The proper names given are mostly those of men on sick call seen passing my tent. A very brief allusion to further study in names, that is, I am interested to note the prevalence of early american names, either of whites of the old tradition (most of the early presidents for example) or of descendants of slaves who took the names of their masters. Interesting in contrast to the relative scarcity of melting-pot names.
   (1945)[4]

N:

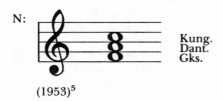

Kung.
Dant.
Gks.

(1953)[5]

O: A. Dominated by the emotions.
   B. Constructive effort—Chinese Emperors and Adams, putting order into things.
   C. The domination of benevolence. Theme in Canto 90. Cf. the thrones of Dante's "Paradiso."

There will be 100 or 120 cantos, but it looks like 112. First 50 cantos are a detective story. Looking around to see what is wrong.
Cantares—the Tale of the Tribe. To give the truth of history. Where

Dante mentions a name, E.P. tries to give the gist of what the man was doing.

Then he talked about the frescoes of Del Cossa in the Palazzo Schifanoia (the name means "chase away care") in Ferrara, which E.P. saw after World War 1:

Schifanoia frescoes in three levels.
Top. Allegories of the virtues. (Cf. Petrarch's "Tr ionfi") study in values.
Middle. Signs of the Zodiac. Turning of the stars. Cosmology.
Bottom. Particulars of life in the time of Borso d'Este. The contemporary.

a) What is there—permanent—the sea.
b) What is recurrent—the voyages.
c) What is trivial—the casual—Vasco's troops weary, stupid parts.
(*c.* 1955)[6]

P: There is a turning point in the poem towards the middle. Up to that point it is a sort of detective story, and one is looking for the crime. The Usura Cantos[7] would be more comprehensible if people would understand the meaning of the term "usury." It is not to be confused with legitimate interest which is due, teleologically, as Del Mar says, to the increase in domestic animals and plants. Consider the difference between a fixed charge and a share from a proportion of an increase. Now *usura* is a charge for the use of purchasing power levied without regard to production, often without regard even to the possibilities of production. The famous Medici Bank went bust when they started taking more deposits than they could invest in legitimate commerce and started making loans to princes—which were non-productive loans.
     (1958)   from B.B.C. Interview with D. G. Bridson[8]

Q: I began the *Cantos* about 1904, I suppose. I had various schemes, starting in 1904 or 1905. The problem was to get a form—something elastic enough to take the necessary material. It had to be a form that wouldn't exclude something merely because it didn't fit. In the first sketches, a draft of the present first canto was the third.
     Obviously you haven't got a nice little road map such as the middle ages possessed of Heaven. Only a musical form would take the material, and the Confucian universe as I see it is a universe of interacting strains and tensions.
     ...the first thing was this: you had six centuries that hadn't been packaged. It was a question of dealing with material that wasn't in the *Divina Commedia*. Hugo did a *Legende des Siècles* that wasn't an evaluative affair but just bits of history strung together. The problem was to build up a circle of reference—taking the modern mind to be the mediaeval mind with wash after wash of classical culture poured over it since the renaissance. That was the psyche, if you like. One had to deal with one's own subject.
     ...There has been a good deal of work thrown away because one is attracted to an historic character and then finds that he doesn't function within my form, doesn't embody a value needed. I have tried to make

the *Cantos* historic...but not fiction. The material one wants to fit in doesn't always work. If the stone isn't hard enough to maintain the form it has to go out.

....

Interviewer: Can you say what you are going to do in the remaining cantos [those following *Thrones*]?

It is difficult to write a paradiso when all the superficial indications are that you ought to write an apocalypse. It is obviously much easier to find inhabitants for an inferno or even a purgatorio. I am trying to collect the record of the top flights of the mind. I might have done better to put Agassiz on top instead of Confucius...

...this is provisionally what I have to do: I must clarify obscurities; I must make clearer definite ideas and dissociations. I must find a verbal formula to combat the rise of brutality—the principle of order versus the split atom...

An epic is a poem containing history. The modern mind contains heteroclite elements. The past epos has succeeded when all or a great many of the answers were assumed, at least between author and audience, or a great mass of audience. The attempt in an experimental age is therefore rash. Do you know the story: "What are you drawing, Johnny?"

"God!"

"But nobody knows what He looks like."

"They will when I get through!"

That confidence is no longer obtainable.

There *are* epic subjects. The struggle for individual rights is an epic subject, consecutive from jury trial in Athens to Anselm versus William Rufus, to the murder of Becket and to Coke and through John Adams.

Then the struggle appears to come up against a block. The nature of sovereignty is epic matter, though it may be a bit obscured by circumstance. Some of this *can* be traced, pointed; obviously it has to be condensed to get into the form. The nature of the individual, the heteroclite contents of contemporary consciousness. It's the fight for light versus sub-consciousness; it demands obscurities and penumbras. A lot of contemporary writing avoids inconvenient areas of the subject.

I am writing to resist the view that Europe and civilisation is going to Hell. If I am being "crucified for an idea"—that is, the coherent idea around which my muddles accumulated—it is probably the idea that European culture ought to survive along with whatever other cultures, in whatever universality.

...The title *Rock-Drill* was intended to imply the necessary resistance in getting a certain main thesis across—hammering. I was not following the three divisions of the *Divine Comedy* exactly. One can't follow the Dantescan cosmos in an age of experiment. But I have made the division between people dominated by emotion, people struggling upwards, and those who have some part of the divine vision. The thrones in Dante's *Paradiso* are for the spirits of the people who have been responsible for good government. The thrones in the *Cantos* are an attempt to move out from egoism and to establish some definition of an order possible or at any rate conceivable on earth. One is held up by the low percentage of reason which seems to operate in human affairs. *Thrones* concerns the states of mind of people responsible for something more than their personal conduct.

... There's need of elaboration, of clarification, but I don't know that a comprehensive revision is in order. There is no doubt that the writing is too obscure as it stands, but I hope that the order of ascension in the Paradiso will be toward a greater limpidity.

(1960)   from *Paris Review* interview with Donald Hall[9]

R: The best introduction to the *Cantos* and to the present selection of passages might be the following lines from the earlier draft of a Canto (1912), reprinted in the fiftieth memorial issue of *Poetry* (Chicago):

> Hang it all, there can be but one 'Sordello'!
> But say I want to, say I take your whole bag of tricks,
> Let in your quirks and tweeks, and say the thing's an artform,
> Your Sordello, and that the modern world
> Needs such a rag-bag to stuff all its thought in;
> Say that I dump my catch, shiny and silvery
> As fresh sardines slapping and slipping on the marginal cobbles?
> (I stand before the booth, the speech; but the truth
> Is inside this discourse—this booth is full of the marrow of wisdom.)

(1966)   Preface to *Selected Cantos*

---

[1]Cantos VIII–XI.
[2]Cantos XLII–XLIII.
[3]Cantos XIV and XV.
[4]First published in *Paris Review*, Vol. 7, No. 28 (Summer-Fall 1962).
[5]Donald Pearce relates that when he asked Pound to describe the structural principle of the *Cantos* in 1953, he sketched the above major chord.
[6]James Laughlin says that Pound dictated these notes on the *Cantos* to him in the middle fifties. ("Gists and Piths," *Poetry*, January 1982.)
[7]Cantos XLV and LI.
[8]D. G. Bridson, "A B.B.C. Interview with Ezra Pound," *New Directions* 17 (1961).
[9]Published in *Paris Review*, Vol. 7, No. 28 (Summer-Fall 1962).

Guide to the *Cantos*

Abbreviations

I have used the following abbreviations for languages in the glossaries to each canto:

A:	Arabic	J:	Japanese
C:	Chinese	L:	Latin
F:	French	ME:	Middle English
OF:	Old French	OE:	Old English
Gk:	Greek	P:	Portuguese
G:	German	Pr:	Provençal
H:	Hebrew	R:	Russian
I:	Italian	S:	Spanish

In the glossaries, the boldface figures at the left-hand margin refer to page numbers in the New Directions edition.

A Draft of XXX Cantos

I

Epic poetry "evokes and recalls" and the first canto sets the poem firmly in the Homeric tradition. In Book X of the *Odyssey*, Circe tells Odysseus that he has to voyage across "the stream of Ocean to where there is a narrow shore and the groves of Persephone—tall black poplars and willows." There he must beach his ship, before he goes to the "house of Hades" to consult the shade of Tiresias in order to learn how to find his way home. Much later, Circe's words are quoted directly in Greek (XXXIX, 194) and they form the opening of XLVII, emphasizing that the basic theme of the poem is a voyage after knowledge:

> Knowledge the shade of a shade,
> Yet must thou sail after knowledge
> Knowing less than drugged beasts
> (236).

Canto I forms as dark a beginning to the *Cantos* as Dante's *selv' oscura* (dark forest, *Inferno*, I, 2). It is concerned, like the first part of David Jones's *Anathemata*, with "rite and foretime." Odysseus/Pound sails to explore the "dark backward and abysm of time" and meets the shades. It also obliquely foreshadows the course of Pound's life and of his poem. For example, Tiresias's prophecy, "Lose all companions," became reality for him nearly thirty years after the line was written, in the prison camp at Pisa (LXXIV, 432).

The parallels with the *Odyssey* (unlike Joyce's *Ulysses*, they are more of subject, theme, and literal text than of structure) continue, becoming increasingly integrated with other material from the *Pisan Cantos* onward. In *Rock-Drill* and *Thrones*, Odysseus/Pound reaches Phaeakia, but Ithaka is never mentioned, probably because the poem's voyage after knowledge and perception does not cease until Pound stopped writing the *Cantos:* "I cannot get to the core of my thoughts any more with words."[1]

The main source for Canto I is a Renaissance Latin translation of the *Nekuia* ("The Book of the Dead")—Book XI of the *Odyssey:* "In the year of grace 1906, 1908, 1910 I picked up from the Paris quais a Latin version of Andreas Justinopolitanus (Parisiis, In officina Christiani Wecheli, MDXXXVIII), the volume containing also...the *Hymni Deorum* rendered by Georgius Dartona Cretensis" (*Literary Essays*, page 259).

Pound considered the *Nekuia* probably the oldest part of the *Odyssey*: "The Nekuia shouts aloud that it is *older* than the rest, all that island, Cretan, etc., hinter-time, that is not Praxiteles, not Athens of Pericles, but Odysseus" (*Selected Letters*, page 274).

Pound uses an approximation of Anglo-Saxon metre to render Divus's Latin. The choice of metre is the first example of the overlayering of times and traditions in the *Cantos*. Pound uses this device with increasing skill and assurance as the poem progresses, so that in the late cantos he can leap thousands of years between lines or half-lines with the swiftness of thought and without incongruity. What he does in Canto I is comparatively simple as the overlayering consists of only four main elements: Greek foretime translated via Renaissance Latin into a twentieth-century form of Anglo-Saxon heroic verse.

Though only a fragment from one book of the *Odyssey*, Canto I gives more of the feel of Homer than any other rendering. It is full of his rhythmic energy; for example, the movement of words in lines 5-6 physically expresses the forward thrust of Odysseus's ship: "So winds from sternward/Bore us out onward with bellying canvas."

Canto I closes with some Latin phrases from G. D. Cretensis's translation of the second Homeric hymn to Aphrodite. That the juxtaposition is partly intended to be critical is clear from the comment Pound included in the rejected first draft of this canto which was published as Canto III in the August 1917 issue of *Poetry:* "(The thin clear Tuscan stuff/Gives way before the florid mellow phrase)."

But the last five lines also harbinger future themes. It is not for nothing that Aphrodite is invoked, as she will become the presiding deity of later, paradisal parts of the *Cantos* "written under the domination of benevolence." And, as Hugh Kenner has pointed out, the theme of money is hinted at: "Gold and copper...ornament Aphrodite. Later, gold coins and (in XII) copper pennies will be the material for financial coups."[2] There is a comparable foreshadowing of themes in the first canto of *La Divina Commedia.*

Glossary

3:   **Circe:** a beautiful witch. A daughter of Helios (the sun god), she lived on the island of Aiaie where Odysseus spent a year with her.

Kimmerian lands: legendary lands where people "on whom the sun never looks" live near the entrance to Hades.

Perimedes and Eurylochus: companions of Odysseus.

ell-square pitkin: little pit, 45 inches square.

Tiresias: wise man, dead before the Trojan War. He alone of all the shades retains his consciousness ("Who even dead yet hath his mind entire," XLVII), but even he needs the draught of blood in order to prophesy to Odysseus.

Erebus: primeval darkness; the underworld.

4:   **dreory:** bloody (OE, "dreorig").

Pluto: Dis, the god of the underworld.

Proserpine: Koré, Persephone. Queen of the Dead and wife of Pluto from September until spring.

Elpenor: companion to Odysseus.

Avernus: the underworld.

Anticlea: the mother of Odysseus.

bever: drink.

5: **Divus:** Pound is here addressing the shade of Andreas Divus, who made the Latin translation which he used for this canto.

In officina Wecheli: (L) at the print-shop of Wechtel (see *Homeri Odyssea,* adverbum translata, Andrea Divo Iustinopolitano interprete, Paris 1538, title page).

Venerandam: (L) worthy of reverence.

Cypri munimenta … est: (L) the citadels of Cypress are her destined home.

orichalchi: (L) of copper.

Argicida: (L) slayer of Argus. One of the names of Hermes, the guide of souls to the underworld.

---

[1] Interview in *Epoca* (1963).

[2] "Drafts & Fragments & the Structure of the *Cantos*," Agenda, Vol. VIII, Nos. 3-4 (Autumn-Winter 1970).

II

The theme is metamorphosis. "The undeniable tradition of metamorphosis teaches us that things do not always remain the same. They become other things by swift unanalysable process." (*Literary Essays,* page 431.)

The rhythms are those of "The murmuring surge,/That on th'unnumbred idle Pebble chafes" (*King Lear,* IV, v) and this sound is often heard in the *Cantos.* Pound made several attempts to find words for "the rush of waves on the sea-beach and their recession," from Mauberley's "imaginary/Audition of the phantasmal sea-surge," to an adaptation of the Homeric phrase *para thina poluphloisboio thalasses* (*Iliad,* I, 34): "the turn of the wave and the scutter of receding pebbles" (*Selected Letters,* page 274). In II the sound echoes in the murmuring voices of the old men of Troy, "fed up with the whole show and suggesting Helen be sent back to Greece" (*ibidem,* page 210).

At line 23, we shift to the myth of Tyro, one of the queens Odysseus meets in Book XI of the *Odyssey.* She was loved by Poseidon, who visited her in the shape of the Thessalian river Enipeus:

> taking his likeness, the god who circles the earth and shakes it
> lay with her where the swirling river finds its outlet,
> and a sea-blue wave curved into a hill of water reared up
> about the two, to hide the god and the mortal woman;[1]

Pound's treatment of this story is one of many examples of his ability to make a myth come alive in the course of three or four lines.

"And by Scios,/to left of the Naxos passage" (7) introduces the next sea-change, and the central myth of II. The source is the third book of Ovid's *Metamorphoses* in Golding's (1567) translation. A group of sailors attempt to kidnap the boy Dionysus and sell him as a slave. He asks to be taken to Naxos, and when the sailors take the ship off course, he bewitches it and turns them into fishes. The story is told by Acoetes, the pilot, who alone among the sailors recognized the god. Bacchus rewards him by making him a priest of his cult. Acoetes tells his story to King Pentheus of Thebes who has taken him prisoner and denied the divinity of Dionysus.

Canto II expresses the "moment of metamorphosis, bust through from quotidien [everyday] into 'divine or permanent world'"—see Item C, page xvii. The rhythms take on an electric energy so that the power of the god seems to be materially present in the words.

Dionysus (Zagreus) is one of the central deities of the *Cantos* and in a sense his presence is felt in all the animals (particularly the cat family), plants, and trees that shine throughout the poem, making its cosmos living and numinous. For Pound, myth is a way of expressing perennial truth, it is never ornament—"A god is an eternal state of mind" (*Selected Prose*, page 47).

A passage in Professor Dodds's introduction to his edition of the *Bacchae* defines the nature of Pound's Dionysus with clarity:

> To the Greeks of the classical age Dionysus was not solely, or even mainly, the god of wine. Plutarch tells us as much, confirming it with a quotation from Pindar, and the god's cult titles confirm it also: he is Δενδίτης or Εὔδενδρος, the Power in the tree; he is Ἄνθιος the blossom-bringer, Κάρπιος the fruit-bringer, Φλεύς or Φλεως, the abundance of life. His domain is, in Plutarch's words, the whole of the ὑγρὰφὑσις, not only the liquid fire in the grape, but the sap thrusting in a young tree, the blood pounding in the veins of a young animal, all the mysterious and uncontrollable tides that ebb and flow in the life of nature.

The sailors are motivated by avarice and consequently fail to recognize the god. This is the first appearance in the *Cantos* of avarice, or *usura*, the most potent force of evil and destruction in the poem. The sailors are destroyed because it has blinded them to the living power of nature. This conflict between the splendour of the universe ("and that the universe is alive," XCIV, 637) and those who exploit it for the sake of money-lust, is at the core of the *Cantos*.

After Acoetes has finished his story, with a warning to King Pentheus which the latter is not to heed, the rhythms embody another sea-change as Pound introduces a myth of his own invention. This tells how Ileuthyeria, a sea-nymph, flees from a band of Tritons and is transformed into coral: "The swimmer's arms turned to branches" (9), recalling Daphne's change to laurel, "Laurel bark sheathing the fugitive" (CX, 779), when she fled Apollo. This leads back to Tyro and the rhythms become slower and infused with sleep, as the images turn into shapes seen and sounds heard in half-dream.

Glossary

6:     **"Sordello"**: a long poem by Browning, published in 1840. For the qualities Pound had in common with Browning, see the passage from *Sordello* quoted in *A.B.C. of Reading*, pages 188–91.

    Lo Sordels ... Mantovana: (Pr) Sordello was from Mantua. He was a troubadour, born *c*. 1200. He is important in the *Cantos* (as he is in Dante's *Purgatorio*, Canto VI et seq.) and, as often happens in Pound's poem, one or two lines here introduce a person or theme that is to receive more detailed treatment later—this is part of the fugal construction of the *Cantos*.

So-shu: Pound told his daughter that So-shu is a Chinese mythological figure. This is possibly a Chinese myth of Pound's invention, just as Ileuthyeria is a Greek one.

Lir: "Celtic cult-deity whose son was the Celtic sea-god and the fate of whose daughters was all of storm and the drag of waters" (David Jones).

Eleanor, ἐλέναυς (Elenaus) and ἐλέπτολις (Eleptolis): destroyer of ships and destroyer of cities—with a pun on Helen of Troy and Eleanor of Aquitaine. The Greek is from Aeschylus, *Agamemnon*, 689-90.

"Let her go back...Grecian voices": These lines are based on *Iliad*, III, 155-160. The old men of Troy sit under the wall complaining about Helen.

Schoeney's daughters: Golding's spelling of Schoneus, one of whose daughters was Atalanta.

7: **Scios:** Golding's spelling of the Greek island of Chios. It was reputed to have been the birthplace of Homer.

Naxos: largest and most fertile of the Cyclades, famous for its wine and worship of Dionysus.

8: **Lyaeus:** name of Dionysus.

9: **Lycabs:** sailor turned into a porpoise by Dionysus.

Medon: sailor turned into a fish (John Dory).

Pentheus: King of Thebes. He flouts Tiresias, who warned him not to oppose Bacchus.

Ileuthyeria: This name, of Pound's invention, was probably connected in his mind with the Greek for 'freedom': Ελευθερία.

10: **Proteus:** old man of the sea. Sea-god, herdsman of the flocks of the sea, seals, etc. He has the power to take all shapes, but if held till he resumes the true one, he will answer questions. It is fitting that he should come at the close of this canto of metamorphosis (see *Odyssey*, IV, 365–570).

---

[1]Richmond Lattimore's translation.

III

Venice, city most central to I-XXX, is here introduced via a fragment of autobiography. Pound had come to Venice in 1907 and published his first book, *A Lume Spento*, there in 1908. He remembers in the first line sitting on the Dogana (customs house) steps, just as Browning had sat "on a ruined palace step/At Venice" considering how to continue *Sordello*. Pound is struck by "one face," where Browning had seen a group of peasant girls ("those girls," *Sordello*, III, 698).

Pound returns in vision to the Greek gods, just as Venice is again seen with them in XVII, XXI and XXV. The landscapes of the *Cantos* live in the mind—this is one reason that the world of the poem has such tangible reality. Line 19 describes the approach to a Chinese temple.

Canto III then shifts to present episodes from the Spanish *Poema del Cid* (c. 1201-1207). Pound has given a prose account of the poem:

> After the ride from Bivar, Myo Cid comes to his town house...in Burgos, but the King's letters have been before him, and everything is closed against him; even in his own house they are afraid to meet him, when he comes up the narrow cobbled street, and beats at the door with his mailed heel, they send a child out to a balcony or window, and she repeats, parrot-wise, the exact words of the King's writ.... Martin Antolinez...despite the King's orders, brings supplies to Ruy Diaz (the Cid), going into voluntary exile by this act. He and the Cid then arrange a hoax on two Jews, Raquel and Vidas. The Cid has been exiled on the false charge of malversation of booty taken at siege; he and Antolinez now turn this to their advantage, and repair their lack of funds. Two chests, covered with vermilion leather and studded with gold nails, are carefully filled with sand and offered for pawn, on condition thát they be not disturbed for a year.
>
> (*The Spirit of Romance*, pages 67–68)

Canto III ends with images of desolation. Eliot was to write years later, in *East Coker*, "the tattered arras woven with a silent motto." As Daniel Pearlman has said, "the decay of the Renaissance is most powerfully suggested in the final line...'Silk tatters,"nec Spe Nec Metu"' in which the stoic motto of the Este family, 'With neither hope nor fear,' is contrasted with the decay that supervened when the Estes fell away from this noble precept." The Este family is one of the main historical subjects presented in I-XXX.

Glossary

11:    **Una niña de nueve años:** (S) a nine year old girl.

       voce tinnula: (L) with ringing voice (Catullus, LXI, 13).

12:    **Ignez da Castro murdered:** "Her position was the cause of jealousy, and of conspiracy; she was stabbed in the act of begging clemency from the then reigning Alfonso IV. When Pedro [her husband] succeeded to the throne, he had her body exhumed, and the court did homage, the grandees of Portugal passing before the double throne of the dead queen and her king, and kissing the hand which had been hers." (*The Spirit of Romance*, page 218—the source for the story is Camoens's *Os Lusiadas*.)

IV

Cantos IV-VII to some extent form a group and concern passion—"people dominated by emotion"—Aphrodite as destroyer, violence and jealousy, just as XC-XCV express paradisal love.

Canto IV opens with the destruction of Troy but then shifts to a vision of dawn and "the original world of the gods." As Peter Levi has said, there is "something April-like" about Pound's work—in purity of image he is excelled by no other poet, and just as night occurs so often in Shakespeare, dawn flashes through the *Cantos*.

From line 12, we enter the world of Provence, in some ways a sacred place for Pound, where the tradition of the gods persists, permanent. Much of IV overlays classical myth with Provençal themes. An old man (a subject rhyme with the old men of Troy in II) quotes Horace's poem to Spring in telling the story of Guillem da Cabestan, a late 12th century Provençal troubadour, which connects with the myth of Philomela, Procne and Tereus:

In Greek mythology, Procne was married to Tereus, king of Thrace. He raped her sister, Philomela, cutting out her tongue to prevent her telling what he had done, and imprisoning her in a remote place. She sent a piece of needlework depicting her misfortunes to Procne, who in revenge killed her own son, Itys, and had his flesh served up to Tereus. When she told him what he had eaten, he tried to kill both sisters, but Philomela changed into a nightingale and Procne into a swallow.

Guillem da Cabestan loved Marguerite, wife of Raymond of Château Roussillon. He killed Guillem and had his heart cooked and served to Marguerite. When she learned what she had eaten, she said that since she had eaten such noble food, her lips would touch no other and she threw herself out of a window.

"Only emotion endures" (*Literary Essays*, page 14). An ancient sadness permeates these lines. The theme of jealousy will recur and the story of Marguerite is remembered near the end of the poem—one of many cases where images return with increased power: "Without jealousy/like the double arch of a window/Or some great colonnade" (CXVII, 801).

As "the wind out of Rhodez" catches in Marguerite's sleeve before she falls from the window, the swallows are imagined still crying "Ytis" (with a pun on "It is Cabestan's heart in the dish") as Procne did to Tereus after he'd eaten his son; and then, in mid-line, Pound shifts to the myth of Actaeon.

Actaeon was a hunter. One day he came upon Artemis bathing; angered at being seen naked by a man, she turned him into a stag and he was chased and killed by his own hounds. Artemis, "the wood queen" (XCI, 612), goddess of nature, chastity and hunting, is a recurrent "eternal state of mind" in the cosmos of the poem.

In Canto IV, the myth of Actaeon is first treated directly, and then (as with Itys) seen through Provençal eyes. The troubadour, Piere Vidal (1175-1215), mutters Ovid as he stumbles through the wood. (Actaeon's story is told by Ovid in *Metamorphoses*, III, 138 ff.) Pound's note on his early poem, "Piere Vidal Old" (1909), makes clear the link with Actaeon: "It is of Piere Vidal, the fool *par excellence* of all Provence of whom the tale tells how he ran mad, as a wolf, because of his love for Loba of Penautier, and how men hunted him with dogs through the mountains of Cabaret..."

Vidal's muttering of Ovid embraces other myths of metamorphosis and the line, "The empty armour shakes as the cygnet moves" (15), recreates Achilles' combat with Cygnus the invulnerable (*Metamorphoses*, XII) when Achilles' adversary is changed to a cygnet, defining the moment of transformation with

9

rhythmic subtlety. It declares "eloquently," as Walter Baumann has said, "the vanity of violence" (*The Rose in the Steel Dust*, page 35).

The following lines are flooded with paradisal light anticipating the light imagery of the late cantos. The rhythms express the movement of whirling water, and with tree images, what Pound described as "our kinship to the vital universe; to the tree and the living rock. We have about us the universe of fluid force, and below us the germinal universe of wood alive, of stone alive." (*The Spirit of Romance*, page 92.)

After the wind-song (see glossary), the imagery becomes that of dusk: "Sound drifts in the evening haze" (16), so the canto has run "From the dawn blaze to sunset" (LXXXVII, 572).

Glossary

13: **ANAXIFORMINGES!:** (Gk) Lords of the Lyre (Pindar).

Aurunculeia: the bride in Catullus's marriage hymn, *Collis o Heliconii*.

Cadmus: see glossary to XXVII (132).

Et ter flebiliter: (L) and thrice with tears (Horace, *Odes*, IV, 12, 5).

15: **Pergusa:** lake near Enna where Dis carries off Persephone.

Gargaphia: the valley where Actaeon is killed.

Salmacis: pool where a nymph of that name and Hermaphroditus are changed into one bi-sexual being.

e lo soleills plovil: (Pr) and the sun rains (Arnaut Daniel). "Where the rain falls from the sun" (*Translations*, page 155).

Takasago: sea-port in S. Honshu, Japan, where two pines grow that are inhabited by the spirit of an old man and his wife. Link with Baucis and Philemon (XC, 605).

Isé: sacred Shinto shrine to the Sun Goddess at Ujiyamada, S. Honshu. Recurs XXI (99) where the parallel growth of the pines of Takasago and Isé are linked to the river Delos, Inopos, which rises and falls at the same time as the Nile.

And Sō-Gyoku...: These lines are extracted from a rendering of the *Feng Fu*, "Rhyme-prose on the Wind," attributed to Sung Yü (Chinese original of 'Sō-Gyoku') of the 4th century B.C. Notes on this poem were discovered by Pound amongst the Fenollosa mss. Hsiang is King Hsiang of Ch'u who is addressed by the poet. A translation by Arthur Waley is included in his *170 Chinese Poems*, page 41. (J. C.) As in *Lear*, these lines express an old theme, that no king can control the elements, but in the original (and much in line with Pound's intentions) they are part of a conscious and gently forceful satirical allegory calculated to admonish the king.

16: **Ecbatan:** capital of the Medes; founded 6th century B.C. by their legendary first king, Deioces. The city recurs in V and in *The Pisan Cantos* becomes "The city of Dioce whose terraces are the colour of stars" (LXXIV, 425).

Danae: Daughter of Acrisius, King of Argos, and mother of Perseus by Zeus who came to her in the form of a golden shower. This foreshadows "Merlin's moder" who was visited by a spirit "in cloth of gold" (XCI, 613).

10

Grey stone-posts leading: anticipates the vision of Elysium in XVI: "The grey stone posts,/and the stair of grey stone" (69).

Sennin: Japanese for Chinese 'Hsien-jen,' usually translated "immortal(s)." Pound understood them as "Chinese spirits of nature or of the air" (*Selected Letters*, page 189). (J.C.)

Père Henri Jacques: a Jesuit who showed reverence for Chinese religion.

Polhonac: Héracle III, Viscount of Polhonac. Guillaume de Saint-Didier addressed love songs to his wife, who agreed to accept him, if so urged by her husband, and so Guillaume wrote a song in which a husband intercedes with his wife in the interests of a rejected lover. Héracle admired the song, sang it to his wife, and thus "set the feast" for Guillaume.

Gyges: a Lydian, secreted by King Candaules, so that he could see the beauty of the naked queen; discovering his presence, the queen forced Gyges to kill Candaules and marry her.

"Saave!": (OF?) Hail! The lines describe a procession in which an image of the Madonna is borne through the crowd by the river Garonne in the South of France and this is juxtaposed with the light and clarity of the river Adige, where, at Verona, there is another, more beautiful, *Madonna in hortulo* (Madonna in the garden) painted by Stefano of Verona.

Cavalcanti: the Italian poet (*c.* 1255-1300) and friend of Dante. XXXVI is mainly a translation of his canzone, *Donna mi priegha*.

arena: the Roman arena at Verona. This recurs XI (50), XII (53), XXI (98), XXIX (105) etc. Pound said, "Four of them 'sat there' [1920 or 1921], one of the group being T. S. Eliot, and...they had felt that past time, history, was present around them" (Louis Dudek, *A Visit to Ezra Pound*). The arena thus makes a kind of setting for the early cantos.

V

The emotion at the core of this dark, complex canto is expressed by the line from Dante which occurs on its last page: "Al poco giorno ed al gran cerchio d'ombra" ("To day drawn in, great ring of shadow").[1]

Among themes introduced here are: the light imagery of neo-Platonism (Iamblichus) which will give radiance to later, paradisal parts of the poem, and perhaps even more important, the motif of Time. Mechanical time dominates the events of V: "on the barb of time" (17) which foreshadows a later line, "Time is the evil" (XXX, 147).

Canto V is built out of violent events, and contrasts, most obviously between light and shade, but also, as Daniel Pearlman has shown, it "is constructed on an interesting directional metaphor, movement upward contending with movement downward in physical, aesthetic and moral terms" (*The Barb of Time*, page 58.)

The upward movement is expressed by light rising like birds which will

11

become a recurrent image—it last appears in Notes for CXVII: "or a field of larks at Allègre... so high toward the sun and then falling" (802).

After dealing with sexual themes ranging from Sappho and Catullus to Provence, V presents two murders: (a) that of Giovanni Borgia ("John Borgia is bathed at last," 18) who was killed in 1496, according to rumour by his brother Cesare, and (b) that of Alessandro, tyrannical duke of Florence, by his cousin Lorenzo (Lorenzaccio) Medici in 1537. It is by means of images that these old crimes are brought alive—the description of the Tiber where Giovanni's body was thrown is memorable: "Tiber, dark with the cloak, wet cat gleaming in patches" (18).

Glossary

17:   **Ecbatan:** see glossary to IV (16).
   Iamblichus: Neo-Platonic philosopher (*c.* A.D. 330)—for Pound's comments on him see *Guide to Kulchur*, page 223.
   ciocco: (I) log; refers to Dante's "ciocci" (*Paradiso*, XVIII, 100) where "Poi come nel percuoter de' ciocchi arsi/surgendo innumerabili faville" (as when burning logs are struck rise innumerable sparks); Dante's simile describes the ascent of spirits from the heaven of Mars to that of Jupiter, the star from which justice proceeds.
   "Et omniformis": (L) and every shape—from Porphyrios, *De Occasionibus* (Concerning Chances), which is included in Iamblichus's *De Mysteriis Egyptiorum, Chaldeorum, Assyriorum*. The full sentence is quoted at the start of XXIII (107): "Et omniformis, omnis intellectus est" (and every intellect is capable of assuming every shape).
   Aurunculeia: see glossary on IV (13).
   "Da nuces!/Nuces!": (L) Give nuts! Nuts! (Catullus, LXI, 131—a wedding rite).
   Sextus: Sextus Propertius (*c.* 50-*c.* 16 B.C.) the Latin poet—see *Homage to Sextus Propertius*.
   and from "Hesperus...": the evening star. This introduces Sappho, "the older song" whom Catullus translated—see Sappho, 149, in *Lyra Graeca*, Vol. 1, and Catullus, LXII.

17-18:   **"Fades light... Atthis, unfruitful:** an adaptation of Sappho's poem to Atthis, one of her followers, who deserted her, with a pun on Attis, priest of Cybele (see Catullus, LXIII). Both Atthis and Attis suggest infertility.

18:   **The talks ran long in the night.... He kept Tyndarida .... de Maensac:** The stories about troubadour poets alluded to in these 22 lines are given in *Literary Essays*, pages 94–108.
   romerya: (Pr) pilgrimage to Rome.
   Lei fassa furar a del: (Pr) had herself carried off by him.
   dreitz hom: (Pr) straight man.

19:   **Varchi of Florence:** Pound's source for the story of Alessandro's murder is Benedetto Varchi's *Storia Fiorentino* (History of Florence).
   "Σίγα μαλ'αῦθις δευτέραν: Siga, mal'authis deuteran, Silence, once more a second time! (Aeschylus, *Agamemnon*, 1344-1345). "Silence" is the cry of the Chorus; the rest is Agamemnon's cry as he is stabbed.

Lorenzo stabbed Alessandro de Medici with an accomplice in 1537.
Se pia? O empia: (I) If pious? Or impious? The source is Varchi, who
went to visit Lorenzo "one wanting the facts" to get a first-hand account
of the murder.
Caina attende: (I) Caina waits (*Inferno*, V, 107—Caina, a lake of ice,
is the region of hell reserved for those who have murdered a relative).
Del Carmine: astrologer who foretold the murder, but Alessandro,
"the tall indifference" (VII, 27), ignores all warnings.
abuleia: loss of will power.
"O se morisse,...da sè": (I) Or if he should die, believed killed by
himself.
Schiavoni: Church on the Tiber where watchman saw the body of
Giovanni Borgia; his cloak was seen to float and the assassins threw
stones on it to make it sink: "Sink the damn thing" (20).

20:    **"Se pia,...terribile deliberazione":** (I) If pious, or impious, but decided and [with] terrible deliberation. Varchi's full sentence is: "For
myself, I do not believe that any of these reasons [for doing the murder]
considered alone and separate from the others, is an adequate explanation, but I believe all of them together were powerful enough to
lead him on to a decision which I cannot call either pious or impious
but which in all truth was terrible and resolute."
Ma se morisse: (I) But if he should die.

---

[1]Dante, *Rime* 78. Peter Dale's translation (*Agenda*, Vol. 17 Nos. 3-4, Vol. 18 No. 1).

VI

Pound's phrase, "a preparation of the palette" (see Item B, page xvii),
applies especially to VI. It is a cluster of Provençal and mediaeval material,
with glances at parallels in Greek mythology (Odysseus and Theseus). It returns to characters already introduced, in particular Eleanor of Aquitaine and
Sordello, and at the same time announces themes and people who will be
prominent later.

The main event on the first page is Eleanor of Aquitaine's marriage to Louis
VII of France, their journey to Acre in Palestine, "went over sea till day's end"
(paralleling Odysseus's voyage in I, 3), on the crusade which Louis led in
1147, and subsequent divorce in 1152. She then married Henry Plantagenet,
going to England to be "spoiled in a British climate" (VII, 24). Bernart de
Ventadour's poem lamenting her crossing the Channel is to be quoted in
XCIII (624).

Two subjects introduced here, which often recur in the poem, are sex and
fertility as the source of artistic creation (Guillaume de Poitiers, Bernart de
Ventadour, Sordello) and, near the end, the story of Cunizza da Romano (*c*.
1198-1279) who was for a time Sordello's lover, and who in old age freed her
slaves. One of the most memorable women in the *Cantos*, her shade visits the

13

poet in the prison camp at Pisa (LXXIV, 437, 443; LXXVI, 452 and LXXVIII, 483). She also appears twice in *Rock-Drill* where her granting of freedom to her slaves, "liberavit masnatos," is juxtaposed with the Greek phrase ἡγάπησεν πολύ, "loved much." Dante placed her in the heaven of Venus (*Paradiso*, IX) and this is where she is last referred to in the *Cantos:* "fui chiamat'/e qui refulgo" [Cunizza], "I was called and here I shine" (XCII, 620). Pound expresses what she meant to him in the *Guide to Kulchur* (pages 107–8):

> Cunizza, white haired in the House of the Cavalcanti, Dante, small gutter-snipe, or small boy hearing the talk in his father's kitchen or, later, from Guido, of beauty incarnate, or, if the beauty can by any possibility be brought into doubt, at least and with utter certainty, charm and imperial bearing, grace that stopped not an instant in sweeping over the most violent authority of her time and, from known fact, that vigour which is grace in itself. There is nothing in Créstien de Troyes' narratives, nothing in Rimini or in the tales of the antients to surpass the facts of Cunizza, with, in her old age, great kindness, thought for her slaves.

Glossary

21:    **Guillaume:** IXth Duke of Aquitaine and VIIth Duke of Poitiers (1071-1127). Grandfather of Eleanor. Probably the first troubadour.

"Tant las fotei . . . . . . et veit vetz: (Pr) "I fucked them often, as you will hear, one hundred and eighty-eight times..." From poem by Guillaume in which he describes how travelling once in Auvergne he met two women of noble birth. Because they believed him to be mute he was invited to make love to them. He remained with them more than eight days.

The stone is alive in my hand: echoed in LXXIV: "stone knowing the form which the carver imparts it/the stone knows the form" (430).

the crops will ... death-year: see XLVII, "doth thy death year/Bring swifter shoot?" (238).

e maire del rei jove: (Pr) and mother of the young king.

Theseus: Parallels between Helen of Troy and Eleanor , started in II, are continued—Theseus wanted to marry Helen when she was a young girl.

Et quand lo reis ... mout er fasché: (OF) And when King Louis heard it he was very angry.

22:    **domna jauzionda:** (Pr) joyous lady. From a poem by Bernart de Ventadour (1148-1195), probably addressed to Eleanor.

"My Lady of Ventadour . . . . sheds such light in the air": lines addressed by Bernart de Ventadour to Eleanor of Aquitaine after joining her court, probably not long before she left for England. Bernart is pleading with her to use her influence to free Alice of Montpellier, wife of Eblis III, vicomte of Ventadour. When Eblis discovered Bernart making songs to his wife, he banished him, and locked Alice in a tower.

'Que la lauzeta mover': (Pr) When I see the lark move. The first line of one of Bernart's songs. Pound translates it in *The Spirit of Romance* (pages 41–42).

Masnatas et servos: (L) domestics and slaves; refers to Cunizza freeing her slaves.

23: **A marito subtraxit ipsam...Sordellum concubuisse:** (L) He took her away from her husband...it is said that Sordello slept with her.

Theseus from Troezene: When Theseus's father Aegeus left Troezene, he left instructions with Aethra (Theseus's mother) that when her son was able, he should lift a certain rock, under which Aegeus had hidden a sword and sandals. Theseus narrowly escaped an attempt by Medea to poison him, thanks to Aegeus seeing the sword, and thus recognizing him in time. (Apollodorus, *Epit.* I, 5.)

VII

The time span extends from Homer to the twentieth century. To adapt a phrase of Joyce, VII "traces the curve of an emotion" by presenting "luminous details" from the *Iliad*, the Roman poets, Provence, Dante, Liu Ch'e, Camoens, Flaubert and Henry James.

"Titter of sound about me, always" (V, 17). Murmurous voices, and old houses, form the dark ground tone: the old men of Troy, the sea-surge, Henry James, and the modern living dead. The latter foreshadow a line from CXV, "the living were made of cardboard" (794)—"moved by no inner being" (26)—they are much the same as Eliot's *Hollow Men*.

Contrasted with these are the passionate ("Only emotion endures," *Literary Essays*, page 14): Helen/Eleanor, Arnaut Daniel ("e quel remir"), Dido, Desmond Fitzgerald, "The live man, out of lands and prisons," who is remembered again in XCII (618) for his honour, and finally the murderer of Alessandro de Medici, Lorenzaccio, "being more live than they, more full of flames and voices" (27).

The tone is elegiac; parts of VII concern Pound's return to Paris, after a seven years' absence, "We also made ghostly visits..." (25), to visit a friend whom he finds to be dead: "But *is* she dead as Tyro? In seven years?" VII is resistant to being pinned down to a single interpretation, but the theme of "devouring time," and poetry's fitful power to brave it, is one strand for the reader to hold onto. The rhythms have a *gravitas*, and subtlety, which remain in the mind, accurately rendering the complexity of its emotions. In a sense it is a coda to the first group of cantos, ending memorably with "the stiff, still features" of the indifferent tyrant, Alessandro.

Glossary

24: **Eleanor...British climate):** She went with her husband, Henry II, there in 1154; after bearing him eight children, she returned to France, but was forced to go back to England in 1174 where she languished as a virtual prisoner until Henry's death in 1189.

'Ελανδρος and 'Ελέπτολις: see glossary to II (6).

The phantom of Rome: The idea of Rome as merely a shadow of Greece recurs in XXV (118): "And as after the form, the shadow..."

"Si pulvis...tamen excute": (L) Even if there is no dust, brush it off.

Ovid tells how to make a pass at a girl on the "marble narrow for seats" of the Colosseum (*Artis Amatoriae*, I, 151).

Then file and candles, e li mestiers ecoutes: (OF) And heard the mysteries. The line depicts a procession, and refers to the mediaeval practice of saying mass before a battle.

y cavals armatz: (Pr) and horses in armour (Bertrans de Born, *Bien me plait le doux temps de printemps*, a war song which Pound translated in *The Spirit of Romance*, page 47).

ciocco: see glossary to V (17).

Un peu moisi .... sous le baromètre ...: (F) A bit mildewed, floor lower than the garden. Against the panelling, a straw armchair, an old piano, and under the barometer. From the fourth paragraph of Flaubert's *Un Coeur Simple*. Modern realism and precise description lead naturally to the homage to Henry James (who had learnt so much from Flaubert) which follows.

The modish and darkish walls ...: probably Lamb House, Rye, Surrey which James leased in 1897 and later bought. See the essay "Henry James" (*Literary Essays*, page 295) for a fuller portrait.

con gli occhi onesti e tardi: (I) with eyes honest and slow. Dante, *Purgatorio*, VI, 63; Pound has transferred Dante's description of Sordello to Henry James.

Grave incessu: (L) grave in movement.

25:    **Ione, dead the long year:** see poem of this title (*Collected Shorter Poems*, page 122; *Personae*, page 112).

My lintel, and Liu Ch'e's lintel: See "Liu Ch'e" (*Collected Shorter Poems*, page 118; *Personae*, page 108), an elegy for a dead courtesan by Liu Ch'e (156–187 B.C.). With reference to "lintel" compare: "And she the rejoicer of the heart is beneath them:/a wet leaf that clings to the threshold."

Elysée: The name carried on is Elysium, the home of the blessed dead.

Erard: French make of piano. These lines refer back to Flaubert's *Coeur Simple* already quoted.

Smaragdos, chrysolithos: (L) emerald, chrysolite (Propertius, II, xvi, 43–46).

De Gama wore ... in Africa: a parody of Camoens's *Os Lusiadas*, II, xcviii, 3–4, where Da Gama's trousers are described as slashed with gold. The next line also parodies Camoens's rhetoric.

Tyro: see my commentary on II.

The scarlet curtain ...: see Golding's Ovid: "a scarlet curtaine streynd against a playstred wall/Doth cast like shadowe, making it seeme ruddye therewithall" (*Metamorphoses*, X, 694–695).

26:    **Lamplight at Buovilla:** "And he [Arnaut Daniel] loved a woman of high degree of Gascony, wife of William of Buovilla, but it was not believed that the lady yielded to him any direct pleasure of love" (*Biographies des Troubadours*).

e quel remir: (Pr) and that I may look at her. Daniel's "Doutz brais e critz," line 32 (*Translations*, pages 172–175). See also *The Spirit of Romance* (pages 87–100), "Consider in such passages in Arnaut as, 'E

16

quel remir contral lum de la lampa' [And that I may look at her against the light of the lamp], whether a sheer love of beauty and a delight in the perception of it have not replaced all heavier emotion, whether or no the thing has not become a function of the intellect."

Nicea: perhaps an allusion to Helen.

"Toc": (F) sham.

O voi che siete in piccioletta barca: (I) Pound translates this line in XCIII (631) and at the close of CIX: "You in the dinghy (piccioletta) astern there!" (774). Dante, *Paradiso*, II,1: Dante is addressing his readers.

Dido...Sicheus: Dido's husband Sichaeus was murdered by her brother Pygmalion for his riches (*Aeneid*, I, 341–356).

27: **Passion to breed a form...rain-blur:** Compare: "...of Love appearing in an ash-grey vision..." (*The Spirit of Romance*, page 88).

Lorenzaccio: see commentary on V.

Ma se morisse!: see glossary to V(19).

And the tall indifference: Alessandro de Medici. See V.

E biondo: (I) He is blond. Dante, *Inferno*, XII, 110. The first round of the seventh circle where the tyrants are placed. Anticipates VIII, line 4.

VIII-XI

The clearest statement about this group is by Pound himself. (See Item H, page xviii.) After the "obscurities and penumbras" of V-VII, which closed with the "tall indifference" of Alessandro who moved to his death without willing otherwise, one of the major turning points in the poem is reached with the introduction of Sigismundo Malatesta, whose personality was will incarnate, and whose energy changed events.

"The history of a culture is the history of ideas going into action" (*Guide to Kulchur*, page 44). Pound said of Dante, "The whole of the *Divina Commedia* is a study of the 'directio voluntatis'," direction of the will (*Jefferson and/or Mussolini*, page 17). This remark also applies to the *Cantos* and this becomes clear in VIII-XI.

Sigismundo is the first historical character to receive detailed treatment in the poem. Once the reader has become familiar with the way history is presented in VIII-XI, he should not have difficulty in following the later historical sections in the *Cantos*. Clark Emery has described Pound's basic methods:

> In his study of history, the effort will be to recapture the intensity of life being lived, and, instead of bringing history to the reader, to bring the reader into history. That is, the reader will not witness an event as an accomplished fact but will seem to be a participant in the event. He will therefore often receive fragmentary information, thus being as confused or ignorant or misled as the original actors. He will often have to speak the language of the time, the dialect of the place. On the other hand, though pressed into action, he will simultaneously maintain his perspective

as reader and will be able to draw inferences from startling juxtapositions
or apparently divergent times, persons, places, events, ideas.
(Ideas into Action, page 94)

Sigismundo Pandolfo Malatesta (1417-1468), Lord of Rimini, Fano and Cesena, was an Italian Renaissance *condottiere* who out of a life of chaos, violence and intrigue ("confusion/Basis of renewals," XX, 92) left the perdurable monument of his Tempio: "If you consider the Malatesta and Sigismundo in particular, a failure, he was at all events a failure worth all the successes of his age. He had in Rimini, Pisanello, Pier della Francesca . . . If the Tempio is a jumble and junk shop, it nevertheless registers a concept. There is no other single man's effort equally registered." *(Guide to Kulchur,* page 2.)

Sigismundo, like Pound, would probably have wished to revive ancient Greek religion. With the help of his architect, Alberti, he transformed the cathedral of Rimini into a Tempio with images of gods and goddesses by Agostino Duccio and others. Particularly beautiful is the figure of Diana with the crescent moon which Pound will remember at Pisa while looking at the actual moon: "(Cythera, in the moon's barge whither?/ how hast thou the crescent for car?" (LXXX, 510).

Canto VIII presents Sigismundo as ruler, and by quoting a letter concerning the painter Piero della Francesca, ideal patron of the arts. Then follow fragments about his life as a *condottiere* leading the armies of Florence and Venice; a snatch of his love poetry: "Ye spirits who of olde were in this land . . ." (30); an account of a festival in Rimini to mark the visit of Francesco Sforza and his bride Bianca Visconti in May, 1442 (31); the conversation of Sigismundo's friend, the Neo-Platonist Gemisthus Plethon at the Council of the Eastern and Western Churches in Ferrara, and finally the general background of violence and disorder against which Sigismundo's positive achievement was made.

Canto IX is the apex of the sequence, and at its centre is the building of the Tempio. It is a good example of Pound's documentary method of presenting history, with its extracts from letters found by the Sienese in Sigismundo's postbag. They captured this when they suspected him of double-dealing, having hired him to attack Count Pitigliano Orsini—Sigismundo doesn't seem to have taken this exploit seriously, but its failure was to play a large part in his downfall. It antagonised the bishop of Siena who later became Pope Pius II and Sigismundo's most powerful enemy.

Canto X opens with the abortive siege of Sorano (Count Pitigliano's stronghold). Sigismundo seems to have angered the Sienese by making a truce with him. He declines to go to Siena to discuss the situation as he suspects he'll suffer the same fate as the *condottiere* Carmagnola (executed by the Venetians). Sigismundo only just manages to escape and in the rest of X his enemies gather. He is burnt in effigy in Rome. Then extracts are given from Andreas Benzi's bloated rhetoric against Sigismundo. Benzi had been ordered by Pius to present the case against him to the College of Cardinals. Canto X closes with Sigismundo's preparations for a battle with the Papal forces where he is greatly outnumbered.

In Canto XI he wins this battle, but things soon go badly for him. He loses Fano and Cesena, and the rest of the canto traces his decline. Near the end

(51), his positive achievement is summed up by the memorable line: "In the gloom the gold gathers the light against it."

Glossary

28: **Calliope:** the muse of epic poetry.
Frater tamquam ... tergo: (L) Like a brother and most dear companion ... written on back.
Maestro di pentore: (I) master of painting (Piero della Francesca).

31: **godeva molto:** (I) much enjoyed
Gemisthus Plethon: (1355?-1450?) Neo-Platonic Byzantine philosopher. He is introduced here attending (as a representative of the Eastern Church) the Council between Pope Eugenius IV and the Eastern Patriarch which attempted to resolve their differences. It moved from Ferrara to Florence because of the plague. This Council, which took place in 1438, receives fuller treatment in XXVI (123-124).

Gemisto, like Pound and Sigismundo, wished to reconcile Christianity and ancient Greek religion. He did much to revive Greek mythology and learning.
POSEIDON: "Gemisto stemmed all from Neptune" (LXXXIII).
concret Allgemeine: (G) the concrete universal. Hegelian term, meaning, roughly, that we can only reach general truths through knowledge of particulars. The *Cantos* is built on this principle.

32: **templum aedificavit:** (L) he built a temple.
Parisina: Her story is told in XX (90-91) and XXIV (112).
Atreides: sons of Atreus. Reference is to the doomed house of Atreus, the murder of Agamemnon (introduced V, 19) and the revenge of Orestes.

36: **casus est talis:** (L) that's how it is.
Poliorcetes: (Gk) taker of cities. The artist Pisanello's epithet for Sigismundo.
POLUMETIS: (Gk) many minded. Homeric epithet for Odysseus.

37: **m'l'ha calata:** (I) he's tricked me in this.
Pitigliano: Count Aldebrando Orsini.

41: **et amava ... decus:** (I and L) and he loved Isotta degli Atti to distraction/ and she was worthy of it/constant in purpose/She delighted the eye of the Prince/lovely to look at/pleasing to the people (and an adornment to Italy).
San Vitale: 6th century Byzantine church in Ravenna.

42: **Carmagnola:** (1380-1432), a distinguished *condottiere*. He changed his allegiance from the Visconti family of Milan to join the Venetians, who later suspected him, probably unjustly, of having been bribed by the Visconti. Having invited him to lunch to give a progress report on his campaign, the Venetians executed him between two ancient columns which had been brought from Syria in 1128. Carmagnola will be met with again, with Sigismundo and Borso d'Este, in the paradise of XVII (78-79).
"anno messo ...: (I) they got the better of Sigismundo.

43: **Borso ...:** Borso d'Este (1413-1471), son of Niccolo d'Este, here tries unsuccessfully to reconcile Sigismundo with Federigo d'Urbino. He followed his father's wishes in becoming a peace-maker: "Keep the peace, Borso" (XX, 91; 95, and repeated at the start of XXI).

'Te cavero...corpo!': (I) I'll tear your guts out!

El conte...te!': The count rises: 'I'll tear your liver out!'

INTEREA PRO GRADIBUS.....FLAGRAVIT: (L) Meanwhile in front of the steps of the Basilica of St. Peter, from dry stuff, a huge pyre was built and on top of it was placed an effigy of Sigismundo, imitating so exactly the man's features and style of dress that it seemed rather to be the real person than his effigy; but so that the effigy could not fool anyone, some writing came from his mouth which said: here I am, Sigismundo Malatesta, son of Pandolpho, king of traitors, naked before God and men, by decree of the sacred senate condemned to the flames. Many read the words. Then as the people stood by, a fire was lit beneath it, and the pyre of a sudden set the likeness on fire. (*Annotated Index* translation.)

44:    **Stupro,** etc.: There isn't space here to translate Benzi's rhetoric, and, besides, most of the words exist in English!

46:    **Borso:** After his violent death, Borso d'Este enters the paradise of XVII (79) together with Carmagnola and Sigismundo. This is one of several examples of historical characters who are treated factually in the *Cantos* and also transfigured to the world of myth and the imagination.

50:    **Sub annulo...OLIM de Malatestis:** (L) Under the seal of the Pope, the palace and council chamber, ONCE of the Lords Malatesta. This loss of the palace at Fano, "the long room over the arches," by the writs made the property of the Pope, recurs with a deeper sadness in *The Pisan Cantos* (LXXVI, 462; LXXX, 501; LXXXIII, 529).

   d'''e b'''e colonne: (I) of the beautiful columns. These are those of the Hospital of the Holy Cross which was built by Sigismundo's younger brother Novello.

   Vogliamo,/che le donne: (I) We wish that the women...

51:    **sexaginta...plures:** (L) sixty-four, nor is he to have more. (Pius II drew up an agreement in 1466 allowing him only 64 soldiers. Sigismundo died three and a half months after signing, aged 51.)

52:    **Henry:** Enrico Aquadelli, steward to Sigismundo.

   Actum...Aquabello: (L) Done in the Castle of Sigismundo in the presence of Roberto Valturio, willingly and with good understanding. His sense of humour never deserted him.

XII

The "merely haphazard or casual" (see Item D, page xvii) is here presented with Chaucerian robustness and humour. The American businessman, Baldy Bacon, whom Pound probably met *c.*1910, is a sort of anti-hero, a parody of Odysseus.

This is the first canto to deal directly with commercial cunning, and usury, which Pound was later to define as "a charge for the use of purchasing power, levied without regard to production; often without regard to the possibilities of production" (XLV, 230). Pound follows Dante in linking usury with sodomy as they are both "evil against Nature's increase" (Addendum for C, 798) and this connection is made clear in the story of the "pore honest sailor" which Jim X... (John Quinn) tells to the bankers' meeting (56–57).

Glossary

53: **Arena romana... en calcaire:** (L and F) Roman arena of Diocletian, the steps, 43 tiers made of limestone. See glossary to IV (16).
Guardia regia: (S) royal guard.

54: **Pollon d'anthropon iden:** (Gk) And of many men he saw [the cities and knew their mind] (*Odyssey*, I, 3). Makes connection between Baldy and Odysseus.
Habitat cum Quade: (L) Live with Quade. See *Pavannes and Divagations*, pages 45–46.
e tot lo sieu aver: (Pr) and all his possessions.

XIII

The philosophy of Kung (Confucius, 551-479 B.C.) gives the universe of the *Cantos* an order, made out of "strains and tensions," which is not imposed, but organic. XIII is drawn from the *Analects* and indirectly the *Ta Hsio* (Great Digest); the last three lines are by Pound himself.

Chinese themes do not recur until XLIX, but LII-LXI, LXXXV, XCVIII and XCIX deal almost exclusively with the Confucian tradition, from its gestation, long before the birth of Confucius, to the neo-Confucianism of the 18th century Emperor Yong Ching. From *The Pisan Cantos* onwards, the Chinese material is closely woven into the texture of the poem—without the limpidity of XIII, this integration could not have been achieved.

The best way to understand the Confucian elements in the *Cantos* is to read Pound's translations, *The Unwobbling Pivot, The Great Digest, The Analects* and *The Classic Anthology defined by Confucius* (The Odes).

Pound believed that a just world order could only be built on the principles of the *Ta Hsio*. I quote a salient paragraph from his version of this as it illumines XIII, and also Pound's intentions in writing the *Cantos:*

> The men of old wanting to clarify and diffuse throughout the empire that light which comes from looking straight into the heart and then acting, first set up good government in their own states; wanting good government in their states, they first established order in their own families; wanting order in the home, they first disciplined themselves; desiring self-discipline, they rectified their hearts; and wanting to rectify their hearts, they sought precise verbal definitions of their inarticulate thoughts [the tones given off by the heart]; wishing to attain precise verbal definitions, they set to extend their knowledge to the utmost. This completion of knowledge is rooted in sorting things into organic categories.
>
> (*Confucius*, pages 29–31)

Canto XIII expresses Pound's innate tolerance and *humanitas* —a quality which the rage and fanaticism of some of his writing can never wipe out.

XIV-XV

Cantos XIV-XV anticipate the usury canto, XLV , and are an unambiguous attack on the false values the *Cantos* was written to combat. Pound provides his own commentary (see Item J, page xviii).

Glossary

61: **Io venni in luogo...muto:** (I) I came into a place of all light silent (Dante, *Inferno*, V, 28).

62: **sadic mothers...:** Compare, "It hath brought palsey to bed..." (XLV, 230).
 EIKΩN ΓΗΣ: *EIKON GES*, image of earth.

63: **pets-de-loup:** (F) academics (literally: wolf-farts).
 Invidia: (L) Envy.

64: **laudatores temporis acti:** (L) praisers of past days (Horace, *Ars Poetica*, V, 173).

65: **et nulla fidentia inter eos:** (L) and no confidence among them.
 bolge: (I) infernal circle (from Dante).

66: **Andiamo:** (I) Let's go!
 Plotinus: (A.D. 205-269), Neo-Platonic philosopher of light, author of the *Enneads*. His work is related to that of Iamblichus—he is the source for the phrase, "Iamblichus' light..." (V, 17) and is often quoted in the late cantos (XCVIII, XCIX, C etc.).
 "Whether in Naishapur or Babylon": FitzGerald, *Rubáiyat of Omar Khayyám*, VIII.

67: **'Ηέλιον τ' 'Ηέλιον:** *Helion t' helion*, the Sun, the Sun. The first of many invocations of the Sun God. Compare XCVI (663) and CXIII (790), "Out of dark, thou, Father Helios, leadest". The *Cantos* is, in a sense, an expression of this theme.

XVI

Pound wakes to a Purgatorial landscape—a Dantescan passage, the images clear-cut: "the stiff herbage/the dry nobbled path" (69). Then, via Lake Nemi and Virgil's Golden Bough (*Aeneid*, VI, 136 ff.), he journeys into the earth, to Elysium, the land of the blessed dead, where he encounters founders of cities, Sigismundo and his younger brother Novello. But the serenity does not endure—Pound sleeps on the grass and hears voices telling of wars.

The rest of XVI is mainly concerned with the horror and waste of the First World War. "War is the highest form of sabotage, the most atrocious form of sabotage," Pound was to write in 1944. After the 1914-1918 war , a quixotic attempt to prevent another by seeking to understand and publish the common causes underlying all wars, became the central passion of Pound's life and work. XVI closes with the Russian Revolution.

Glossary

68: **Peire Cardinal:** 13th century troubadour. "Peire Cardinal is extremely lucid on the imbecility of belligerents and the makers of wars" (*The Spirit of Romance*, page 48).
Il Fiorentino: (I) The Florentine (Dante).
crimen est actio: (L) judgement is action.

69: **Palux Laerna:** (L) the marsh of Lerna where Herakles killed the Hydra.
aqua morta: (L) dead water.
The grey stone posts: see IV (16).
patet terra: (L) the earth opens.

70: **Galliffet:** French army commander who led the charge of the Chasseurs d'Afrique at Sedan in the war of 1870.

72-74: **Et ma foi, ... soit bien carré, exact:** (F) And really, you know all the strong men [with a pun on nervous ones]. No,/there is a limit; animals, the animals are not/made for that, a horse is of little importance. Men aged 34 on all fours/who cried "Mummy." But the tough ones/at the end, there at Verdun, there were only those big boys/and they saw extremely clearly./What are they worth, the generals, the lieutenants,/ they weigh a centigramme,/they are nothing but wood,/Our captain, all closed in on himself like/the old technocrat he was [this is similar to the way Iago taunts Cassio in *Othello* as being an "Arithmetician," i.e., an officer who knows all about the strategy of war, but nothing of its reality], but he's a block-head. There, you know/all, all functions, and the thieves, all the vices,/But the vultures,/there were three in our company, all killed./They went out to plunder a corpse, for nothing,/ they would have gone out for nothing but that./And the Jerries, you can say anything you want,/militarism, etc./All that, but, BUT,/the Frenchman, he fights when he has eaten./But those poor chaps/in the end attacked each other so they could eat,/without orders, savage beasts, they were taken prisoner; those who could speak French said, "Why? We attacked so that we could eat."/It's the fat, the fat/their trains ran at six kilometres an hour/and they creaked, they grated, one could hear them five kilometres away./(That's what finished the war.)/The official list of dead: 5 million./He tells you, well, all stank of oil./But no! I yelled at him./I said to him: You're an idiot! You missed the war./Oh yes! all the men of taste, I agree,/all of them in the rear/But a chap like you!/He's a man, a type like that!/What he could have made!/He was in a factory./What, burying squad, ditch diggers, with their heads/behind, who looked like this,/they risked their lives for a lump of dirt,/Must be nice and square, just right ... [This passage should be read in conjunction with section IV of *Hugh Selwyn Mauberly*, "These fought in any case, ... "].

75: **Pojalouista:** (R) If you please.

23

XVII

Cantos I-XVI, originally published as a group, cover a time span from Homer to the Russian Revolution. Canto I's closing phrase, "So that:" (5) is here taken up to open XVII, which celebrates an earthly paradise, and, like II, Dionysus, "So that the vines burst from my fingers." The place is Venice, but transfigured, and, as in III, it is seen in connection with "the original world of the gods."

Glossary

76:   **ZAGREUS:** Dionysus.
     IO: (Gk) Hail.
     Nerea: from the Greek, Nereid; sea nymph, daughter of Nereus.
77:   **Memnons:** Memnon, son of Tithonus and Eos (the dawn).
78:   **Borso, Carmagnola:** see glossary to XI (42; 43; 46).
     i vitrei: (I) the glass-makers.
     sistrum: rattle used in the worship of Isis.
     Aletha: sea deity, probably Pound's invention.
     Koré: Persephone. This relates XVII to I, where she first occurs. XVII is, in part, another journey to the underworld, this time to the land of the blessed dead. "The bright meadow" is the Elysian fields. The Persephone myth, Dionysus, and the rites of Eleusis are at the centre of the cosmos of the *Cantos:* XXI (100); XXXIX, XLV, XLVII; LXXIX; LXXXII; XC and CVI. Sir Paul Harvey's *Oxford Companion to Classical Literature* is helpful here:

> ...the 'Eleusinian Mysteries'... were celebrated at Eleusis in Attica in honour of Demeter and Persephone, with whom was soon associated Dionysus, worshipped under the name of Iacchos [LXXXIX, 490-91]. They arose from an agrarian festival...and appear to have been originally a feast of purification and fertility having reference to the Autumn sowing of the corn. With this came to be connected the ideas of the gods of the lower world, the descent into Hades, and the future life. The mysteries culminated in a rite carried out in a darkened hall, where the worshippers were shown visions in flashes of light. The nature of these visions is not known. They were probably mythological scenes with some bearing on the doctrine of life after death. [Page 283]

"The truth having been at Eleusis? and a modern Eleusis being possible in the wilds of a man's mind only?" (*Guide to Kulchur,* page 294).

XVIII-XIX

Fraud is the binding theme of these two cantos, and related to this, the economic causes of war: "War, one war after another,/Men start 'em who couldn't put up a good hen-roost" (83). The contrast with the serenity and stillness of XVII could not be more sharp.

Canto XVIII opens with the beginnings of paper money. The source is *The Travels of Marco Polo* (Vol. I) where Polo describes how Kublai Khan issued and controlled his currency: "The Emperor's Mint is in this same city of Cambalac [Peking], and the way it is wrought is such that you might say he hath the Secret of Alchemy in perfection, and you would be right!" Pound commented: "What we see on closer examination of the text is that Polo regarded the issue of paper money as a sort of clever hoax, backed up by tyrannical power. The real tyranny resided, of course, in the Khan's control of credit. The parallels are fairly obvious." (*Selected Prose*, pages 174–76; *204–5*.)

The control and issue of money is a major theme in the *Cantos*. It is introduced here for the first time; at this stage Pound is groping to understand the subject. He was to write later: "Sovereignty inheres in the power to issue money, or to distribute the power to buy (credit or money) whether you have the right to do so or not" (*Selected Prose*, page 325: *355*).

Related to this was Pound's lifelong attempt to discover the true causes of war. "Bellum cano perenne.... [I sing perennial war]...between the usurer and any man who/wants to do a good job" (LXXXVI-LXXXVII, 568-69). Much of XVIII deals with the machinations of the munitions manufacturers and sellers who are presented as one of the hidden makers of wars. This subject receives more detailed treatment in XXXVIII.

Canto XIX is a collection of anecdotes. Continuing the theme of fraud, it opens with the story of how a big company sabotaged a new invention by paying the inventor half a million dollars to keep it quiet, which shows how monopoly capitalism can destroy man's creative intelligence.

Most of XIX belongs to the "casual," but certain phrases become important repeats later, in particular the words of Arthur Griffiths (the leader of Irish Sinn Fein): "Can't move 'em with a cold thing, like economics" (85), which recurs in LXXVIII (481) and XCVII (678), and Lincoln Steffens's remark about revolutionaries (86) is repeated with tragic force on the last page of *The Pisan Cantos* (540).

Glossary

80: **Kublai:** Kublai Khan (1214-1294) became Emperor of the Mongols in 1260 and of all China in 1280.
hyght: (ME) is called.
There was a boy in Constantinople: Sir Basil Zaharoff (whom Pound renames Sir Zenos Metevsky) (1849?-1933), munitions magnate. Started selling arms *c.* 1876 for Nordenfeldt & Co., joining later with Hiram Maxim (probably the *Biers* referred to in XVIII), and both joined Vickers in 1913. Zaharoff also had interests in oil, international banks and newspapers.
83: **King Menelik:** (1844-1913), Emperor of Ethiopia 1889-1913.

XX

After two cantos which deal with "the casual," XX concerns "the permanent." Its chief constituents are Provence, Renaissance Italy, and the Lotus Eaters of the *Odyssey*.

The tone of the first two pages is fresh and spring-like. In the opening eight lines, Pound puts together luminous words about love, from Latin, Greek Provençal, and Italian—a good example of how his subtle ear can make a rhythmic unity out of phrases from different languages.

Then, in an autobiographical passage, Pound visits the scholar, Emile Lévy, who was compiling a Provençal dictionary, to consult him about a phrase by Arnaut Daniel whose meaning had been puzzling him. This leads to an evocation of Provence as an earthly paradise. But this beauty is shattered by an abrupt switch to the confused and tortured state of mind of Niccolo d'Este, after he has executed his wife Parasina and his natural son, Ugo, having discovered they were lovers. This event will be treated more realistically in XXIV (112). (In rapid changes of tone, Pound is more akin to Villon than any other poet.) Pound provided a commentary on this section, and the rest of XX, in a letter to his father (1927):

> Nicolo d'Este in sort of delirium after execution of Parasina and Ugo...
> '"And the Marchese
> was nearly off his head
> after it all."'
> Various things keep cropping up in the poem. The original world of the gods; the Trojan War, Helen on the wall of Troy with the old men fed up with the whole show and suggesting she be sent back to Greece.
> Rome founded by survivors of Troy. Here ref. to legendary founding of Este (condit [founded] Atesten, Este).
> Then in the delirium, Nicolo remembers or thinks he is watching the death of Roland. Elvira on wall of Toro (subject rhyme with Helen on Wall)...
> The whole reminiscence jumbled or 'candied' in Nicolo's delirium. Take that as a sort of bounding surface from which one gives the main subject of the Canto, the lotophagoi: lotus eaters, or respectable dope smokers; and general paradiso. You have had a hell in Canti XIV, XV; purgatorio in XVI etc.
> The 'nel fuoco' is from St. Francis' 'cantico': "My new spouse placeth me in the flame of love." Then the remarks of the opium smoker about the men who sailed under Ulysses.
> 'Voce profondo': with deep voice.
> And then resumé of the Odyssey, or rather of the main parts of Ulysses' voyage up to the death of all his crew.
> For Elpenor, vide Canto I.
> Ear wax, ears plugged so they couldn't hear the sirens.
> (*Selected Letters,* pages 210–211)

A moving section of XX, different from the way Homer treats the subject, is the chorus of Odysseus's companions: "Feared neither death nor pain for this beauty..." (93-94) which foreshadows both the words of tovarisch (the exploited common man) in XXVII (132) and the opening line of the *Pisan Cantos:* "The enormous tragedy of the dream in the peasant's bent shoulders" (425).

As Louis Zukofsky said, "The movement of the *Cantos* is that of fire and wind." XX, one of the most rhythmically haunting, concerns "people dominated by emotion" and defines states of dream and delirium.

Glossary

89: **quasi tinnula:** (L) as if ringing. An adaptation of Catullus's *Epithalamium* (LXI).

Ligur' aoide: (Gk) Pound, in the letter quoted above, translates this "keen, or sharp singing (sirens), song with an edge on it" (*Odyssey*, XII, 183).

Si no'us ... val: (Pr) Pound translates these lines, by Bernart de Ventadour, in *Rock-Drill:* "And if I see her not,/no sight is worth the beauty of my thought." XCII (619) and XCV (645).

viel: (Pr) a lute-like instrument.

s'adora: (I) She is worshipped. Cavalcanti, Sonnet XXXV, "My lady's face is it they worship there" (*Translations*, page 95).

Possum ego ... tuae: (L) Can I not remember your nature! (Propertius, II, xx, 28).

Qui son ... Ovidio: (I) Here are Propertius and Ovid.

Arnaut's, settant'uno .... Ambrosiana: (I) a catalogue number in the Ambrosian Library (Milan) which locates the ms. of the Daniel poem, in which the word *noigandres* occurs, which prompted Pound to consult Lévy.

noigandres: (Pr) from *Er vei Vermeills vertz, blaus, blancs, gruocs;* the last line of the first strophe ends: *E jois le grans, e l'olors d'enoi gandres,* which probably means: "the seed of her love is joy, and her perfume wards off pain or boredom." It seems that Pound adopted Lévy's reading of *d'enoi gandres* (a description of love) as "a warder-off of pain or boredom."

90: **Agostino:** A. di Duccio (?1418-1481), sculptor who did the bas-reliefs in Sigismundo's Tempio.

Jacopo: J. Sallaio (1422-1493), Florentine painter.

Boccata: Giovanni B. (?1435-?1480), Umbrian painter.

Sandro: S. Botticelli (1444-1510), Florentine painter.

e l'olors: (Pr) and the scent.

remir: (Pr) I gaze. For a note on what the use of Daniel's word is intended to convey, see glossary to VII (26).

91: **"Peace! keep the peace, Borso":** Borso was the third son of Niccolo d'Este, ruler of Ferrara (1384-1441). Ferrara, a small city state, surrounded by Mantua, Padua, Verona and Bologna, with Venice and Milan also nearby, was not in a good position to get involved in a war—hence Niccolo's advice to his son, which Pound repeats at the end of XX (95) and the opening of XXI. XXIV deals in greater detail with the Este family.

Ganelon: one of the 12 peers in *The Song of Roland;* prompted by jealousy, he betrayed Roland's rear-guard forces to the Moslems.

Tan mare fustes: "... Roland's remark to moor who comes up to finish him off, ... he smashes the moor over the head with his horn (*olifans:* elephant: olifant tusk) and then dies grumbling because he has damaged the ornaments on the horn and broken it. *Tan mare fustes:* colloquial: you came at a bad moment. Current cabaret song now: *J'en ai marre:* I'm fed up." (*Selected Letters*, page 210.)

27

Toro, las almenas: (S) the battlements of Toro, a town in Zamora province, N.W. Spain. For this and references to *Elvira, Sancho, Alfonso* and *Ancures*, see Lope de Vega's play, *Las Almenas de Toro*, and Pound's comments on it in *The Spirit of Romance* (pages 191–93).

Epi purgo: (Gk) on the wall (*Iliad*, III, 153). Refers back to II (6).

peur de la hasle: (OF) fear of sunburn.

telo regido: (L) with rigid javelin. A bawdy pun.

Neestho: (Gk) Let her go back (*Iliad*, III, 159). See II (6).

92:    **HO BIOS:** (Gk) Life.

cosi Elena vedi: (I) As Pound explained to his father: "thus I saw Helen, misquote of Dante." See *Inferno*, V, 64 where Virgil names the carnal sinners—the movement of XX has affinity with *Inferno*, V.

olibanum: (L) frankincense.

Aeolus: lord of the winds (*Odyssey*, X and *Aeneid*, I).

styrax: (L) resin or gum.

spilla: (I) pin or brooch.

94:    **Circe Titania:** Circe, daughter of the sun. See Ovid, *Metamorphoses*, XIV, 382, 438, and Shakespeare's *Midsummer Night's Dream*.

neson amumona: (Gk) "narrow island: bullfield where Apollo's cattle were kept" (*Selected Letters*, page 210).

Salustio / And Ixotta: Sigismundo's son and wife.

Ac ferae familiares: (L) and tamed beasts.

Somnus: Roman god of sleep—it's fitting he should be evoked in this canto of dream and reverie.

95:    **chiostri:** (I) cloisters.

le donne e i cavalieri: (I) the ladies and the knights (Dante, *Inferno*, V, 71 and *Purgatorio*, XIV, 109).

Cramoisi: (F) crimson cloth.

diaspre: (I) jasper.

XXI

Canto XXI begins with details of the rise of the Medici family—in many ways the founders of modern banking—showing how, by control of credit, the Medici were able to force the governments of Venice and Naples to make peace with Florence. In contrast to the tyranny of Kublai (XIX), here the control of the money supply is in the hands of private individuals, not the state.

Pound's attitude to the Medici is not wholly hostile—he clearly admires Cosimo as a patron of learning who fostered the revival of the study of Greek. But the hidden, often irresponsible power of private bankers over governments, is to become a major theme, and Pound later became convinced that it is one of the causes of wars.

From the intrigues of the Medici and their opponents, XXI shifts to America: first, there is a line introducing Pound's grandfather, Thaddeus Colman Pound, who built a railway not for personal profit, an implied contrast to the Medici. He is to open XXII and will recur in XXVIII (138); LXXXVIII (581) and XCIX (699) etc. (For details, see *Selected Prose*, page 295:*325*.) Secondly, there is an extract from one of Thomas Jefferson's letters which introduces Jefferson as patron of the arts (a subject-rhyme with Sigismundo) and sets his frugal way of living against the Italian luxury which, in XXI, precedes and follows it. Not just the first eleven, but the first thirty cantos, are "a preparation of the palette"—the quotation from Jefferson introduces American history which plays an increasingly important part as the poem proceeds (XXXI-XXXIV, XXXVII, LXII-LXXI, LXXXVIII-LXXXIX).

The rest of XXI is in lyric form, and concerns "the permanent." It returns us to Venice, "the original world of the gods," and the myths of Persephone and the underworld.

Glossary

96: **"Keep on..."**: words of Giovanni de Medici to his son Cosimo. By developing their business interests the Medici increased their power, not by gaining political office. Subject-rhyme with Niccolo's advice to his son Borso (see glossary to XX).

di sugello: (I) with seal.

In carta di capretto: (I) on rich parchment.

97: **E difficile.... stato:** (I) It is difficult/In Florence it is difficult to live richly/Without status./"And not having status, Piccinino/Had to fear whoever had status."

affatigandose per suo piacer o non: (I) Pound translates this in VII: "So that he can work as he likes,/or waste his time as he likes" (29). Links Jefferson with Sigismundo.

98: **Placidia's:** tomb of Galla Placidia (*c*.388-450), Empress of the Western Roman Empire; buried in Ravenna. "Every self-respecting Ravennese.... receives spirit or breath of life, in the Mausoleum of Galla Placidia" (*Selected Prose*, page 292:*322*). It is one of the sacred places in the *Cantos*.

palazzo: the Palazzo Ducale, Venice. Its building is central to XXV (117).

nel tramonto: (I) in the sunset.

99: **Gignetei kalon:** (Gk) a beautiful thing is born.

Actium: site of the battle between Octavius and Anthony and Cleopatra.

Midas...Pan: the legendary king of Phrygia whose touch turned things to gold. Avarice destroys nature—the root of Pound's vision is memorably expressed by what the old leaf-sweeper says.

Isé...Inopos: see glossary to IV (15).

Phoibos: Apollo.

turris eburnea: (L) tower of ivory (from the *Litany of the Blessed Virgin*).

100: **Titania:** see glossary to XX (94).

Phaethusa: another daughter of the sun (*Odyssey*, XII, 132-33). She recurs XXV (118).

Dis: god of the underworld. "Dis spide hir: lovde hir: caught hir up" (*Metamorphoses*, V, 495). "Her" is Persephone.

XXII

Canto XXII opens with Pound's grandfather (already introduced in XXI) and contrasts him with a different kind of American railway builder: the capitalist who exploits nature for profit. "I have never believed that my grandfather put a bit of railway across Wisconsin simply or chiefly to make money..." (*Jefferson and/or Mussolini*, page 33). The rest of XXII presents "the casual," in a series of humorous anecdotes, including memories of Pound's visit to Gibraltar in 1908.

Glossary

101:   **C.H.:** Clifford Hugh Douglas (1879-1952), the founder of Social Credit. His ideas will be presented in XXXVIII (190). For his importance to Pound see *Selected Prose* (pages 177−182:*207−212*).

       Mr. Bukos: John Maynard Keynes (1883-1946), the English economist. Keynes *was* an "orthodox economist" in the 1920s, when this conversation took place. He said later, "I myself held with deep conviction for many years the theories which I now attack." He never accepted Douglas, but did write in 1936, "Major Douglas is entitled to claim, as against some of his orthodox adversaries, that he at least has not been wholly oblivious to the outstanding problem of our economic system" (*General Theory*, pages 370−71).

       H.C.L.: the high cost of living.

102:   **Standu nel...d'Adamo:** (I) Standing in the earthly paradise/Thinking how to make Adam's mate!!

       Come si fesse? E poi...volpe: How make?/And then he saw a vixen.

       e pensava.../Corre,...rabbia: and he thought...She runs, the vixen runs, Christ runs,...and he gave a leap, and caught the tail/of the vixen...and from this she was made,/and for this reason/woman is a fury,/A fury-and-a-rage.

103:   **Freer:** surname of Pound's great aunt who first took him to Europe (1906), in whose company he first met Yusuf, the Jewish tourist guide who remembers him (by his great aunt's name) and here takes him around Gibraltar.

       Gibel Tara: Gibraltar.

105:   **e faceva bisbiglio:** (I) and whispered, as in gossip.

XXIII

Canto XXIII presents science and myth as complementary aspects of the poem's voyage after knowledge. In concision and complexity of reference, it foreshadows the method of the late cantos. Among many themes woven together are: Odysseus's voyage to the underworld (here connected with the mythical journey of the sun after it has set, and to Dante's dark wood), Niccolo's delirium (XX, 90-91), and the world of the troubadours.

Glossary

107: **Et omniformis:** see glossary to V (17).

Gemisto: see glossary to VIII (31).

Peloponesus: south part of Greece where Gemisto lived. He urged the Emperor, Manuel II, to build a wall on the Isthmus of Corinth to shut out the Turks and Eastern Christianity.

Novvy: Malatesta Novello, younger brother of Sigismundo. He sent for Greek books for the library he founded in Cesena which were lost at sea.

Irol: French motor fuel.

Houille blanch/Auto-chenille: (F) water power/caterpillar tread vehicle.

Invention-d'entités... consister: (F) " 'Science does not consist in inventing a number of more or less abstract entities corresponding to the number of things you wish to find out', says a French commentator on Einstein" (*A.B.C. of Reading*, page 18).

J'ai obtenu... guérison: I got a burn... from which it took me six months to recover. Pierre Curie (1859-1906), the French chemist and physicist, is quoted as an example of courage in the pursuit of knowledge.

Tropismes: (F) responses to stimulus.

'Άλιος δ' 'Υπεριονίδας.... περάσας: *Alios d'Hyperionidas depas eskatebaine chryseon/Ophra di okeanoio perasas*, The sun, Hyperion's child, stepped down into his golden bowl and after crossing the stream of Ocean. (The source of this and the following Greek and Latin quotations is J. Schweighaeuser's bi-lingual [Greek and Latin] edition of Athenaeus which contains Stesichorus's fragment on the voyage of the sun. For an English translation, see Loeb *Lyra Graeca*, II.)

ima vada noctis obscurae: (L) the lowest depths of dark night.

"ηλιος, ἅλιος... μάταιος: *helios, alios, alios = mataios*, sun, of the sea, or fruitless = empty, vain.

alixantos, aliotrephès, eiskatebaine: (Gk) worn by the sea, sea-reared, he went down into.

108: **ποτι βένθεα.... κατάσκιον:** *poti benthea/nuktos eremnas,/poti matera, kouridian t'alochon/paidas te philous..... eba daphnaisi kataskion*, [and then, after crossing the stream of Ocean, he reached] the depth of black [and holy] night, and joined his mother, his faithful wife and dear children. [Meanwhile the son of Zeus] entered [on foot] the laurel-shaded [grove].

selv' oscura: (I) dark wood (Dante, *Inferno*, I, 2).

'Yperionides: (Gk) son of Hyperion: Helios.

Capriped: goat-footed, satyr.

As we lay there... arras: a return to the Niccolo d'Este delirium scene (XX, 90-91).

De Maensac...: This story first introduced in V (see *Literary Essays*, pages 94—108).

109: **Mount Ségur:** the stronghold of the Albigensians where the Catholics massacred them in 1244. Formerly the site of a temple of Apollo, it is a sacred place in the *Cantos*.

Simone: Simon de Montfort (1160-1218), leader of the crusade against the Albigensians 1209-1229.

they were sailing: Aeneas, son of Aphrodite and Anchises, en route to founding Rome after the sack of Troy.

Tethnéké: (Gk) He is dead.

King Otreus: When Aphrodite took human form to lie with Anchises, she told him that her father was King Otreus, in order to keep her identity secret. Anchises and Venus recur LXXVI (456-57).

and saw then.....: This vision of the birth of Venus is a recurrent image—it last occurs in XCI (611):
"Crystal waves weaving together toward the gt/healing."

XXIV

The Este family is now treated factually in contrast to the partly mythical treatment it received in XX and XXIII. The central episode is a journal of the voyage of Niccolo d'Este to the Holy Land in 1413—this parallels Odysseus's voyage in I and that of Hanno in XL. Niccolo's behaviour after the execution of his son Ugo is then presented and XXIV closes with references to the subsequent decadence of Ferrara.

Glossary

110: **mandates:** mandates of the Este family.
barbarisci: (I) wild horses.
un libro franxese...: (I) a French book called Tristan.
...verde colore predeletto: (I) green beloved colour.

111: **dove fu Elena rapta da Paris:** (I) where Helen was taken by Paris.
Ora vela, ora a remi,...vespero: (I) Now sailing, now rowing, until the hour of sunset. Compare Canto I.

112: **hic est medium mundi:** (L) here is the centre of the world.
Ego, scriptor cantilenae: (L) I, the writer of this canto.
Benche niuno cantasse: (I) although no one was singing.
Fa me hora...Ugo: (I) Now let my head be cut off/since you've so quickly beheaded my Ugo.
Rodendo con denti...in mani: (I) Chewing with his teeth a stick he had in his hands.
ter pacis Italiae auctor: (L) three times author of the Italian peace.

113: **E fu sepulto nudo:** (I) and was buried naked. The phrase is translated in LXXXII (526).

114: **Ferrara, paradiso...stomagose:** (I) Ferrara, heaven of tailors, "disgusting festival."
"Is it likely...my crib": The infant Mercury said this to Apollo after he had discovered Mercury had stolen his cattle (Homeric Hymn, IV, *To Hermes*).

Albert made me...tannery: Alberto d'Este, father of Niccolo, built the Schifanoia Palace in Ferrara, which contained the frescoes of Cosima Tura and Francesco del Cossa. Pound considered them to have an affinity with the *Cantos:* "The Schifanoia does give—there is an analogy there. That is to say, you've got the contemporary life, you've got the seasons, you've got the Zodiac and you have the *Triumphs* of Petrarch in different belts..." (Bridson, "A B.B.C. Interview with Ezra Pound.") After the decline of the Este family the Schifanoia Palace was used as a tobacco factory; the Italian verb *coniciare* means to tan hides, or to cure tobacco, hence the confusion of "tannery" in the text.

XXV

We return to Venice. (The last Venetian canto was XVII.) The first two and a half pages, and the last, are taken from decrees concerning the Palace of the Doges. At the centre is the building of the Palazzo Ducale; this leads into a lyric presenting the Roman poet Sulpicia's love for Cerinthus. Love is here seen as creator of form and radiance, anticipating *Rock-Drill* XC-XCV. Contrasted with this clarity are dead forms, "dead concepts," and vain dogmas, like the disputes about the Trinity which took place in Ferrara in 1438 (see XXVI). A vision of the birth of Venus recurs (similar to that in XXIII) but the tone shifts abruptly and the canto closes with an account of the corrupt behaviour of Titian.

Glossary

115: **In libro pactorum:** (L) in the book of the contracts.
et/quod publice innotescat: (L) and which may be published.
simul commorantes: (L) lingering together.

116: **Donna Sorantia Soranzo:** Exiled because her husband was leader of a plot against the government, she was only allowed to return to Venice to attend her sick father.

117: **Sulpicia:** (*c.*40 B.C.) poet whose work is included in Vol. III of the works of Tibullus. The lines Pound quotes are from an unknown author (perhaps Tibullus himself) who wrote in her name about her love for Cerinthus.
"Pone metum Cerinthe": (L) Put aside fear, Cerinthus.

118: **"deus nec.../dies sanctus:** nor does God harm lovers./This day a holy one for me.
Sero, sero...: (L) Too late, too late.
bolge: one of the ditches in the eighth circle of the *Inferno.*
Phaethusa: see glossary to XXI (100).
Phlegethon: river of fire in Hades. "...that hydrophobic river" (Beddoes).

119: **Napishtim:** Utnapishtim, Sumerian equivalent of Noah, is granted immortality by the gods after he survived the Flood (see *Epic of Gilgamesh*).
νους: *nous*, mind as the active principle in the universe.

XXVI

Like III, XXVI opens with a memory of Pound's stay in Venice in 1907-8. The rest of the canto consists mainly of annals of the city taken from different centuries. Most of the characters involved have already appeared in the poem.

The main events are: (1) The release of Matteo de Pasti (c.1470), Veronese sculptor and medalist, who had been sent by Sigismundo to make a portrait of the Turkish Emperor Mohammed II, and was arrested because he was suspected by the Venetians of being in league with the Turks. (2) The Venetians charge Nicolo Segundino to attempt to make peace between Pius II (Pio) and Sigismundo, a mission later accomplished by Bernard Justinian. (3) Details of early Doges, in particular a description of the festivities at the installation of Lorenzo Tiepolo (Doge 1268-1275). (4) The festivities at the marriage of Niccolo d'Este's son Leonello to Margherita Gonzaga, 25 April 1435. (5) The gathering of delegates to a Council of the Eastern and Western Churches convened by Pope Eugenius IV (see glossary to VIII-XI, 31). (6) The last 4 pages consist mainly of letters which are self-explanatory.

Glossary

121: **"Relaxetur!":** (L) Let him be released!
"caveat ire ad Turchum: (L) let him beware of going to the Turk.
124: **Te fili Dux...anulo:** (L) You, my son the Duke, and your successors with a golden ring.
Balista: (I) catapult.
Per animarla: (I) to animate him.
126: **Lorenzo de Medicis:** "Lorenzaccio" of V and VII.

XXVII

The first one and a half pages consist of fragments and anecdotes, chosen with satirical intent, illustrating aspects of the first quarter of the twentieth century. The courage of scientists and doctors risking their lives in the pursuit of knowledge, a theme introduced in XXIII, is set against the darkness and stupidity of Europe at this time.

The rhythm then suddenly comes alive with the co-operative energy that went into building the Cathedral at Ferrara and by implication all other cathedrals, "All rushed out and built the duomo" (130), and this leads, by contrast, to the blind chaos of the Russian Revolution and the suffering of the exploited common man (Tovarisch), from the myth of Cadmus to the present. He speaks, echoing the bones of Odysseus's companions (XX, 93-4), and the Graces bend over him in compassion.

Canto XXVII links back to the last page of XVI. As Kenner has pointed out, XVII-XXVII forms a sequence which is carefully matched with I-XVI; like the latter, "it begins (XVII) with Renaissance classicising and ends (XXVII) with the Russian Revolution."

Glossary

129: **Formando di ... persona:** (I) Forms a new person from desire. Cavalcanti, Ballata XII (*Translations,* page 125).

Et quant.... le reverra pas: (F) And as to the third/he has fallen into the/of his wife/and won't be seen again.

oth fugol ouitbaer: a misquotation of the Old English poem *The Wanderer* which was not misquoted in English editions of the *Cantos* until Faber started using the American text in 1975. The line should read: *Sumne fugel othbaer:* one a bird bore off.

130: **Sed et universus...:** (L) And the whole population of the church, too.

ciptadin: (I) citizen.

131: **Brumaire, Fructidor:** French revolutionary months (October 22– November 20 and August 18–September 16).

Petrograd: Leningrad, formerly St. Petersburg, was called Petrograd when the Russian Revolution broke out.

Tovarisch: (R) comrade.

And three forms...: the Xarites, or Graces. Attendant on Venus, they personify beauty and grace and were probably originally vegetation goddesses. This is partly how they are seen here.

132: **Cadmus:** founder of Thebes. A dragon guarding a spring killed his companions. He killed it and sowed its teeth. From them armed warriors sprang up who were set fighting each other until only five remained, the Sparti, ancestors of the noble families of Thebes. Cadmus was probably of Phoenician origin—hence his connection with "golden prows" here and in IV (13).

Eblis: see glossary to VI (22). Pound visited the castle where Alice of Montpellier was imprisoned, finding it in ruins.

XXVIII

This is the first canto to deal wholly with "the casual" since XXII. It is a string of mainly humorous anecdotes, in part illustrating the stupidity of the American abroad, bound together by the common theme of space and travellers.[1]

Glossary

133: **Boja d'un Dio:** hangman of a God (an oath in Romagnola dialect).

Aso iqua me: This is me here (Romagnola dialect).

137: **"Je suis ... le poids":** (F) I am stronger than/the Buddha/.... I am/ stronger than/Christ.... I would have/abolished/gravity!

"... sont ... KOH-lon-i-ale": (F) It's the old marines.

voce tinnula: see glossary to III (11).

139: **Sic loquitur eques:** (L) Thus speaks the knight.

---

[1]Pound used the words "Space (Travell.)" to define the theme of XXVIII—see note by Kenner in *Paideuma,* Vol. II No. 2.

XXIX

Canto XXIX concerns the metaphysics of love and sex, and the nature of woman. It closes with sunrise and a return to the paradisal landscape of XVII.

Glossary

141: **Pearl,...:** The lake is Garda. See an early poem, "The Flame," for the significance of the opening image: "Sapphire Benacus, in thy mists and thee/Nature herself's turned metaphysical..." (*Personae*, page 50).

Pernella...: Penelope Orsini, mistress of Aldobrando Orsini, Count of Pitigliano. His son, Nicolo, killed her and her son in 1465, when he discovered she had poisoned his younger brother hoping that her own son would inherit the rule of Pitigliano.

ainé...: (F) elder; **puiné:** younger.

Liberans et... liberatos: (L) And freeing from every chain those who have been liberated (from the Will of Cunizza). See commentary on VI.

142: **nimium amorata in eum:** (L) too much in love with him.

"The light of this star...": "perche mi vinsi il lume d'esta stella" (Dante, *Paradiso*, IX, 33).

And he looked from the planks...: planks to make coffins, lying "Before the residence of the funeral director."

Juventus: a personification of the spirit of youth.

143: **O-hon...vi'-a-ge:** (F) It's sometimes said in the village.

The cicadas continue uninterrupted: The old men's voices on the wall of Troy, echoing II (6), VII (24) and XX (91).

144: **Deh! nuvoletta...:** (I) Ah, little cloud.

Wein, Weib, TAN AOIDAN: (G & Gk) wine, women and song.

Our mulberry leaf, woman...: "She is the passive 'mulberry leaf' which the creative will transforms into the silk of art (TAN AOIDAN, song)" (Pearlman, *The Barb of Time*).

Ailas e que'm....vuelh: (Pr) Alas, what good are my eyes/For they see not what they wish (Sordello).

Nel ventre....mente mia: (I) Inside your womb or in my mind.

Faziamo...due: (I) Let's do it both together.

145: **She is submarine,...:** See *"Sub Mare"* (*Collected Shorter Poems*, page 82; *Personae*, page 69).

Arnaut: A. Daniel, the Provençal poet, here used as pseudonym for T. S. Eliot. The "wave pattern cut in the stone" of the castle of Excideuil where Eliot spoke to Pound of his fear of the life after death, recurs in LXXX (510), CVII (758) and CV (717).

nondum orto jubare: (L) before sunrise.

Phoibos: Apollo.

XXX

The "Compleynt" of Artemis expresses her "eternal state of mind" with Chaucerian clarity. Forming a coda to the first thirty cantos, it anticipates the canto against usury (XLV, 229).

Artemis's statement of values is set against unnatural events: the story of Ignez da Castro (see glossary on III) and the mercenary marriage of Lucretia Borgia.

The Borgia subject is continued with a letter from the printer Soncinus, concerning an edition of Petrarch's *Rime*, which he produced at Fano for Cesare Borgia in 1503.

Canto XXX closes with the death of the Borgia Pope Alexander VI in the same year; from now on, the Italian Renaissance (central to I-XXX) is no longer such a major theme in the *Cantos*.

Glossary

147: **Paphos:** shrine of Aphrodite in Cyprus. Leaving her lover Mars, she returns out of pity to her lame husband, Hephaestos (Vulcan), the smith of the gods. Compare XLV: "It hath brought palsey to bed, lyeth/between the young bride and her bridegroom/CONTRA NATURAM" (230).

148: **Came Madame 'YΛH:** Pound translates 'YΛH, (*ULE*) as "uncut forest, and the stuff of which a thing is made, matter as a principle of being" (*Selected Prose*, page 97:*83*). The word is used in XXX ironically for "matter" against spirit, "things grown awry," as Madame 'YΛH is Lucretia Borgia, daughter of Pope Alessandro. At the instigation of his son, Cesare, the Pope arranged for her marriage with Alfonso d'Este (grandson of Nicolo). Because of her bad reputation, the Este family said their "Honour" demanded a large dowry, to be paid in cash before the ceremony. Alfonso visited his future wife secretly during her journey to Ferrara and was reputed to have spoken to no one either coming or going.

Fano Caesaris: the Fano of Caesar. See glossary to XI (50).

Cantos XXXI–XLI

XXXI-XXXIV

These four cantos, presenting the beginnings of U.S. civilization, mark a major shift in the poem's emphasis. The jump from the decline of the Renaissance (XXX) to the New World is refreshing. That Pound's epic is as American as Homer's was Greek is here manifest for the first time.

Cantos XXXI-XXXII are composed of extracts from the letters of Thomas Jefferson and John Adams, the second and third Presidents of the U.S.A. The latter will have ten cantos devoted to him (LXII-LXXI). The intelligence, energy and curiosity of these two men, in contrast to the stupidity and decadence of the European rulers of their time, are conveyed vividly by the same methods Pound used to present the life and times of Sigismundo. They had a unique opportunity to create a new civilization and they took it. The clearest commentary on this section is Pound's essay, "The Adams-Jefferson Letters as a Shrine and a Monument," where he says: "From 1760 to 1826 two civilised men lived and to a considerable extent reigned in America. They did not feel themselves isolated phenomena." (*Selected Prose*, page 117:*147*.)

Canto XXXIII opens with a letter from John Adams against all forms of absolute power, which expresses the political values Pound believed in. The *Cantos* record the fight to preserve the individual human spirit, and "to keep the value of a local and particular character" against all forms of oppression and blurring of distinctions throughout history. They deal with the perennial struggle of man's creative intelligence against the exploiters of "the abundance of nature" (LII, 257). These themes, which become clearer as the poem proceeds, are at the core of the Adams and Jefferson cantos. Pound's espousal of Mussolini's Fascist programme seemed to him compatible with the ideas of the American Founding Fathers; those who label Pound's political thought as "fascist" in the sense in which the word is popularly used or misused, have failed to see the drive of his work entirely.

The rest of XXXIII juxtaposes fragments illustrative of the evils of capitalism, drawn, in part, from Marx, and British factory inspectors' reports concerning child labour in the 19th century; the canto closes with more recent quotations showing the corruption of the Federal Reserve banking system.

Canto XXXIV concludes this first sequence of American cantos with extracts from the *Diary of John Quincy Adams 1794-1845*. He was the son of John Adams and President from 1825 to 1829. Out of the mass of detail, certain things emerge clearly: the flaws in the American system and early signs of decay; the evils of slavery, and related to this, the fraud and barbarity which the state of Georgia used to deprive the Indians of their land.

Glossary

153: **Tempus ... tacendi:** (L) A time to speak, a time to be silent. Sigismundo inscribed this motto on the tomb of his wife, Isotta; a reversal of the Vulgate's *Tempus tacendi, et tempus loquendi* (Ecclesiastes III:7), quoted in LXXIV, 429. In XXXI it establishes a link between these four Jefferson/Adams cantos and the four devoted to Sigismundo.

157: **et des dettes.... moyens:** (F) and of the debts of the said Echelles.../ ... in the principal decrees of the Council, December, '66/weapons and other implements which can only be for/the government's account... M. Saint-Libin/well-versed in the languages of the country, known by the Nabobs..../ ... to excite him, and to follow hot upon the enemy, the English/little delicate about the means....

159: **a guisa de leon ... posa:** (I) like a lion ... when he rests (Dante, *Purgatorio*, VI, 66, describing Sordello who shows Dante and Virgil the vale of negligent princes—hence his relevance here to Jefferson's contempt for contemporary kings and queens). The description of Sordello is intended also to apply to Jefferson.

161: **AGATHOS:** (Gk) good.
kalos k'àgathos: (Gk) beautiful and well-born. See Marx, *Das Kapital*, 259-260, where he says that the owner of the means of production lives off surplus labour no matter what he is.
Literae nihil sanantes: (L) Literature curing nothing. From John Adams's letter to Jefferson, June 28, 1812. This phrase recurs with tragic force in CXVI (795).

169: **but I perceived ... planted:** compare XCIX, "watched things grow with affection" (695).

171: 信 "Fidelity to the given word. The man here standing by his word" (*Confucius*, page 22).
Constans .... Tenacem: (L) Constant in purpose .../Just and enduring (Horace, *Odes*, III, 3). In 1844 J. Q. Adams was presented with an ivory cane bearing this inscription. *Constans proposito* was quoted previously IX (41)—another link with Sigismundo.

XXXV

From the New World we shift to 20th century European decadence. The satire, directed against Viennese Jewish society, is not narrowly racialist—exceptions are pointed, as for example, "the young lady..." who "seemed to have been able to mobilize..." (173). Set against these anecdotes are moves towards creating a just bank to aid production in the cloth trade in North Italy. This anticipates the central episode of XLII-LI, the founding of the Monte dei Paschi in Siena.

Glossary

172: **Mitteleuropa:** (G) Central Europe.
175: **inficit umbras:** (L) tinges with a darker shade (Ovid, *Metamorphoses*, X, 596).
   una grida: (I) a proclamation.
   When the stars...: small flowers of olive tree which drop in midsummer. Recurs XLVII (237).
   ύλη: see glossary to XXX (148).
   omnes de...ultramarinis: (L) from all overseas regions.
176: **Mocenigo:** Doge of Venice 1414-23.

XXXVI

This is a radiant, still centre, its rays extending to later, paradisal sections.
   Apart from 32 lines at the end, it is a translation of Cavalcanti's canzone *Donna mi priegha*, which attempts to define a mystery: the origin and nature of love.
   Pound's own writings on Cavalcanti provide a lucid commentary: "It is only when the emotions illumine the perceptive powers that we see the reality" (*Translations*, page 24). "Guido thought in accurate terms;...the phrase corresponds to definite sensations undergone" (*Literary Essays*, page 162). The essay just quoted illumines not only XXXVI, but later cantos, particularly XC-XCV.

Glossary

177: **affect:** emotion or passion.
   virtu: "the potency, the efficient property of a substance or person" (*Translations*, page 18).
   Where memory liveth: the original, *dove sta memora*, is quoted LXIII (353) and LXXVI (452 and 457).
   diafan: translucent form. Pound uses Cavalcanti's word, which the latter may have drawn from Bishop Grosseteste's treatise, *De Luce*. A phrase from this, *Per plura diafana* (through many translucent forms), recurs in the late cantos, from Pisa onwards, when the poem is often pervaded by paradisal light.
178: **Deeming intention:** see Richard of St. Victor: "*Nisi bona intentio, mens moritur.* Without good intention the mind dies." (*Selected Prose*, page 73:71.)
   forméd trace: see LXXVI, "nothing matters...trace in the mind" (457).
   divided from all falsity: see LXXX, "'With us there is no deceit'" (500). The moon nymph says this to the fisherman in the Noh play, *Hagoromo* (*Translations*, 312). Pound intended to connect Cavalcanti's

line with the Noh play—he placed the word *hagoromo* in the margin of the earlier English edition.

179: **"Called thrones...topaze":** based, in part, on the final words of Cunizza (*Paradiso,* IX, 61), "*voi dicete Troni,*" and other passages in the *Paradiso.* The Thrones are the third of the angelic orders: spirits of divine judgement. A different version of the line occurs LXXXVIII (581). **Balascio:** ruby (*Paradiso,* IX, 69). The whole line foreshadows Pound's paradise and in particular *Thrones,* XCVI-CIX.
Eriugina: Johannes Scotus (*c.*800-877), Irish philosopher and theologian. Part of his thought stems from Greek sources and Neo-Platonic imagery of light. He appears in the *Cantos* as part of a persistent tradition of religious intelligence which was at times, but not always, opposed to the dogmas of the Church, and whose roots, tentatively, can be traced to the Eleusinian mysteries. Much of Pound's paradise is made from inklings of this tradition. Pope Honorius III ordered Erigena's work to be burnt in 1225 as he may have suspected that it was influencing the Albigensians. Pound thought the latter were not Manicheans, but possibly part of this hidden tradition. (See XXIII, etc.)
"Authority comes...way on": "*Auctoritas ex vera ratione processit, ratio vero nequaquam ex auctoritate*" (Erigena, *De Divisione Naturae*). This work is quoted again in *The Pisan Cantos: "Omnia quae sunt, lumina sunt":* "All things that are lights," LXXIV (429) and LXXXIII (528). Erigena is often mentioned in the later cantos.

180: **Sacrum, sacrum...coitu:** (L) Sacred, sacred, the illumination of coitus. "Paganism included a certain attitude toward; a certain understanding of, coitus, which is the mysterium" (*Selected Prose,* page 70). This line anticipates XXXIX and XLVII, which are both concerned with "in-luminatio coitu."
Lo Sordels...Mantovana: see glossary to II.
Goito: castle where Sordello was born.
Five castles...: Sordello was given these, and a dye-works, as a reward for his services as a soldier.
Dilectis...Thetis: (L) Most beloved and familiar soldier...the fort of Monte Odorisio/Monte San Silvestro with Pagliete and Pila.../In the region of Thetis.
pratis nemoribus pascuis: (L) meadows, woodlands, pastures.
Quan ben...ric pensamen: (Pr) When I think deep in my rich thought (Sordello).

XXXVII

"The intensely Jeffersonian drive of Van Buren" (*Jefferson and/or Mussolini,* page 14).

Canto XXXVII continues the presentation of American history started in

XXXI-XXXIV. Its main source is *The Autobiography of Martin Van Buren* (see Bibliography).

Van Buren (1782-1862) was eighth President of the U.S.A. (1837-41). He was a democrat and active campaigner against slavery and for liberty of the working class. Pound summarised the period covered by this canto: "1830-40—The war of the people against the Bank, won by the people under the leadership of Jackson and Van Buren. The most interesting decade in American history: a decade that has practically disappeared from the school books." (*Selected Prose*, page 279:*309*.)

Van Buren wanted to set up an "independent treasury" freeing the government from involvement in the credit system of banks and businesses. The aim was to have the state free of debt, and to maintain the rights of the elected government over the money supply, as they are set down in the Constitution: "The Congress shall have power: to coin money, regulate the value thereof and of foreign coin and to fix the standards of weights and measures." Jackson and Van Buren successfully prevented the renewal of the Charter of the Bank of the U.S.A. because they wished America to avoid the situation of England where the private Bank of England had gained control of the nation's credit.

Banks, good and bad, will be central to XLII-LI. XXXVII gives the first detailed treatment of the struggle between governments and private banks—a subject at the root of many of the history cantos. The Jackson/Van Buren period is presented again in LXXXVIII-LXXXIX, through the speeches and writings of Thomas Hart Benton.

Glossary

185: **Villa Falangola:** where Van Buren lived in Sorrento after his retirement, and where his *Autobiography* was written.

in the mirror of memory: This phrase recurs in introducing John Adams's memoirs, LXX (410).

186: **HIC/JACET/FISCI LIBERATOR:** (L) Here lies the liberator of the treasury. A phrase probably invented by Pound.

XXXVIII

The theme of XXXVIII is the hidden causes of war. At its centre is a summary of C.H. Douglas's diagnosis of what is wrong with the capitalist financial system.

Glossary

187: **il duol...moneta:** (I) the suffering which he is bringing on the Seine by debasing the coinage. Philip the Fair debased the coinage to one-third its value to finance his Flemish wars.

Metevsky: see glossary to XVIII (80).

189: **Der im Baluba...hat:** (G) This sentence, translated in the next line, is quoted from Leo Frobenius (1873-1938), the German anthropologist. He travelled extensively in Africa and is the source for most of the African elements in the *Cantos*. "....Frazer worked largely from documents. Frob. went to *things*, memories still in the spoken tradition, etc." (*Selected Letters*, page 336.) In the incident referred to here, tribesmen in Biembe believe that Frobenius has raised a tempest and consequently cease to be hostile to him (*Erlebte Erdteile*, V, pages 49-53). *Baluba* is Pound's error for *Biembe*.

190:    **A factory/has another aspect....prices at large:** These lines are a paraphrase of C.H. Douglas's "A + B Theorum" which is one of the main ideas of Social Credit:

> Payments may be divided into two groups: Group A—All payments made to individuals (wages, salaries and dividends). Group B—All payments made to other organizations (raw materials, bank charges, and other external costs). Now the rate of flow of purchasing power to individuals is represented by A, but since all payments go into prices the rate of flow of prices cannot be less than A + B. The product of any factory may be considered as something which the public ought to be able to buy, although in many cases it is an intermediate product of no use to individuals, but only to subsequent manufacture; but since A will not purchase A + B, a proportion of the product at least equivalent to B must be distributed by some form of purchasing power which is not comprised in the descriptions grouped under A. It will be necessary at a later stage to show that this additional purchasing power is provided by loans credits (bank overdrafts) or export credit. (*Credit, Power and Democracy*, page 22.)

Douglas believed that "Systems were made for men, not men for systems..." (*Economic Democracy*, page 18) and that the capitalist financial system was based on the fundamental error of treating money as a commodity. He also believed, like Pound, that "for the purpose of good government" money "is a ticket for the orderly distribution of WHAT IS AVAILABLE...it is NOT in itself abundance" (*Selected Prose*, page 265:*295*). Douglas further proposed that a National Dividend be distributed to all citizens from the surplus wealth of a nation, "so that while there is real *wealth* to be distributed, nobody shall lack for want of money with which to buy" (*The Monopoly of Credit*, page 99).

192:    **"faire passer...la nation":** (F) "to put these matters/before those of the nation."

XXXIX

The first part concerns Circe and is based on Book X of the *Odyssey*. Exploring the island of Aeaea, Odysseus's men come upon her "house of smooth stone," surrounded by fawning animals she has bewitched with "evil drugs." She invites the men in, feeding them with drugged honey, barley, cheese and wine which turns them into pigs. Odysseus later escapes this fate, as Hermes has given him the herb, Moly, which prevents the drugs from acting.

The wilderness survives. The "eternal elements," the seasons, and Odysseus's long stay with Circe before he departs on his voyage to meet the dead, are powerfully evoked: "Spring overborne into summer/late spring in the leafy autumn" (193).

Circe's words to Odysseus, saying that he must journey to the Underworld, are quoted directly in Greek (194), recalling the voyage in I, and anticipating XLVII. XXXIX closes with a ritual dance to spring and fertility.

"*Inluminatio coitu*" (XXXVI, 180)—XXXIX expresses the perennial power and mystery of sex and nature. It is one of the very few great erotic poems in English.

Glossary

193:    **kaka pharmak edōken:** she had given them evil drugs (*Odyssey*, X, 213).

      lukoi oresteroi ede leontes: mountain wolves and lions (*Odyssey*, X, 212).

      born to Helios...Pasiphae: Circe was the daughter of Perse and Helios, the sun god. Her twin sister was Pasiphae, the Queen of Crete.

      Venter venustus...cultrix: beautiful belly, priestess of the cunt (Pound's Latin).

      ver novum: (L) new spring, full of song, new spring (*Pervigilium Veneris*, line 2).

      KALON AOIDIAEI...thasson: sweetly singing...either a goddess or a woman...let us call to her right away (*Odyssey*, X, 227-28).

194:    **illa dolore...vocem:** (L) she hushed with grief, her voice likewise (Ovid, *Metamorphoses*, XIII, 538-40).

      ’Αλλ’ ἄλλην....Περσεφόνεια: Circe's words to Odysseus (*Odyssey*, X, 490-4) which Pound translates at the start of XLVII: "Who even dead....road's end" (236).

      Hathor: the Egyptian fertility goddess.

      Che mai da....diletto: (I) so that the delight will never part from me (Dante, *Paradiso*, XXX, 62).

      Glaucus: fisherman who became a sea-god after eating a magic herb.

      nec ivi...sum: (L) nor did I go to the pigsty/nor into the pigsty did I enter. Adapted LXXIV (436).

      Euné kai...thalamon: Making love in bed said Circe/into the bedroom (*Odyssey*, X, 335-36, 340).

      Eurilochus, Macer: companions of Odysseus.

195:    **Ad Orcum....pervenit:** (L) Has anyone yet been to Orcus [the Underworld]? Has not yet come in a black ship.

      Sumus in fide...canamus: (L) We are protected [by Diana] and girls we sing (Catullus, XXXIV, 1-4).

      sub nocte: (L) under night (Virgil, *Aeneid*, VI, 268).

      Flora: Roman goddess of flowers.

      ERI MEN...KUDONIAI: (Gk) In the spring the quinces (Ibycus, *Lyra Graeca*, 84).

      By Circeo...: Monte Circeo near Terracina (north of Naples) was once, before the sea receded, thought to be Circe's island. "Given the material means I would replace the statue of Venus on the cliffs of Terracina" (*Selected Prose*, page 53).

"Fac deum!" "Est factus.": (L) Make god! He is made. A variation on "Homo factus est" (St. John's Gospel, Chapter I).

196:    **A traverso le foglie:** (I) Through the leaves.

        Sic loquitur...nupta: (L) So the bride speaks/So the bride sings.

XL

The first half presents details of 19th century financial conspiracies and the cultural effects of usury, which illustrate the statement, by Adam Smith, with which the canto opens.

Then, as an escape from this corruption, the voyage of the Carthaginian navigator, Hanno, is presented. He led an expedition (*c.* 470 B.C.) through the straits of Gibraltar and founded seven cities on the Atlantic shore of Morocco. This fourth voyage in the poem is a subject rhyme with the voyages in I, II, XXIII, XXIV, LXV and XCIV.

Glossary

197:    **Morgan:** John Pierpont M. (1837-1913). "The great Morgan, during the Civil War, bought on credit a certain quantity of damaged rifles from the War Department in Washington, and sold them to a Military Command in Texas, and was paid by the latter before he had to pay the former. He made $75,000 profit. Later he was even tried and convicted, but this did not prevent his becoming the great Mahatma of Wall Street, and a world politico-economical power." (*Selected Pros₍,* page 141:*171.*)

199:    **HANNO:** All but the last six of the remaining lines of XL are adapted from the Greek source, *The Periplus of Hanno.*

        Entha hieron Poseidōnos: (Gk) there a temple of Poseidon.

201:    **NOUS:** see glossary to XXV (119).

        Karxèdoniōn Basileos: (Gk) King of the Carthaginians.

XLI

Cantos XXXI-XLI began with Jefferson and the American Revolution. The section closes with a juxtaposition of Mussolini and Jefferson showing that Pound intended the *Cantos* to be directly involved in the present.

> Nobody can understand the juxtaposition of the two names Jefferson-Mussolini until they are willing to imagine the transposition:
>
> What would Benito Mussolini have done in the American wilderness in 1770 to 1826?
>
> What would Tom Jefferson do and say in a narrow Mediterranean peninsula containing Foggia, Milan, Siracusa, Firenze, with a crusted conservatism that no untravelled American can even suspect of existing.
>
> (*Jefferson and/or Mussolini,* page 23.)

45

It was not because he was a dictator, but for his constructive actions, that Pound placed Mussolini among the heroes of the *Cantos:* "I believe in a STRONG ITALY as the only possible foundation...for the good life in Europe." "...I assert again my own firm belief that the Duce will stand not with despots and the lovers of power but with the lovers of ORDER." (*Jefferson and/or Mussolini*, pages 35 and 128.)

It is probably impossible to have the kind of acute perception which Pound possessed without a counterbalancing blindness. In politics he missed much which was obvious to people not "afflicted with genius." But it needs to be pointed out that despite Pound's admiration for Mussolini, the political thought of the *Cantos* represents an attempt to restore the Anglo-Saxon heritage—it is against unlimited sovereignty and therefore fundamentally anti-fascist. Of such contradictions poems are made.

The Mussolini section of XLI is followed by satire of the English and German society which ended with the First World War. Jefferson recurs, and finally there are a few lines about arms dealers foreshadowing the second European war, which, six years later, was radically to change Pound's life and the course of his poem.

Glossary

202:   **Ma questo ... divertente:** (I) But this is amusing. Pound met Mussolini 30 January 1933 and this was the Duce's comment on looking through *A Draft of XXX Cantos* which Pound had presented to him. Mussolini's assassination is recorded in LXXIV (425) and there are several references to him from then on—he last appears in CXVI (795).
   confine: (I) exile.
   "Noi ci facciam...: (I) We'd have our throats cut for Mussolini.

204:   **ordine, contrordine .... qualunque":** (I) Order, counter order and disorder/"Some kind of peace."

205:   **Monte dei Paschi:** (I) The Mountain of the Pastures. Sienese bank founded in 1624. This line introduces the central episode of the next group of cantos.
   And Woergl in our time?: see glossary to LXXIV (441).

Cantos XLII-LI

XLII-XLIII

These cantos give details of the founding of the Sienese bank, the Monte dei Paschi (Mountain of the Pastures), briefly introduced in XLI.

Embedded in the historical detail, giving it poetic validity, is a four line lyric, of strong simplicity, reminding of man's mortality: "Wave falls and the hand falls... not over an hundred" (210).

Pound's prose provides an explanation of the significance of the Monte:

> Two kinds of bank have existed: the MONTE DEI PASCHI and the devils.
>
> Banks built for beneficence, for reconstruction; and banks created to prey on the people.
>
> Three centuries of Medici wisdom went into the Monte dei Paschi, the *only* bank that has stood from 1600 till our time.
>
> Siena was flat on her back, without money after the Florentine conquest.
>
> Cosimo, first duke of Tuscany, had all the Medici banking experience behind him. He guaranteed the capital of the Monte, taking as security the one living property in Siena, and a certain amount of somewhat un-handy collateral.
>
> That is to say, Siena had grazing lands down toward Grosseto, and the grazing rights worth 10,000 ducats a year. On this basis taking it for his main security, Cosimo underwrote a capital of 200,000 ducats, to pay 5% to the shareholders, and to be lent at 5½%; overhead kept down to a minimum; salaries at the minimum and all excess profit over that to go to hospitals and works for the benefit of the people of Siena. That was in the first years of the seventeenth century, and that bank is open today...
>
> And the lesson is the very basis of solid banking. The CREDIT rests *in ultimate* on the ABUNDANCE OF NATURE, on the growing grass that can nourish the living sheep.
>
> (*Selected Prose*, page 240:270.)

Glossary

209: **'And how this people... monument!':** H.G. Wells's comments on the monument to Queen Victoria outside Buckingham Palace.

Lex salica! lex Germanica: Salic law, Germanic law.

Antoninus: Roman Emperor, 137-161 A.D. He said the law of Rhodes,

47

rather than Roman law, should apply at sea. Pound regarded Antoninus's reign as the "apex" (LXXXVII, 581) of the Roman Empire—a view shared by Gibbon who wrote, "Antoninus diffused order and tranquility over the greatest part of the earth."

Bailey: *Balia,* ruling authority in Siena in the early 17th century.

210: **wave falls...hundred:** compare "So light is thy weight on Tellus..." (XLVII, 238).

213: **ACTUM SENIS:** (L) done at Siena.

OB PECUNIAE...: (L) because of the scarcity of money.

215: **et omnia alia juva:** (L) and all other rights.

eiusdem civitatis Senén: (L) of the same city.

videlicet alligati: (L) that is to say under obligation.

217: **kallipygous:** (Gk) with beautiful buttocks.

quocunque aliunde: (L) from anywhere else.

220: **Orbem bellis...implevit:** (L) Urban VI filled the world with wars, the city with taxes.

XLIV

Canto XLIV continues to present Sienese history and in particular the Reforms of Pietro Leopoldo, grand duke of Tuscany 1765-1790. "The real history went on. 1760-90 in Tuscany with the work of Pietro Leopoldo and Ferdinand III of Hapsburg Lorraine, wiped out by the Napoleonic flurry and the name Hapsburg defiled and become a synonym for reaction..." (*Guide to Kulchur,* page 263.)

The list of Leopoldo's reforms (227-29) is a clear statement of the *Cantos'* political values. Details of further Leopoldine reforms are given in L (246).

Canto XLIV closes with a reference to the fact that the Monte dei Paschi was set up to "keep bridle on usury," which directly introduces XLV, and the theme at the root of XLII-LI.

Glossary

223: **Ferdinando:** Ferdinand III (1769-1824), the second son of Pietro Leopoldo, was grand duke of Tuscany from 1790 to 1799, and later, from 1814 until his death.

225: **Dovizia annonaria:** (I) abundance of food.

Frumentorum...conservit: (L) Free grain/dole restrictions relaxed for the good of the poor and rich.

227: **gabelle:** (I) taxes on goods.

XLV

Canto XLV is a passionate denunciation of the most potent force of evil in the *Cantos.* Usury, or avarice, which treats money as a commodity which can be bought and sold, rather than as "a ticket for the orderly distribution of

WHAT IS AVAILABLE," destroys civilization and degrades the mysteries of sex and nature.

Glossary

229:    **With Usura:** " 'With' in English derives from Ang-Saxon and has oppositive aroma. As in 'withstand' meaning 'stand against.' " (*Selected Letters*, page 303.) This pun applies only to the first line, which is really the title of the canto.

harpes et luz: (OF) harps and lutes. From Villon's "Ballade for his Mother" (*Le Testament*).

with usura the line grows thick: "—means the *line* in painting and design. Quattrocento painters still in morally clean era when usury and buggary were on a par. As the moral sense becomes... incapable of moral distinction... painting gets bitched. I can tell the bank-rate and component of tolerance of usury in any epoch by the quality of the *line* in painting. Baroque, etc., era of usury becoming tolerated." (*Selected Letters*, page 303.)

demarcation: "... is intellectual. It is also boundary of field if you like, but demarcation is universal. The bastid Cromwell and —— Anglican bishops and bankers obscure every hierarchy of values." (*Selected Letters*, page 304.)

Pietro Lombardo: Italian architect and sculptor (1435-1515). He carved the mermaids on the pillars of Santa Maria dei Miracoli (Venice) mentioned in LXXIV (430) and LXXXIII (529).

230:    **'La Calunnia':** title of painting by Botticelli (Uffizi Gallery, Florence).

Adamo me fecit: (L) Adam made me. Signed column on pillar of church of San Zeno, Verona.

St Trophime: church in Arles, France, built 11th to 15th century.

Saint Hilaire: church in Poitiers, 11th century.

None learneth to weave gold...: "... in Rapallo Middle Ages, industry of weaving actual gold *thread* into cloth" (*Selected Prose*, page 304). Echoes V, "Weaving with points of gold" (17).

It hath brought palsey to bed: "I.e., palsied old man. Shakespeare's language is so resilient." (*Selected Letters*, page 304.)

Eleusis: town in Attica where the Eleusinian Mysteries were celebrated. " 'Eleusis' is *very* elliptical. It means that in place of the sacramental—in the Mysteries, you 'ave the 4 and six-penny 'ore. As you see, the moral bearing is very high, and the degradation of the sacrament (which is the coition and *not* the going to a fatbuttocked priest or registry office) has been completely debased largely *by* Xtianity, or misunderstood of that Ersatz religion." (*Selected Letters*, page 303.) See the end of glossary on XVII for further notes on Eleusis.

XLVI

The usury theme is continued into the present. One of the main causes of the rot is traced to the foundation of the Bank of England in 1694. A statement by the founder of the Bank, William Paterson, is placed at the centre of XLVII: *"Hath benefit of interest on all/the moneys, which it, the bank, creates out of nothing"* (233). Thus, in contrast to the Monte dei Paschi, the Bank of England is shown to have no "true base of credit" in "the abundance of nature." This part of the *Cantos* is the "turning point" Pound refers to in the B.B.C. interview (Item O, page xx).

Glossary

231: **Seventeen/Years on this case...:** Pound is recalling the beginning of his fight for monetary reform which stemmed from his meetings with C.H. Douglas in the *New Age* offices *c.* 1918.

An' the fuzzy bloke: a humorous description of Pound in talk with Douglas. The latter had proposed that governments should distribute the surplus of the national wealth in dividends to all citizens.

Decennio: 10th anniversary celebration of Italian fascism.

Il Popolo: newspaper started by Mussolini in 1914.

5 millions: "Liste officielle des morts 5,000,000" (XVI, 73). Usury is here seen as a cause of the First World War.

Debts to...New York: "Owing to the tariff the whole South was going into debt. We must never forget the important statistic.... that southern debtors owed at least $200,000,000 to money lenders in New York City alone." (Christopher Hollis, *The Two Nations*, page 208.) Usury thus possibly caused the Civil War more than the issue of slavery.

232: **Orage:** A.R. Orage (1873-1934). Editor of *The New Age* and, later, *The New English Weekly.* (See *Selected Prose*, pages 407–421: *437–451*.)

233: **Said Paterson:** William P. (1658-1719), founder of the Bank of England. (See C. Hollis, *The Two Nations*, Chapter 2.)

"Very few people....interest": John Sherman quoted in letter from Rothschild Brothers to Messrs. Ikleheimer, Morton and Van Gould, June 25, 1863. (See *Selected Prose*, page 281:*311*.)

234: **Si requieres monumentum:** (L) If you would see a monument. (*Si monumentum requires, circumspice.* If you would see his monument, look around. The inscription over the North Door in St. Paul's Cathedral, London, referring to its architect, Sir Christopher Wren.

Hic est hyper-usura: (L) This is usury beyond measure.

'Hic nefas'...'commune sepulchrum': (L) Here is infamy...the common sepulchre.

Aurum est...sepulchrum: (L) Gold is a common sepulchre. Usury, a common sepulchre.

235: **helandros...helarxe:** (Gk) destroyer of men and destroyer of cities and destroyer of governments.

Hic Geryon est: (L) This is Geryon. He is a monster and symbol of Fraud in Dante's *Inferno*, where he is associated with usurers and described as *"colei che tutto il mondo appuzza"* ("he who pollutes the whole world," *Inferno*, XVII, 3). "The usurers are there against nature, against the natural increase of agriculture or of any productive work. Deep hell is reached via Geryon (fraud) of the marvellous patterned hide, and for ten cantos thereafter the damned are all of them damned for money." (*Literary Essays*, page 211.)

XLVII

Canto XLVI stated that Pound was drawing "to a conclusion,/of the first phase of this opus" (233-34), so XLVII is a new beginning, and a return, with deepened understanding, to the original voyage after knowledge of Odysseus/Pound in I.

Closely related to XXXIX, it expresses sexual mysteries ("*Sacrum, sacrum, inluminatio coitu*"), harmony with "the times and seasons," vegetation rituals associated with "the yearly slain" Adonis/Tamuz, and through these, man's relationship to death and the universe. Canto XLVII thus embodies the living forces which usury destroys and degrades.

Glossary

236:   **Who even dead ... road's end:** adapted from *Odyssey*, X, 490-94, which was quoted in XXXIX (194). "I hope that elsewhere I have underscored and driven in greek honour of human intelligence" (*Guide to Kulchur*, page 146).

Ceres: Demeter, the corn goddess.

Proserpine: see glossary to I.

phtheggometha thasson: see glossary to XXXIX (193).

The small lamps ... bay: During the festival of the Madonna at Montallegro above Rapallo, Pound saw local women set votive lights adrift in the sea which he related to vegetation rites for the death of Adonis. See "Statues of Gods" (*Selected Prose*, page 71, not in U.S. edition).

Tamuz: Babylonian name of Adonis. He was loved by Aphrodite. After he had been killed by a boar, both she and Proserpine claimed him and Zeus decreed he should spend part of the year with each. He is thus a god of vegetation, who, like Proserpine, dies each Autumn and returns with the Spring. (See Adonis section of Frazer's *The Golden Bough*.)

By this gate art thou measured: gate of the womb; gate also of death. Chaucer uses "gate," in the same sense, in *The Pardoner's Tale:* "And on this ground, which is my moodres gate, I knokke with my staf, bothe erly and late,/And seye 'Leeve mooder, leet me in!...'" See also XCIV, "And that all gates are holy" (634).

Scilla: sea-monster whose cave was opposite Charybdis (*Odyssey*, XII, 80-100).

TU DIONA...ADONIN: (Gk) You Dione (Aphrodite) and the Fates weep over Adonis (Bion, "Lament for Adonis," 93-94.)

236:   **The sea is streaked red with Adonis:** "Every year, in the belief of his

51

worshippers, Adonis was wounded to death on the mountains, and every year the face of nature itself was dyed with his sacred blood. So year by year the Syrian damsels lamented his untimely fate, while the red anemone, his flower, bloomed among the cedars of Lebanon, and the river ran red to the sea, fringing the winding shore of the Mediterranean, whenever the wind set inshore, with a sinuous band of crimson." (J. Frazer, *The Golden Bough*, abridged edition, page 329.)

237: **What shoots rise new by the altar:** "Perhaps the best proof that Adonis was a deity of vegetation, and especially the corn, is furnished by the gardens of Adonis.... baskets or pots filled with earth, in which wheat, barley, lettuces, fennel, and various kinds of flowers were sown.... Fostered by the sun's heat, the plants shot up rapidly, but having no root they withered as rapidly away, and at the end of eight days were carried out with images of the dead Adonis, and flung with them into the sea... All these Adonis ceremonies... were originally intended as charms to promote the growth or revival of vegetation." (*The Golden Bough*, page 341.)

Moth is called over mountain: the first of many moth and butterfly images. As Richard Sieburth (*Instigations: Pound and Rémy de Gourmont*, page 158) has said, "the Odyssean moths of Canto XLVII, called over mountain, *naturans*,.... at last reach shore" on the last page of the *Cantos*: "That the kings meet in their island..." (802).

naturans: (L) obeying its nature.

Molü: magic herb given by Hermes to Odysseus which prevented Circe's drugs from acting.

Begin thy ploughing.... Two oxen...: adapted from Hesiod, *Works and Days*, 383-391; 448.

Pleiades: seven stars in the constellation of Taurus (the seven daughters of Atlas).

238: **Tellus:** (L) the Earth.

cunnus: (L) cunt.

Zephyrus... Apeliota: West wind.... East wind.

239: **almond bough... flame:** the rebirth of Adonis in the spring.

XLVIII

In contrast to the intensity of the preceding canto, the first two and a half pages of XLVIII consist of a jumble of historical anecdotes, ironic and humorous. It is these sharp contrasts which make it possible to read the *Cantos* in large chunks at a time. The thread binding the stories together, as Michael Alexander has pointed out, is "monopolists against adventurers" (*The Poetic Achievement of Ezra Pound*, page 130).

Then, after an account of a village festival in the Italian Tyrol based on a letter Pound received from his daughter Mary in 1934, the canto closes with a lyric passage recalling the massacre of the Albigensians and describing things seen during the walking tour Pound and Eliot took in Provence in 1919. The descriptions of insect life anticipate the minute observation of the natural world in *The Pisan Cantos.*

Glossary

241:    **DIGONOS:** (Gk) twice born. Dionysus was twice-born, once from his mother, Semele, and then from the thighs of his father, Zeus.
     Mr Rhumby: pseudonym for Woodrow Wilson's Secretary of State, Bain-Colby—humorous contrast between the care taken to choose a dog for Queen Victoria, and the way Colby was chosen: "three senators; four bottles of whiskey."

242:    **Athelstan:** Anglo-Saxon king (924-940). His laws governing merchants are here contrasted with corrupt modern practice. He is mentioned in the later cantos for introducing gilds, "And yilden he gon rere" (XCI, 613, etc.).

243:    **Mt Ségur:** see glossary to XXIII (109).
     Savairic;...Gaubertz: troubadour poets, S. de Mauleon and G. de Poicebot, who first appear in V (18).
     Falling Mars in the air...: "The flying ant or wasp or whatever it was that I saw cut up a spider at Excideuil may have been acting by instinct, but it was not acting by reason of the stupidity of instinct" (*Jefferson and/or Mussolini,* page 18).

XLIX

The still centre of the *Cantos:* the images speak with quiet power, expressing the repose and harmony with the universe of Pound's Confucianism. It takes up the Chinese theme introduced in XIII and anticipates the Chinese history cantos (LII-LXI) which form the first half of the next section.

There are three sources: (1) the first 32 lines are based on a 16th century ms. of Chinese and Japanese poems and drawings which came into Pound's possession via his father; (2) a Japanese transcription of an ancient Chinese poem ascribed to the Emperor Shun (2255-2205 B.C.); and (3) "Sun up; work," a Chinese folk song, deriving (like Shun's poem) from a poem recorded by E. Fenollosa, the Sinologist, whose manuscripts Pound inherited.

The closing two lines, by Pound himself, stress XLIX's kinship to the previous union with nature canto, XLVII.

Glossary

244:    **no man:** perhaps a pun on Odysseus's OY TIΣ (no man), the name he gives to deceive the Cyclops. The poems which make up the early part of XLIX are also anonymous.
     scur: obsolete form of 'shower'; variant of 'skirr,' meaning to pass rapidly over stretch of land or water (O.E.D.).

245:    **Tsing:** The 'Ch'ing' or Manchu dynasty as embodied in its 2nd emperor, Kang Hsi (A.D. 1662-1722), who appears elsewhere in the *Cantos* as 'Kang Hi.'

State by creating riches...debt: a return to the usury motif, "the state need not borrow" (LXXIV, 441).

Geryon: see glossary to XLVI (235).

KEI MEN RAN KEI...: an ancient song traditionally attributed to the legendary emperor Shun, and sung on the occasion of his abdication in favour of Yü (*c.* 2205 B.C.). (J.C.) Pound made an attempt to translate this song when he reread the Fenollosa mss. in 1958:

> Gate, gate of gleaming,
> knotting, dispersing
>   flower of sun, flower of moon
> day's dawn after day's dawn   new fire

L

Canto L opens with three lines from John Adams, repeated from XXXII, making a parallel between the American Revolution and the reforms of Pietro Leopoldo which were being introduced at the same time. Reforms further to those listed in XLIII are given, and the rest of L deals mainly with the reasons for the fall of Napoleon, which is seen as a victory for usury. It is interesting to note that the American historian Brooks Adams, whom Pound did not read until 1940, also held this view: "Probably Waterloo marked the opening of the new era, for after Waterloo the bankers met with no serious defeat" (*The Law of Civilization and Decay*, page 268).

Following all the political intrigue, the last four lines present an image of dawn and stillness, connecting with the paradisal five lines which open LI.

Glossary

246: **Zobi:** Antonio Zobi, *Storia civile della Toscana*, is the main source for L.

247: **MARENGO:** near Alessandria, Piedmont, N.W. Italy. Napoleon's victory (1800) against the Austrians here gave him control of Italy.

248: **'From the brigantine....Flanders:** refers to the "Hundred Days" when Napoleon tried to recover his Empire. **'Incostante':** the name of the ship on which he left Elba. He was defeated at Waterloo (in Flanders).

249: **Dirce:** Stand close around ye Stygian set
    With Dirce in one bark conveyed;
    Or Charon, seeing, may forget
    That he is old, and she, a shade.
            (Landor)

LI

Canto LI is a recapitulation of the main theme of XLII-LI: usury against the natural order and splendour of the universe. It has, as Pound pointed out, "a prologue and finale which fit the denunciation into the poem as a whole."

Glossary

250: **Shines in...our eye:** adapted from stanzas 4 and 5 of *Al cor gentil repara sempre amore* by Guido Guinicelli (*c.* 1230-1272). For a translation, see D.G. Rossetti, *Poems and Translations.*

Fifth element; mud; said Napoleon: see, "The sun, as Guinicelli says beats on the mud all day/and the mud stays vile" ("Notes for Cantos," *Agenda,* Vol. VIII, Nos. 2-3).

251: **Blue dun....take Granham:** fishing fly. These lines give details on how to make the fly and when to use it. "Granham" is a trade name for a type of fly.

That hath the light of the doer...to it: "...meant an ACTIVE pattern, a pattern that sets things in motion" (*Polite Essays,* page 51).

Deo similis...adeptus: (L) Godlike in a way/this intellect has grasped (Albertus Magnus).

Zwischen die...vivendi: (G & L) Between the two peoples a modus vivendi is achieved. Rudolf Hess, Hitler's deputy, said this in a broadcast from Königsberg, 8 July 1934.

circling in eddying air; in a hurry: Geryon. Compare hurry of usurers with the patience and close observation of the "times and seasons" needed for fishing.

Geryon: see glossary to XLVI (235).

the regents: Pound told Daniel Pearlman that they were bankers (*The Barb of Time,* page 218n.).

252: **League of Cambrai:** short-lived alliance of states against Venice (1508-1510). It looked as if it would succeed, but Venice soon recovered.

正 名 :The two ideograms serve to introduce the Chinese cantos which are to follow. They are *Cheng:* 'correct' and *Ming:* 'name(s)'—i.e., to define the correct terms—the rectification of language. Pound saw it as "true definition" (LXVI, 382), to "Call things by their names" (LII, 261).

Cantos LII–LXXI

LII

Following a restatement of the positive achievements related in the previous section and of the usury theme, LII consists of an adaptation of part of the *Li Ki* (Book of Rites), one of the Five Chinese Classics. Its compilation was begun in the 1st century B.C. and completed in the 2nd century A.D. from documents said to come from Confucius and his disciples, but incorporates both much earlier and later material. The section Pound uses is in some ways an Eastern equivalent of Hesiod's *Works and Days*, so LII continues, like XLVII and XLIX, to show man's kinship to the "vital universe" and need to reverence "the times and seasons." The passage runs from the beginnings of summer, until winter's end, forming a kind of natural overture to the long chronicle of Chinese history which is to follow.

Glossary

257: **Schacht:** (1877-1970) President of the Reichsbank under Hitler.
anno seidice: (I) year 16 [of the Fascist era].
neschek: (H) usury.
Vivante: Leone Vivante (1887-1970), Italian philosopher, author of *English Poetry* (1950), whom Pound often visited in his villa near Siena.
——— sin: These and the following black lines indicate that Pound's publishers censored, for fear of libel, a number of references to the Rothschilds. "Hitler jailed no Rothschilds, and Pound thought that the poor Jews whom German resentment drove into concentration camps[1] were suffering for the sins of their inaccessible coreligionists" (Kenner, *The Pound Era,* page 465).
goyim: (Yiddish) gentiles.
Johnnie Adams: Adams said: "All the perplexities, confusion, and distress of America arise, not from defects in their constitution or confederation, not from want of honour or virtue, so much as from downright ignorance of the nature of coin, credit and circulation."
Remarked Ben: A document attributing this remark to Benjamin

Franklin has, I believe, subsequently been proved to have been a forgery.

258:    **of the two usuries...put down:** adapted from Shakespeare, "Twas never merry world since of two usuries the merriest was put down, and the worser allow'd by order of law" (*Measure for Measure*, Act III, ii). The merriest is whoring.

Between KUNG and ELEUSIS: A key phrase, as the universe of the *Cantos* is one of creative tension between the rational civic order of Confucius and the mysteries of ancient Greek religion.

Burgos: "Only twice in my life have I heard church music achieve true intensity: once in Burgos, Spain, and again in Cortona" (*Ezra Pound and Music*, page 361).

Know then: introduces Pound's paraphrase of the 'Yüeh Ling' (monthly command) section of Chapter V of the *Li Ki*.

259:    **Ming T'ang:** Temple of Light, where the imperial family worshipped its ancestors.

manes: (L) spirits of the dead.

Lords of the Mountains...rivers: spirits in ancient Chinese religion.

261:    **Heaven's Son:** the Emperor.

止 : point of rest. A place to stop and also to start from. Connected with peace in the *Cantos* and a key ideogram, particularly in the late sections of the poem. Pound's own sense of the word derives from the beginning of *The Great Digest* (see *Confucius*, pp. 29; 39–45).

---

[1]Places not yet (1938) committed to a policy of extermination. News of that policy, when it was instituted, no more reached Rapallo than it did most of Germany. (Kenner's footnote.)

LIII–LXI

The only stretch of continuous chronology in the poem, these cantos present the history of China from its legendary beginnings in the 3rd millenium B.C. until the accession of Kien Long in A.D. 1736, soon after John Adams was born, to whom the next section, LXII-LXXI, will be devoted. Pound's source is an 18th century French work, *Histoire Générale de la Chine* by Père de Moyriac de Mailla, who based his work on a neo-Confucian Chinese historian.

Pound told Basil Bunting that LIII-LXI was his equivalent to Homer's catalogue of ships in the *Iliad* (II, 494-877) and intended to relax the reader. The music of these cantos has a quality quite distinct from the rest of the poem; they are best enjoyed if read rapidly, I believe. As Kenner has said, Pound has managed "to improvise with great brilliance a 'Chinese' idiom moving to gongs and cymbals, conveying the shock of clangorous monosyllables and contained radiance of luminous details registered in ideograms, ideas with boundaries" (*The Pound Era*, page 434).

"The history of a culture is the history of ideas going into action" (*Guide to*

Kulchur, page 44). The Chinese history cantos manifest Confucian ideas "going into action" throughout a time span stretching from over 2,000 years before the birth of Confucius, until the middle of the eighteenth century.

> THE LESSON of Chinese history?... might... be of two kinds. By implication, we might more despise and suspect the kind of education which we (my generation) received, and we might acquire some balance in NOT mistaking recurrence for innovation.
>
> My generation was left ham ignorant, and with the exception of a few, mostly tongue-tied and inarticulate specialists, the whole occident still ignores 3000 years of great history.... to call a book "General History," and omit the great emperors, is as stupid as to omit Constantine and Justinian....
>
> Fads and excesses are never new. One might note that Wu Wang in the recent Boxer times and Kung B.C. found beheading prevalent. Nevertheless the Chinese chronicle records "abolition of capital punishment"...
>
> Before thinking that old-age pensions, medical relief, educational endowments etc.etc. are news, one shd. at least glance at a summary of the chinese story.
>
> (Excerpted from *Guide to Kulchur,* pages 274, 275 and 276.)

Pound provides his own table of the main dynasties and events on pages 255–56.

Glossary

262: **YAO:** (2357–2259 B.C.) the first of three successive Chinese emperors—the second was Shun (2255–2205) and the third, Yü (2205–2197)—who became a standard of excellence against which all later emperors were measured. Characters for the three emperors' names appear on pp. 263 and 302 of the *Cantos.*
Ammassi: (I) grain pools.

263: **Chang Ti:** Ruler of Heaven. Originally the first of the ancestral spirits; later comparable to Jehovah. Complementary to 'Heaven' or *Tien,* which, though more of an impersonal force, was also sometimes seen in personal terms. (J.C.)
moving the sun and stars: "L'amor che move il sol e l'altre stelle" (Dante, *Paradiso,* last line).
que vos vers ... conforme: (F) that your verses express your intentions and that the music conforms.

264: **so that in 1760 Tching Tang opened the copper mine...:** This is probably the first recorded example of a ruler understanding the "distributive function of money," LXXVII (468), LXXXV (549) and LXXXVIII (580). "That story is 3,000 years old, but it helps one to understand what money is and what it can do. For the purpose of good government it is a ticket for the orderly distribution of WHAT IS AVAILABLE. It may even be an incentive to grow or fabricate more grain or goods, that is, to attain abundance. But it is NOT in itself abundance." (*Selected Prose,* page 265:*295.*)

265: **hsin jih ... hsin:** the four ideograms mean: make new, by day, make new. Key ideograms, which recur frequently, to express dawn and renewal.

YIN: 18th century B.C., a minister of Tching Tang.

272: **Chung Ni:** Confucius.

273: μεταθεμένων τε τῶν χρωμένων: *metathemenōn te tōn chrōmenōn,* if those who use a currency give it up in favour of another. (Aristotle, *Politics,* 1257b 16.) A recurring phrase.

274: **POLLON IDEN:** (Gk) Of many [men] he saw [the cities] [and knew their minds] (*Odyssey,* I, 3).

周 **Chou:** the dynasty Confucius favoured (268).

276: **Chu king:** *Shu King,* the Book of History which Pound uses as the basis for LXXXV.

Chi king: The Odes (*The Classic Anthology Defined by Confucius* which Pound translated in 1954).

279: **Pretty manoeuvre ... Naples:** refers to exhibition of submarine warfare put on by Mussolini for Hitler in the Bay of Naples, 1938. A comparison between Hitler's visit to Mussolini and that of the Tartar King to the Emperor Han Sieun.

281: **taoists:** The followers of a school of Chinese philosophy and associated popular religion going back to the writings attributed to Lao Tzu (the book is probably *c.* 4th century B.C.). As a philosophy of life Taoism advocates harmony with nature and its mysterious underlying principle. Its followers incline to passivity and a lack of worldly ambition. This contrasts with the pragmatism of Confucian thought which entails a deep involvement in the affairs of men. Following his Confucian source for the Chinese cantos Pound shows his disrespect for the "taozers" in many places. Despite some correspondence between Pound's own (and western based) mystical involvement with nature and a Taoistic pantheism, his Confucian alignment here is more true to his own inclinations as regards personal action and his sense of worldly mission (cf. Kenner who claims to see Taoist elements in the Cantos but who does not make these distinctions: *The Pound Era,* pages 254–58). Confucianism had its own appreciation and, indeed, love of nature as can be seen from parts of the *Analects* (e.g. *Analects,* VI. 21, paraphrased in Canto LXXXIII, 529). (J.C.)

289: **Nestorians:** followers of the ancient Christian Church of Persia, who started sending missionaries to China in 631.
tael: Chinese coin.
corvée: (F) forced labour.

290: **Orbem bellis...implevit:** see glossary to XLIII (220).

仁者以身發財

仁者以財發身不

The Chinese ideograms are from Tseng's comment on Confucius's *Ta Hsio* (Great Digest): "The humane man uses his wealth as means to distinction, the inhumane becomes a mere harness, an accessory to his takings" (*Confucius,* page 83). A paraphrase of the same passage occurs in Canto LII (261): "Good sovereign by distribution/Evil king is known by his imposts."

294: **pourvou que ça doure:** (F) provided that it endures.
298: **Lux enim...partem:** (L) For light of herself, into every region (Grosseteste, *De Luce*).
Tcheou Tun-y: Chou Tun-i (1017-1073), scholar and philosopher; a forerunner of the neo-Confucian movement of Chu Hsi. Pound here links him with neo-Platonic philosophers of light.
seipsum...diffundit: (L) itself, it diffuses itself (Grosseteste).
risplende: (I) it shines (Dante, *Paradiso,* I, 2 and Cavalcanti's *Donna mi priegha,* line 26).
et effectu: (L) and in effect.
master of Nenuphar: Tcheou Tun-y was known as this, because he lived by a stream full of water-lilies.
301: **biglietti:** (I) bank notes, paper money.
Mt Tai Haku...carpet: 3 lines from a poem by Li Po (A.D. 701-62).
310: **Et/ En l'an trentunième....funérailles:** (F) And/in the 31st year of his rule/aged sixty/HONG VOU seeing his faculties weaken/said: May virtue inspire you, Tchu-ouen./You, faithful mandarins, men of letters, soldiers/Help my grandson sustain/The dignity of his power/the weight of his office/And just as for Prince OUEN TI/of HAN in ancient times/make the obsequies for me.

60

313: : the ideogram is *pien*[4]: 'to change.' "The sign of metamorphosis" (*Selected Prose*, page 107:*93*.)

316: **Sinbu:** Jimmu Tenno (711-585 B.C.), first of the legendary emperors of Japan. A direct descendant of the Sun Goddess, he founded the Imperial Dynasty which has remained unbroken to this day.

reges sacrificioli: (L) priest kings.

318: **TO KALON:** (Gk) THE BEAUTIFUL.

322: **Li Sao:** Through Sorrow. This is the title of a famous ancient Chinese poem attributed to Ch'u Yüan (4th century B.C.) and usually translated as "Encountering Sorrow."

Atrox MING, atrox finis: (L) Terrible MING, terrible end.

323: τάδ' ὦδ' ἔχει: *tad ōd echei*, That's how it is. The last words of Klytemnestra's speech (*Agamemnon*, 1401-6): "This is Agamemnon, my husband, dead by my right hand, and a good job. That's how it is."

324: **De libro...censeo:** (L) Concerning the book *Chi King* (The Odes), I think thus.

Ut animum...rationis: (L) To purge our minds, Kung said, and guide them to the light of reason.

perpetuale effecto: (I) perpetual effect (from line 26 of Cavalcanti's *Donna mi priegha*).

CHI KING....servat: (L) The Odes show and exhort. But the just man, and free from lust, serves his master.

obsequatur...deflectat: (L) obeys his parents, never turns aside.

igitur...encomiis: (L) therefore my praises.

periplum: (Gk) coastal voyage. Recurs LXXIV (425) etc. In *The Pisan Cantos* it is sometimes used for voyages of the mind.

334: **YONG TCHING:** Iong Ching; it was during his reign (1723-1735) that the *Sheng U* (Sacred Edict) was produced in the form Pound uses it in XCVIII-XCIX.

339: **and as to the rise of the Adamses:** a linking line, to introduce the next section (LXII-LXXI). John Adams was born in the final year of the reign of Iong Ching.

LXII–LXXI

After the catalogue of Chinese Emperors, LXII-LXXI present in detail the thoughts and actions of one just ruler engaged in creating a new nation. This is Pound's most sustained tribute to human liberty and the quality of early American civilization. John Adams, as G.S. Fraser has pointed out, was "in a sense almost the father of a dynasty,...an example of what the good ruler, seeking to lay the foundations of a stable community, should be. These Adams cantos, which came out in 1940, are a great expression of American patriotism; it is tragic to think that their author, five years later, was nearly put on trial for his life for high treason." (*Ezra Pound*, page 70.)

Tom Scott has written, "I predict that the next century will see, even be dominated by, a dialogue between the U.S. and China in which Pound's poetry will take on an importance and weight not obvious at the moment: that not only has he woven a new wholeness, or at any rate potential wholeness, out of European and American, but also of Chinese elements."

The switch, from an 18th century Frenchman's conception of Chinese history to the world of John Adams, makes good sense, if we remember that Chinese civilization and Confucianism were regarded as an ideal by the French Enlightenment of Voltaire and Bayle, which was perhaps the most significant influence on the thinking of Adams and Jefferson.

This is the most unified section of the *Cantos*, as Pound sticks almost exclusively to his source, *The Works of John Adams* (see bibliography), and he presents the material in the same order as it appears there. Obscurity manifests itself in details, due to Pound's method of "condensation to maximum attainable," but the overall portrait of Adams's integrity and perception throughout his long and interesting political life is conveyed with humour and clarity. It is hard to think of a 20th century statesman with a comparable grasp of the essentials of good government.

Canto LXII and the first quarter of LXIII give some of the main events of Adams's life from the outside, as these pages are based on biographies by his son, John Quincy Adams, and grandson, Charles Francis Adams (Volume 1 of Pound's source).

Canto LXIII, from "Vol Two (as the protagonist saw it:)" (352), LXIV, LXV, and the early part of LXVI are taken from the diary and autobiography of John Adams, as well as an autobiographical account titled "Travels and Negotiations" (Volumes II and III).

Canto LXVI, from "WHERETOWARD THE ARGUMENTS..." (381), LXVII, and the first page and a half of LXVIII present Adams's political writings: *Defense of the Constitution, Discourses on Davilla* and articles he wrote in the *Boston Gazette*. His political beliefs are expressed in this section. (Volumes III, IV and VI.)

Canto LXVIII, from "Commission to France '77" (396), LXIX, and the first one and a half pages of LXX are drawn from Adams's state papers and public correspondence. (Volumes VII, VIII and IX.)

Canto LXX, from "I leave the state with its coffers full..." (410), and the final Adams canto, LXXI, are based on his private correspondence (Volumes IX and X). Here the most important events in his life are seen again "in the mirror of memory" (410), giving the ten cantos a poetic unity, which links them, surprisingly, with *The Pisan Cantos*.

I am indebted to Frederick Sandars, *John Adams Speaking* (see bibliography), for the above summary and for much of the following Chronology. Those who cannot obtain Pound's original source, but wish to understand all the historical details of LXII-LXXI, should consult his book. It gives extracts from the sources for every line.

Chronology

1735:   John Adams born at Braintree, Massachusetts, a village near Boston. He was fourth in line from Henry Adams who had emigrated from Somerset 1636 (LXII, 341).

1755:   Graduated from Harvard.

1757:   Admitted to the Boston Bar. His deep knowledge and respect for English Common Law, and Sir Edward Coke's *Institutes,* is important to the political ideas of the *Cantos.* Law as a safeguard against tyranny is the main theme of the Coke cantos (CVII-CIX). "Common law of England, BIRTHRIGHT of every man here and at home" (LXVI, 384).

1760-1775: "What do we mean by the revolution? The War? That was no part of the revolution; it was only an effect and consequence of it. The revolution was in the minds of the people, and this was effected from 1760-1775, in the course of fifteen years, before a drop of blood was shed at Lexington." (John Adams to Thomas Jefferson, 24 August 1815.) Quoted in XXXII (157) and L (246).

1761:   Writs of Assistance. Adams took notes at the trial where James Otis lost his case against the Writs. They were general search warrants authorizing peace officers to help English port agents to find smuggled goods. They were one of the early causes of resentment against the English. (LXII, 354.)

1764:   Adams marries Abigail Smith.

1765:   Stamp Act passed in English Parliament. Official documents, newspapers, etc. circulated in America are required to be stamped showing that a tax on them has been paid. Adams leads protests against this, arguing that the tax was unconstitutional as the colonies were not represented in Parliament. His argument rested on the principle, "no taxation without representation." (LXIV, 356; LXVI, 383, etc.)

1766:   Stamp Act repealed.

1768-1769: Adams defends John Hancock against charges of smuggling wine in his ship *Liberty.* He secures an acquittal.

1770:   Lord North becomes Prime Minister. Boston Massacre occurs 5 March. Some Boston citizens were baiting a British sentry. His troop came to his support and shot five of them dead. As a result, Captain Preston was indicted for murder. With characteristic courage and integrity, Adams successfully defends Preston and the other British soldiers, an action which must have been unpopular. (LXII, 342-43; LXIV, 359, etc.)

1773:   Lord North tries to help British East India Company by Tea Act which gave them monopoly on transport of tea to America where it would be taxed and sold only by Company agents. (LXXII, 341-2.) 16 December, Boston Tea Party.

1774:   Adams seeks impeachment of Chief Justice Oliver for his refusal to renounce salary grant from the Crown. The Council of Massachusetts House of Representatives refuses to convict, but jurors all over the country refuse to take oath, saying they cannot serve "while Chief Justice of this Court stands impeached" (LXV, 363). September, Adams attends first Continental Congress and takes a large part in drafting a declaration of rights.

1775: Articles by Adams, justifying the constitutional arguments in favour of independence, appear in the *Boston Gazette* under the pseudonym NOVANGLUS. 19 April, Battles of Lexington and Concord. May, Second Continental Congress, where Adams nominates Washington commander-in-chief. (LXV, 364.)

1776: 4 July, Congress adopts Jefferson's draft of the Declaration of Independence. He was to write later: "No man better merited than Mr. John Adams to hold a conspicuous place in the design. He was the pillar of its support on the floor of Congress, its ablest advocate and defender..." (Letter to W.P. Gardner, February 1813.)

1777: November: Congress appoints Adams to join Benjamin Franklin and Arthur Lee as commissioner to France.

1778: France signs treaty of alliance with the United States. With his son, John Quincy, Adams sails to France on the frigate *Boston*, to begin ten years' service in Europe as a diplomat of the U.S. The voyage described LXV (368-71) makes a subject rhyme with other voyages in the *Cantos*. May, Louis XVI gives Adams his first audience.

1779: Adams is recalled to America, but sails again for France in November.

1780: June, Congress appoints him to negotiate Dutch loan, and, on his own initiative, Adams journeys to Holland for this purpose in July, without having yet heard Congress's decision.

1781: Adams is elected, along with Franklin, Jay, Laurens, and Jefferson, to negotiate peace with Britain. Cornwallis surrenders 19 October.

1782: March, Lord North resigns as Prime Minister. June, Adams secures first Dutch loan. Further loans follow in 1784, 1787 and 1788. October, he completes treaty with the Netherlands. (LXVIII, 400-2 and LXIX, 403-5.) November, Adams returns to Paris to negotiate with British and fight for U.S. fishing rights. (LXV, 377-8.)

1783: 3 September, Britain recognizes U.S. independence and signs peace treaty in Paris.

1785: February, Adams is appointed first American ambassador to London. (LXX, 412.)

1786: Jefferson joins him on a tour of English countryside. (LXVI, 300-301.)

1788: Returns, at his request, to Boston.

1789: Washington President. Adams elected Vice President, despite Alexander Hamilton's effort to prevent this.

1791: Adams quarrels with Jefferson after the latter's praise of Tom Paine's *Rights of Man*.

1793: Louis XVI executed. Adams re-elected Vice President. France declares war on England.

1794:	Jay Treaty with Britain signed by John Jay and Lord Grenville.
1796:	Adams elected President; Jefferson Vice President. Hamilton retained as Secretary of the Treasury despite the efforts he had made to prevent Adams from becoming President. He starts to encourage opposition to Adams inside the cabinet and Congress.
1797:	French Directory, angered by Jay Treaty, rejects Charles Pinckney's diplomatic mission.
1798:	Undeclared war between America and France.
1799:	Adams sends William Murray, Oliver Ellsworth and William Davie on a mission to attempt to make peace with France. This angers the Hamilton faction who are pro-British.
1800:	Peace secured with France. (LXXI, 418.) 30 September, a new convention, replacing the treaty of 1783, signed with Napoleon. News of this does not reach Washington in time to affect national election. Jefferson and Aaron Burr win, both of whom receive 73 votes against Adams's 65. (LXX, 410.)
1801:	Jefferson inaugurated President. Adams retires from public life to devote himself to writing.
1812:	Adams and Jefferson become reconciled and resume correspondence. " 'You and I ought not to die before we have explained ourselves to each other.' (Adams to Jefferson, 15 July, 1813). Did Rousseau or Montaigne ever write anything to equal that sentence, given the context (1760 to 1813)?" (*Selected Prose,* page 128:*158.*)
1818:	Abigail Adams dies.
1826:	On the Fourth of July, the fiftieth anniversary of America's independence, Jefferson dies at Monticello; Adams, in Quincy, dies a few hours later. "OBEUNT 1826, July 4" (LXXXVIII, 583).

Glossary

| 341: | **'Acquit of evil ... Europe':** from Charles Francis Adams's Preface, excusing himself of any deliberate faults in writing the life of his grandfather. |
| 341: | **tcha:** (C) tea. |

343: **mens sine affectu:** (L) a mind without passion.
Coke: Sir Edward Coke (1552-1634), the great English lawyer, who fought for the independence of the judiciary against James I, citing Bracton to the king's face: "the king should be subject not to man, but to God and the law." His *Institutes* will be used by Pound in *Thrones,* CVII-CIX.

344: **Novanglus:** New Englander. Pseudonym for Adams.

345: **Schicksal, sagt der Führer:** (G) Destiny, said the Führer.
THUMON: (Gk) spirit, courage.

349: **Hamilton:** Alexander H. (?1757-1804). First Secretary of the Treasury (1789-1795). He established a national fiscal system, largely modelled on the Bank of England. He believed in a strong federal government.

65

He plotted against Adams, both before and during the latter's presidency, and would have liked America to get involved with England in a war against France, whereas Adams and Jefferson believed that America should stay out of European wars. A belief in this principle of non-involvement was one of the reasons for Pound's broadcasts over Rome Radio. Opposed to the agrarianism of Adams and Jefferson, Hamilton seemed to Pound an early representative of the forces of usury in American politics.

350: **ego scriptor cantilenae:** I, the writer of this canto.
ARRIBA: (S) HAIL.

352: **Eripuit caelo fulmen:** (L) He snatched the lightning from the sky. A reference to Franklin's experiments to discover the cause of thunder.

𝕀𝔼 Cheng⁴: see glossary to LI.

353: **in quella parte ... memora:** (I) in that part/where memory lives (Cavalcanti, *Donna mi priegha*).
la qual manda fuoco: (I) which sends fire (Ibidem).

355: **sub conditione fidelitatis:** (L) under condition of faith.

356: **damaged actus ... injuriam:** (L) an act of law does harm to none.

360: **nihil humanum alienum:** (L) nothing human is alien.
SUBILLAM ... apothanein: (L & Gk) Sibyl/at Cumae I with my own eyes/ ... "What do you want?" "To die." Pound relates this passage from Petronius (*Satyricon*, XLVIII, 8) to a visit Adams paid to an old woman of 110 who said much the same as the Sibyl.

369: **ane blasterend bubb ... ding:** adapted from Gavin Douglas's great Scottish translation of Virgil, *Aeneid*, I, 18-19: "Ane blusterand bub out fra the north braying/Gan over the foreship in the bak sail ding" (*bub*: storm; *ding*: beat).

377: **For my part thought .... balances of power:** the Adams cantos were written 1938-1939, so these lines, which Pound emphasised with a black line, are prophetic. He considered Roosevelt had manoeuvred America into the Second World War unconstitutionally and contrary to the principles of Adams and Jefferson. It was, in part, on these grounds that Pound justified his broadcasts from Rome during 1941-1943.

382: **OB PECUNIAE ...:** see glossary to XLII (213).
ching⁴ ming²: see glossary to LI (252). A general attribute of John Adams and his works. (J.C.)

388: **OBSTA PRINCIPIIS:** (L) Resist the beginnings. Adams continues, "nip the shoots of arbitrary power in the bud, is the only maxim which can ever preserve the liberties of any people" (Volume 4, page 43).

393-4: **facilius laudari .... potest esse:** (L) it is more easily praised than discovered/or not lasting/excellently blended in moderation ... /is nevertheless brought about in unison ... a state by agreement/where there is no justice, there can be no law. (Tacitus; Cicero; the final line is from St. Augustine, *Civitas Dei*, XIX, 21.)

394: **ἄρχειν και ἄρχεσθαι:** *archein kai archesthai*, to rule and to be ruled (Solon, Aristotle).

66

jura ordo ... leges: (L) right order ... equity laws (Livy, Annals, III, 63).

395: **Regis ... populique:** (L) Of the king, of the aristocrats and of the people.

396: **MISERIA .... vagum:** (L) Slavery a MISERY where law is undefined.

407: **natural burella:** (I) natural dungeon (*Inferno*, XXXIV, 98).

per l'argine sinistra ... volta: (I) it would turn to the left side (*Inferno*, XXI, 136).

quindi Cocito .... membruto: (I) whereby Cocytus, Cassio with monstrous limbs (*Inferno*, XXXIV, 52 & 67).

410: **pro hac vice:** (L) in return.

formato loco: formèd trace (Cavalcanti, *Donna mi Priegha*, see XXXVI, 178, line 27).

412: **meminisse juvebat:** (L) it will be pleasant to remember (*Aeneid*, I, 203).

413: 中 The ideogram is *Chung:* pivot; point of balance, middle, or centre. Originally more of a "bull's eye," Pound none the less came to see the word in terms of these extended meanings (cf. XIII, 59: "It is easy ... middle." Where character is alluded to). (J.C.) From the Confucian Classic, *Chung Yung*, which Pound translated at Pisa, "Unwobbling Pivot." It recurs, characterising "John Adams, the Brothers Adam" as "our norm of spirit," LXXXIV (540).

DUM SPIRO: (L) while I breathe.

nec lupo ... agnum: (L) not to entrust a lamb to a wolf.

DUM SPIRO AMO: (L) while I breathe I love (Pound adds AMO to Adams's text).

416: **Every bank of discount .... crazy:** Adams wrote: "Funds and banks I never approved, or was satisfied with our funding system; it was founded in no constant principle; it was contrived to enrich particular individuals at the public expense. Our whole banking system I ever abhorred, and I continue to abhor, and shall die abhorring. But I am not an enemy to funding systems. They are absolutely and indispensably necessary in the present state of the world. An attempt to annihilate them would be as romantic an adventure as any in Don Quixote or in Oberon. A national bank of deposit I believe to be wise, just, prudent, economical, and necessary. But every bank of discount, every bank by which interest is to be paid or profit of any kind made by the deponent, is downright corruption. It is taxing the public for the benefit and profit of individuals; it is worse than old tenor, continental currency, or any other paper money. Now, Sir, if I should talk in this strain, after I am dead, you know the people of America would pronounce that I died mad." (Adams to Benjamin Rush, 28 August 1811.) This letter recurs LXXIV (437; 439) and LXXVI (457) and is referred to in XCV (643).

417: **THEMIS CONDITOR:** (Gk & L) Justice the Founder.

The Pisan Cantos

The Pisan Cantos

The Chinese and Adams cantos were finished by the summer of 1939 and Pound started to prepare for what he believed would be the final section of the poem. Soon after the outbreak of war, he wrote, "I've got my time cut out for positive statements. My economic work is done (in the main). I shall have to go on condensing and restating, but am now definitely onto questions of BELIEF..." "I have... got to the end of a job or part of a job (money in history) and for personal ends have got to tackle philosophy or my 'paradise.'" (*Selected Letters*, pages 328 and 331.)

So, while Europe was beginning to tear itself apart for the second time this century, Pound was meditating his "paradise." He had written, as Noel Stock tells us (*The Life of Ezra Pound*, page 375), in Dorothy Pound's copy of LII-LXXI, near the date 11th February 1940:

> To build the city of Dioce
> (Tan Wu Tsze)
> Whose terraces are the colour of stars.

a line he would remember at Pisa (LXXIV, 425).

But as the horror of the war increased, to write a "paradise" became unthinkable, and probably the only fragment of this projected work that exists from the war years is the passage, "Now sun rises in Ram sign" (800), which he sent to a Japanese correspondent in March 1941, "to go into Canto 72 or somewhere." It has a freshness akin to the opening of the *Canterbury Tales*. He added a note to the letter, "All of which shows that I am not wholly absorbed in saving Europe by economics" (*Selected Letters*, page 348). He probably wrote no more cantos until 1944.

As Pound's life and his poem become more interwoven than before in *The Pisan Cantos*, some account should be given of the events which led to his imprisonment in the American Army Disciplinary Training Center at Pisa, where LXXIV-LXXXIV were composed. The best record is the memoir by Pound's daughter, Mary de Rachewiltz, *Discretions*, to which the reader is referred for more information—written with tact and clarity, it provides useful background to the poetry.

Pound visited America in the spring of 1939 in a vain attempt to influence political leaders against war. Roosevelt said he was too busy to see him. The visit is recalled in the *Cantos*, " 'am sure I don't know what a man like you/would find to *do* here'/said Senator Borah" (LXXXIV, 537); " 'Has packed the Supreme Court/so they will declare anything he does constitutional.' Senator Wheeler, 1939" (C, 713).

Pound began to broadcast from Rome Radio in 1941. After America entered the war, he stopped for about a month and tried to return to America, but officials in the U.S. Rome Embassy refused him permission. Another complication was that he would have had to leave his aged parents in Rapallo—his father was in hospital with a broken hip. He resumed broadcasting on 29 January 1942, with a proviso that he would not be asked to say anything contrary to his conscience as an American citizen. An announcer prefaced each speech with this statement.

The broadcasts hammered the same ideas as his writings of the twenties and thirties, and were mainly concerned with the economic causes of war, but the tone was fanatical, due to his increasing isolation at this time. To an extent, his historical and monetary theories had blinded him to what was really happening in Europe. It is more than a pity that he never went to Germany. If he had come face to face with the evil regimentation of Nazism, he would have recognized, as he did later, that it was totally opposed to the passion for liberty which is the mainspring of his poetry and prose.

He attacked certain Jews as agents of usury, but not "the small Jew": "Don't start a pogrom, that is, not an old style killing of small Jews. That system is no good whatsoever." (30 April 1942)..."Above all you cannot blame it on the small Jew for he is in most cases as damned a fool and as witless a victim as you are" (16 May 1943). These statements show that he had no idea of what the Nazis were doing.

There is no doubt that he said much which he subsequently regretted: "How mean thy hates/Fostered in falsity" (LXXXI, 521), and as he was to say in old age to Robert Lowell (*History*, page 140): "That nonsense about the Jews...Olga knew it was shit..." But, having seen Europe destroy itself once, as "Mauberley" movingly records, he fought throughout the thirties, by pamphlets, poetry and correspondence, for a radical monetary reform which he believed would prevent this from happening again. His broadcasts were not treason, but the logical outcome of this struggle.

The view that the banking system was a major cause of the war was not peculiar to Pound. For example, Lord Boothby, who is no economic crank, wrote in *The Times Business News* (20 May 1968), "when all is said and done" the Central Bankers "were primarily responsible for the Second World War."

The clearest statement of Pound's position at this time is a letter which he wrote on 4 August 1943 to the U.S. Attorney General on hearing that he was under indictment for treason: "I have not spoken with regard to *this* war, but in protest against a system which creates one war after another, in series and in system. I have not spoken to the troops, and have not suggested that the troops should mutiny or revolt." (*Selected Prose*, page 15.)

His daughter explained his reasons for speaking: ".... as an American citizen he felt it was his duty to avail himself of the only means open to him to protest against the politics of a President who was exceeding his rights, endangering the Constitution, who had promised American mothers that their sons would not be sacrificed, while actively preparing for war" (*Discretions*, page 152).

Ironically, Pound based his stand on principles he found expressed by the founders of the American nation, such as the lines from John Adams that he marked in the margin in LXV (377) and Jefferson's letter to William Wirt, 30 May 1811: "But for us to attempt, by war, to reform all Europe and bring them back to principles of morality and a respect for the equal rights of nations, would show us to be only maniacs of another character."

Finally, it needs to be said that by broadcasting, Pound was seeking to establish a valid point, that a man should have the right to freedom of speech "wherever placed," as he put it in the letter to the Attorney General just quoted; and he continued, "Free speech under modern conditions becomes a mockery if it does not include right to free speech over the radio." He returned to this theme at Pisa, "free speech without free radio speech is as zero" (LXXIV, 426). Although this right did not exist under Mussolini and his comment therefore has a certain ironic ring, Pound was in dead earnest in making this telling observation.

When Italy capitulated to the Allies in September, 1943, soon after the fall of Mussolini, Pound was on one of his visits to Rome. He headed north, through a country in chaos, travelling 450 miles, mostly on foot, to the Italian Tyrol where his daughter lived. Incidents on this journey are recalled in LXXVIII (478).

He returned to Rapallo several weeks later, probably making brief contact with the new Italian Republic which Mussolini was setting up at Salò, on the southwestern shore of Lake Garda, in collaboration with the Germans, who had rescued him from captivity. There are several references to Salò in *The Pisan Cantos*.

It was during this period that he resumed the *Cantos*, writing LXXII and LXXIII in Italian. These have not yet been incorporated in the collected edition, but thanks to the courtesy of Barbara Eastman, I have been able to read them in her English translation. Pound himself began a translation, but did not complete it.

Just as the First World War canto, XVI, concerned with the battlefields of France, has a long passage in French, it is fitting that LXXII-LXXIII, which mirror the collapse of Italy, should be written in Italian. To a certain extent, the quality of this dark poetry, in particular LXXII, is Dantescan; but the war has made it inevitable that it is the Dante of the *Inferno*, not the *Paradiso*, who is the presiding genius. Eliot wrote the Dantescan section of *Little Gidding*, "In the uncertain hour before the morning," about a year earlier in wartime London.

Until LXXII-LXXIII appear in their proper place in the poem, it must suffice to quote from an essay by Barbara Eastman which clearly defines their nature:

> ...LXXII plummets straight to the depth of an *inferno* that is Dantescan in language and feeling and imagery; and both poems specifically combine the mediaeval and modern hells of Italy at war, as Dante blended the antique and contemporary sufferers in his *bolge*. It is true that there is praise for Italy, but not for Mussolini's Italy alone, nor is there only praise.

In the powerful visionary episodes of Canto 72, Italian greatness is shown to be historically, almost genetically—and certainly fatally—flawed. Both cantos, clearly inspired by the lived Italy, as Dante's were six and a half centuries earlier, speak of a nation of conspirators and patriots, embattled and betrayed.[1]

Canto LXXIII was probably written soon after the fall of Florence to the Allies in August 1944. About six months later, when Pound was working on a translation of Mencius, two partisans came to the door of his home in Rapallo. He put Legge's *Confucius* and a Chinese dictionary into his pockets and was taken away. Soon after this, from 24 May 1945 until six months later, he was a military prisoner at the American Army Disciplinary Training Center at Pisa.

The treatment he received at the beginning was so cruel as to be barbaric. The D.T.C. was known as the "arse hole of the army" (LXXIV, 437). Most of the prisoners were murderers and/or rapists. For three weeks, until he became ill, Pound was put in a wire and concrete cage, six feet by six and a half, reinforced, in his case, with "air-strip" steel ("hast'ou swum in a sea of air strip/through an aeon of nothingness,/when the raft broke and the waters went over me," LXXX, 513). There was no protection from rain and wind. "By night a special reflector poured light on his cage alone.... There were always two guards, with strict orders not to speak to him." (Kenner, *The Pound Era*, pages 461-62.) After his collapse, he was moved to a tent in the Medical Compound.

Kenner has provided the best description of the landscape of *The Pisan Cantos*:

[The D.T.C.]...lay north of Pisa on the coastal plain, near the village of Metato, by the Via Aurelia.... White oxen now shared the Aurelian Way with jeeps, and down a side road past the camp moved...traffic...raising clouds of dust. A half-mile square of barbed wire enclosed the place; birds settled on the strands, the prisoner was to observe, like notes of silent music. North and East stretched mountains, one cone-shaped above delicate trees (he named it Taishan, for China's sacred peak), two to the left of it low and hemispherical (he named them the breasts of Helen). Pisa lay South; peering through the dangling laundry on clear days one could see the Tower. Sun and moon rose over the mountains, set over the invisible sea. Lizards basked in the heat; grass clung to friable earth; one could watch a wasp building her nest, or ants marching or crickets singing, or men at the obstacle fence working out the 14-hour days and looking uncommonly like figures at the grape arbour in the Schifanoia frescoes in Ferrara. He was in a tent in the medical section of the compound, regaining his wits, wits as always shaped by myth: a man of no fortune and with a name to come, Odysseus in the Cyclops' den.

(*The Pound Era*, pages 473-74.)

The Pisan Cantos (together with the translations from Confucius which he also finished at Pisa[2]) are, in a sense, Pound's Testament, as they were written under the imminent threat of execution—treason is, after all, a capital offence. It is not for nothing that Villon's *Epitaph*, which was written under similar circumstances, is quoted in LXXIV, "Absouldre, que tous nous vueil absoudre" (427).

Here present "in the mirror of memory" (XXXVII, 185; LXX, 410), Pound's friends, and the concerns of his life and the previous cantos, come fleetingly to focus with the swiftness of thought; and the themes, gods and images at the core of the poem return, but, to quote Eliot, "renewed, transfigured, in another pattern." They crowd about him, like the shades thronging round Odysseus in I—Pisa is, in some ways, another *Nekuia.*

There is a new *humanitas,* natural speech rhythm and lack of contrivance. The life of the camp is constantly breaking into and changing the flow of the reverie, "[Only shadows enter my tent/as men pass between me and the sunset,]" (LXXX, 515); a black prisoner makes him a table out of a packing case, against regulations (LXXIV, 434; LXXXI, 518-19), and ever present is the delicacy and *hilaritas* of nature, which, apart from Confucius and memory, is the only certain good on which he can rely, so its smallest manifestations take on the greatest magnitude for him: "When the mind swings by a grass-blade/an ant's forefoot shall save you/the clover leaf smells and tastes as its flower" (LXXXIII, 533).

Surprise, as Eliot said, is one of the essential qualities in poetry. It is hard to think of a greater surprise in literature than the change in tone from the Adams cantos to the first line of LXXIV. At Pisa the poet suffered the wreck of the Europe he loved, in actuality, which gives his vision new depth. I think of King Lear, or the "compound ghost" in *Little Gidding* who said, "So I find words I never thought to speak." And, fulfilling the prophecy of Tiresias in I, he has lost "all companions" (5):

> As a lone ant from a broken ant-hill
> from the wreckage of Europe, ego scriptor.
> (LXXVI, 458)

Pound here came to realise the truth of something he had only hinted at in 1938: "...a modern Eleusis being possible in the wilds of a man's mind only?" (*Guide to Kulchur,* page 294). But the vision, "To build the city of Dioce whose terraces are the colour of stars" (LXXIV, 425) remains, strengthened by suffering, "now in the mind indestructible" (LXXIV, 442). As a record of pain, exposure to the elements and deepened understanding and serenity, "in the drenched tent there is quiet/sered eyes are at rest" (LXXXIII, 529), there is little in our poetry with which to compare these pages.

---

[1]*The Gap in the Cantos (Paideuma* and *Agenda,* 1980).
[2]*The Great Digest (Ta Hsio)* and *The Unwobbling Pivot (Chung Yung).* This is the best companion volume to *The Pisan Cantos:* the texts relate at many points.

LXXIV

425: **Manes!:** (*c.*216–276) the Persian founder of the Manicheans. He was executed at the instance of the Zoroastrians.
Ben and la Clara: Mussolini and his mistress, Clara Pettacci, were hung up by the heels in Milan after they had been assassinated by the partisans.
DIGONOS: see glossary to XLVIII (241).

Possum: a bang...whimper: see last line of T.S. Eliot's "The Hollow Men."

To build the city of Dioce...stars: the Ecbatan of IV (16) and V (17). The city which King Deioces built is described by Herodotus: "...the battlements are white, of the next black, of the third scarlet, of the fourth blue, of the fifth orange; all these are coloured with paint. The two last have their battlements coated respectively with silver and gold." (*Histories*, Book I, 98.) George Rawlinson, who translated the above, points out that the seven colours are "precisely those employed by the Orientals to denote the seven great heavenly bodies..."

process: Pound's equivalent for the Chinese word 'Tao,' more often translated 'the Way.' (J.C.) "What heaven has disposed and sealed is called the inborn nature. The realization of this nature is called the process.... You do not depart from the process even for an instant: what you depart from is not the process." (*Confucius*, pages 99 and 101.)

Washed in the Kiang...candor: "After Confucius' death, when there was talk of regrouping, Tsang declined, saying: 'Washed in the Kiang and Han, bleached in the autumn sun's slope, what whiteness can add to that whiteness, what candour?' (Mencius III,1, IV, 13.)" (Note to Pound's translation of *The Analects*.)

periplum: see glossary to LIX (324).

OΫ ΤΙΣ, OΫ ΤΙΣ?: OU TIS, No man? No man? The name for himself that Odysseus gives the Cyclops (*Odyssey* IX, 366).

sorella la luna: (I) sister moon (St. Francis).

426: **T'ang history:** i.e., the time of Tching Taang, who understood the "distributive function of money" (LIII, 264).

im Westen nichts neues: (G) all quiet on the western front.

Wanjina: The son of a god; he created the world by speaking the names of objects, but he made too many things, so his father took away his mouth (an Australian aboriginal legend).

Ouan Jin: (C) man of letters.

427: **in principio verbum:** (L) in the beginning was the word (John I:1).

Mt. Taishan: see general commentary on LXXIV-LXXXIV.

poluphloisboios: (Gk) loud-roarings (Homeric epithet for the sea; *Iliad* I, 34, etc.).

Cosa deve....ginnocchion: (I) Why must it continue? If I fall, I'll not fall on my knees.

Lute of Gassir. Hooo Fasa: Gassir was son of Nganamba Fasa, king of the Fasa tribe. *Hooo:* (Mali [Sudanese]) Hail! This line introduces the folk-song about Wagadu which is an important motif in LXXIV (430-1; 442) and to the *Cantos* as a whole as it concerns the recurrent destruction and rebuilding of a city. The source is Leo Frobenius, *African Genesis:*

> Wagadu appeared four times in the daylight in splendour: four
> times she departed, that men could not see her. Once through
> Vanity, once through the Breaking of Faith, once through Greed,
> and once because of Schism. Four times Wagadu altered her name.
> Once she was called Dierra, next she was called Agada, then
> Ganna, and finally Silla. Four times Wagadu turned her face. Once

she looked to the North, once to the West, once to the East, and once to the South. For Wagadu had, as often as they had been visible to man on earth, four gates: one to the North, one to the West, one to the East, and one to the South. From these quarters comes the strength of Wagadu and to these quarters it extends, whether Wagadu is imaged in stone or in wood or in earth or only exists as a shade in the mind and in her children's yearning. For the essence of Wagadu is not of stone, nor of wood, nor of earth. Wagadu is the strength that lives in the hearts of men. And she is knowable when the heart lets her be seen and the ear hears the strokes of the sword and the clanging on shields: but she cannot be seen when, oppressed and exhausted by the ferocity of Man, she falls asleep. Because of Vanity, Wagadu slept once, a second time for the Breaking of Faith, a third because of Greed, and the fourth time because of the Schism. But, if Wagadu is found again the fifth time, then she will live so strongly in the minds of men that she will never be lost to them, and Vanity, Breaking of Faith, Greed, and Schism will never again have effect on her.

Each time that Wagadu declined through the fault of Man, she rose with new beauty, more splendid than ever. Vanity brought with it the song of the minstrels which everyone imitated and values so highly today. The Breaking of Faith brought pearls and a shower of gold. Greed brought the craft of writing.... But the fifth Wagadu will bring from Schism the permanence of rain that falls in the South and the cliffs that rise from Sahara, for every man will bury Wagadu deep in his heart and every woman deep in her loins.

Ho! Dierra, Agada, Ganna, Silla! Ho Fasa!

(Quoted in translation in Clark Emery's *Ideas in Action*, pages 130–31.)

les six potences...absoudre: (F) the six gallows/Forgive, may you forgive us all (adapted from Villon's *Epitaph*).

428: **el triste....rivolge:** (L) and the sad thought turns/to Ussel. To Ventadour/his counsel goes, time returns.

Kuanon: Indian/Chinese/Japanese goddess of mercy. Recurs frequently in the late cantos.

Linus, Cletus, Clement: early saints and popes whose intercession is sought in the Roman Mass.

429: Ideogram *hsien:* clarity, radiance; in some contexts '(divine) glory.' This is Pound's "tensile light" whose tensility derives from the lower left elements for 'silk.' The light, of course, comes from the sun (upper left). (J.C.)

Erigena: see glossary to XXXVI (179).

Yao...Shun...Yu: see glossary to LIII (263).

Tempus tacendi, tempus loquendi: see glossary to XXXI (153).

tovarish: see glossary to XXVII (131).

430: mo^4: 'not,' 'do not,' 'there is not.' For Pound, the ideogram figures "a man on whom the sun has gone down." The sun appears in the centre of the character and sets through vegetation which is written above it. The lower element was originally more vegetation but does look somewhat like a man with his arms outstretched. (J.C.)

the nymph of the Hagoromo: see glossaries to XXXVI (178) and LXXX (500).

sia Cythera: (I) either Venus.

dell' Italia tradita: (I) of the betrayed Italy.

431: Demeter: Ceres, corn goddess, mother of Persephone.

ch'intenerische...Torre: (I) that softens the Tower on the left.

Che sublia...cader: (Pr) and faint and fall away (Bernart de Ventadour); see glossary to VI (22).

Vai soli: (L) death to the lonely man (quoted in the last poems of Laforgue).

NEKUIA: Canto I, where the dead are called up (*Odyssey*, XI).

'HAION ΠΕΡΙ 'HAION: *helion peri helion*, the sun around the sun.

"Redimiculum Metellorum": Basil Bunting's first book.

432: Est consummatum, Ite: (L) It is finished, go. (A conflation of Christ's last words on the cross and "Ite missa est" towards the end of the Latin Mass.)

these the companions: echoes Tiresias's prophecy in I, "lose all companions" (5):

Fordie: Ford Madox Ford

433: William: W.B. Yeats

Jim: James Joyce.

Uncle George: George Holden Tinkham (1870-1956), Republican representative for Massachusetts 1915-43. Opposed U.S. entry into League of Nations and Roosevelt's efforts to get U.S. into the Second World War.

'ΡΕΙ ΠΑΝΤΑ: *Rei panta*, All things flow (a fragment from Heracleitus (*c.* 500 B.C.) which often recurs in the late cantos).

435: Terracina: see glossary to XXXIX (195).

χθόνια γέα, Μήτηρ: *Chthonia gea, Mater*, Nether earth, Mother. The earth, which Pound slept on after he had been taken from the concrete cage, is a recurrent image in LXXIV-LXXXIV.

ΤΙΘΩΝΩΙ: *Tithōnōi*, to Tithonus (husband of Eos, the dawn, who was granted immortality by Zeus, but not immortal youth).

in coitu: see glossary to XXXVI (182).

staria senza piu scosse: (I) [this flame] would shake no more (*Inferno*, XXVII, 63).

436: der im Baluba...: see glossary to XXXVIII (189).

pouvrette et...lus: (F) poor, old and illiterate (from the Prayer to the Virgin which Villon wrote for his mother, *Le Testament*).

magna NUX animae: (L & Gk) great night of the soul (St. John of the Cross).

ac ego....animae: (L) and I in the pig-sty...I went to the pig-sty and saw spirit corpses. The Circe here is not the beautiful goddess of XXXIX, but an evil enchantress connected with usury.

437: ΘΕΛΓΕΙΝ: *thelgein*, to bewitch; to cheat.

nec benecomata: nor Circe of the beautiful hair—echoes "trim-coifed" in I.

κακὰ φάργακ' 'έδωκεν [sic]: *Kaka pharmak edōken*; see glossary to XXXIX.

old Upward... Sitalkas... shot himself: Allen U. (1863-1926). English author of *The New Word* (1907) and *The Divine Mystery* (1913). See *Selected Prose* (pages 373–82; *403–41*). **Sitalkas:** warrior king of Thrace, c. 431-424 B.C.

437-8: **To study with the white wings.... at harvest:** an adaptation of the Confucian *Analects*, I, i-v.

438: **E al Triedro... Luna:** (I) And in the corner, Cunizza/ and the other [woman]: "I am the moon." Both phrases recur often in LXXIV-LXXXIV. For notes on Cunizza, see commentary on VI.

saeculorum Athenae/γλαύξ, γλαυκῶπις,/olivi: (L, Gk [*glaux, glaukopis*] & I) timeless Athene, little owl with gleaming eyes,/olive trees. "How hard the old cloistered scholarship... has toiled to understand the word glaukopis given to the goddess Athene. Did it mean blue-eyed, or grey-eyed, or by the aid of Sanskrit—merely glare-eyed? And all the time they had not only the word glaux staring them in the face, but they had the owl itself cut at the foot of every statue of Athene.... to tell them she was the owl-eyed goddess, the lightning that blinks like an owl. For what is characteristic of the owl's eyes is not that they glare, but that they suddenly leave off glaring like light-houses whose light is shut off. We may see the shutter of the lightning in that mask that overhangs Athene's brow and hear its click in the word glaukos. And the leafage of the olive whose writhen trunk bears, as it were, the lightning's brand, does not glare but glitters, the pale underface of the leaves alternating with the dark upper face, and so the olive is Athene's tree and is called glaukos." (Allen Upward, *The New Word*, quoted by Pound, *Selected Prose*, pages 377-8:*407-8*.)

Boreas, Apeliota libeccio: North, East and South winds.

"C'e il babao": (I) There's the bugbear.

439: **λιγύρ':** *ligur*, clear (in *Odyssey* XII, 183, describes the sirens' song).

Meyer Anselm: M. Amschel Rothschild (1743-1812), the founder of the House of Rothschild.

440: **METATHEMENON... KRUMENON:** see glossary to LIII (273).

441: **Wörgl.... safe side of the law:** "At about the beginning of the second decade of the Fascist Era, the small Tyrolean town of Wörgl sent shivers down the backs of all the lice of Europe, Rothschildean and others, by issuing its own Gesellist money (or rather the Gesellist variety of Mazzinian money). Each month every note of this money had to have a revenue stamp affixed to it of a value equal to one per cent of the face-value of the note. Thus the municipality derived an income of twelve per cent per annum on the new money put into circulation.

"The town had been bankrupt: the citizens had not been able to pay their rates, the municipality had not been able to pay the school-teachers, etc. But in less than two years everything had been put right, and the townspeople had built a new stone bridge for themselves etc. All went well until an ill-starred Wörgl note was presented at the counter of an Innsbruck bank. It was noticed, all right—no doubt about that! The judaic-plutocratic monopoly had been infringed. Threats, fulminations, anathema! The burgomeister was deprived of his office, but the ideological war had been won." (*Selected Prose*, page 284:*314*.)

442:    **quia impossibile est:** (L) because it is impossible (Tertullian's reason for Faith).

ΚΟΡΗ, 'ΑΓΛΑΟΣ'ΑΛΑΟΥ: *Koré, aglaos alaou,* Koré (Persephone), the blind man's shining (?).

443:    **Περσεφόνεια:** *Persephoneia.* (This, and the previous jumbled Greek echo *Odyssey* X, 490-4, quoted in XXXIX.)

ΣΕΙΡΗΝΕΣ: *Seirenes,* Sirens (*Odyssey,* XII, 42-200).

ΧΑΡΙΤΕΣ: *Charites,* the Graces (see glossary to XXVII, 131).

but this air...borne on the seawaves: an evocation of the birth of Venus.

nautilis biancastra: (I) a white shell.

tira libeccio: (I) the South-West wind blows.

Genji at Suma: In the Noh play, *Suma Genji,* an old woodcutter is the apparition of the hero Genji, "as a sort of place spirit, the spirit of the seashore at Suma" (*Translations,* pages 232-36). The pause, indicated by the space and comma after *Suma,* onomatopoieically expresses the wind-change—the whole passage follows the movement of the winds.

Tiro, Alcmene...: The shades of dead women rise before Pound on the winds, as they rose to Odysseus in *Odyssey* XI. **Alcmene:** the mother of Herakles.

Tyro: see commentary on II.

nec casta Pasiphae: (L) nor chaste Pasiphae (Propertius, II, xxxviii, 52).

Eurus, Apeliota: the South-East and East winds.

Rupe Tarpeia: rock in Rome from which criminals were thrown to their deaths.

"in the name of its god": Micah, 4:5.

Spiritus veni/adveni: (L) Come spirit/come.

444:    **Time is not, Time is the evil...:** echoes XXX (147).

Βροδοδάκτυλος: *Brododaktylos,* rosy-fingered dawn. Pound uses the Aeolic form, from Sappho, rather than the Homeric, 'ροδοδάκτυλος.

le contre-jour: (F) the half-light.

vento ligure, veni: (I) Ligurian wind, come.

φαίνε-τ-τ-τ-τττ-αι μοι: *phainetaimoi* [a god] he seems to me. Sappho's poem to Anactoria, stuttered (*Lyra Graeca,* Loeb Classical Library, Vol. I, page 186).

l'aer tramare: (I) the air to tremble (Cavalcanti, Sonnetto VII, *Translations,* page 38).

446:    **εσσομένοισι:** *essomenoisi,* for generations to come (*Odyssey,* XI, 76). Refers to *Elpenor:* see glossary to I.

aram vult nemus: (L) the grove needs an altar.

"La Nascita": Botticelli's painting, *The Birth of Venus.*

funge la purezza: (I) purity acts ("The *unmixed* functions in time and space without bourne." *Confucius,* page 187).

formato locho: Pound translates this phrase of Cavalcanti "formèd trace" in XXXVI (178).

Arachne mi porta fortuna: (I) The spider brings me good luck.

ΕΙΚΟΝΕΣ: *eikones,* images, ikons.

448: e **"fa di clarita l'aer tremare"**: and make the air to tremble by its clarity (Cavalcanti, *Sonnetto VII*).
"Ecco il te": (I) Here's the tea.
449: **nec accidens est**: (L) and is not an attribute.
Hast'ou seen.... steel dust: "The *forma*, the immortal *concetto*, the concept, the dynamic form which is like the rose pattern driven into the dead iron-filings by the magnet, not by material contact with the magnet itself, but separate from the magnet. Cut off by the layer of glass, the dust and filings rise and spring into order. Thus the *forma*, the concept rises from death..." (*Guide to Kulchur*, page 152.) See also Ben Jonson, *Her Triumph*, where the phrase, *or swansdown ever?* occurs.
Lethe: the river of forgetfulness in Hades. It also runs through the earthly paradise of Dante's *Purgatorio* (XXVIII).

LXXV

450: **Phlegethon**: see glossary to XXV (118).
Gerhart: G. Münch, German pianist, arranger and composer. He regularly took part in the concerts Pound organised in Rapallo during the thirties. The music presented here is the violin line from Münch's arrangement of Clément Janequin's 16th century work, *Chant des Oiseaux*.
Buxtehude: (1637-1707) German composer.
Klages: 19th century French composer.
Sachs: (1495-1576) German Meistersinger.

LXXVI

452: **dove sta memora**: (I) where memory liveth (Cavalcanti, *Donna mi priegha*, XXXVI, 177).
Dryas...Heliades: (L) wood nymphs and Heliads. The Heliads were daughters of Helios, who changed into poplars as they mourned their brother Phaeton. (Ovid, *Metamorphoses*, II, 340 ff.)
e che fu chiamata Primavera: (I) and she who was called Spring (see Dante, *La Vita Nuova*, XXIV, 20-23). A reference to Cavalcanti's love Monna Vanna.
nel clivo ed al triedro: (I) on the slope and at the corner.
la vecchia sotto S. Pantaleone: (I) the old woman under San Pantaleone.
e la scalza: (I) and the barefooted one.
453: **Greif...Schöners...**: restaurants.
454: **Chung**: see glossary to LXX (413).
誠 The ideogram means *sincerity*. Pound glosses it: "The precise definition of the word, pictorially the sun's lance coming to rest on the precise spot verbally. The right hand half of the compound means: to perfect, bring to focus." (*Confucius*, page 20.)

78

455: **Galla's rest:** Placidia's (see glossary to XXI, 98).
456: **Tout dit...fortune:** (F) everything says that fortune does not last.
l'ara sul rostro: (I) the altar on the rostrum.
of following Ponce....florida: Juan Ponce de León (1460-1521) discovered Florida while looking for the Fountain of Youth, Easter Sunday, 1513.
de leon alla fuente florida: (I & S) of Leon to the flowery fountain.
Anchises: father of Aeneas, by Venus. See XXIII (109).
Κύθηρα δεινά: Kuthera deina, dread Aphrodite.
457: **Κόρη, Δελιά δεινά/et libidinis expers:** (Gk & L) Koré, dread Delia (Artemis)/and without lust.
πολλά παθεῖν: polla pathein, to suffer much (adapted from Odyssey, I, 4, where Odysseus is said to have experienced many sufferings on the sea).
ac ferae familiares: see glossary to XX (94).
458: **atasal:** "union with God" (from Avicenna, the Mohammedan philosopher).
Dione: mother of Aphrodite; perhaps here Aphrodite herself, as in XLVII.
Κύπρις: Kupris, Aphrodite.
un terzo cielo: (I) a third heaven (Dante, Paradiso, VIII, 37—the heaven of Venus).
459: **but the crystal can be weighed in the hand:** the first introduction of a central image of Pound's "paradise." It is "an approach to the infinite by form, by precisely the highest degree of consciousness of formal perfection; as free of accident as any of the philosophical demands of a 'Paradiso' can make it" (Literary Essays, page 444, where Pound is referring to the ovoid sculptures of Brancusi).
Thetis: sea nymph, mother of Achilles.
Maya: mother of Hermes.
spiriti questi? personae?: (L) spirits these? people?
οἱ βάρβαροι: hoi barbaroi: the barbarians.
pervenche: (I) periwinkle.
460: **Le Paradis...artificiel:** (F) Paradise is not artificial. An important motif in the late cantos; it is partly a reply to Baudelaire's Les Paradis Artificiels, which were drug-induced.
J'ai eu pitié...assez: (F) I've had pity for others/probably not enough.
l'enfer non plus: (F) hell isn't either.
δακρύων: dakruōn, tears.
L.P.: Pierre Laval; Pétain. **gli onesti:** (I) the honest ones.
la pastorella dei suini: (I) the little shepherdess of the pigs.
benecomata dea: (L) trim-coifed goddess (from Andreas Divus's Odyssey, see I, 3).
le bozze: (I) the rough draft. Memories of Pound's stay in Venice in 1908 when he considered giving up his vocation as a poet and throwing his first book, A Lume Spento, into the tide water.
461: **Arachne...:** see glossary to LXXIV (446).
462: **Olim de Malatestis:** see glossary to XI (50).

lisciate con lagrime...lachrymis: (I & L) smoothed with tears/with polished tears.
la concha: (I) the shell.
ΠΟΙΚΙΛΟΘΡΟΝ', 'ΑΘΑΝΑΤΑ: *poikilothron, athanata,* Richly enthroned, immortal (Sappho, *Hymn to Aphrodite*).
saeva: (L) cruel.
po'eri di'aoli: (I) poor devils.
463: **Knecht gegen Knecht:** (G) Slave against slave.
ΜΕΤΑΘΕΜΕΝΩΝ: *Metathemenon,* see glossary to LIII (273).
ΝΗΣΟΝ 'ΑΜΥΜΟΝΑ: *neson amumona,* see glossary to XX (94).

LXXVII

465: **hennia:** (Japanese *hannya*) evil spirit in Noh drama (see *Awoi No Uye, Translations,* pages 323-331).
466: **ψυχάριον ἀι βάσταζον νεκρὸν:** *Psucharion ai Bastaxon nekron.* Swinburne memorably translated this line from Epictetus, "A little soul for a little bears up this corpse which is man" (*Hymn to Proserpine*).
467: **sumne fugol othbaer:** see glossary to XXVII (129).
Καλλιπλόκαμα: *Kalliplokama,* with beautiful hair.
Ida: hill in the Troad where Aphrodite and Anchises made love, and where their son, Aeneas, was born.
Shun's will and/King Wan's will: "When the aims of Shun and Wan were set together, though after a thousand years interval, they were as two halves of a tally stick.... That things can be known a hundred generations distant, implied no supernatural powers, it did imply the durability of natural process which alone gives a possibility of science." (*Selected Prose,* pages 99-100; *85-6.*) This is based on Mencius, IV,ii, I,3. The characters for a 'seal' or 'tally stick' appear on the next page (468).
directio voluntatis: (L) direction of the will (Dante, *De Vulgari Eloquentia,* II, 2). The character, 'chih,' associated with this concept from Dante, appears beside the line. (Cf. LXXXVII, 572.)
468: **and as to the distributive function...of the unit of money:** these 12 lines are a summary of the economic themes of the preceding cantos: (a) Tching Tang's discovery of the "distributive function of money" (LIII, 264)—as Pound says elsewhere, money should merely be "a ticket for the orderly distribution of what is available" (*Selected Prose,* page 265;*295*)—which leads to the fact that "the state can lend money"; (b) "the true base of credit" (*Monte dei Paschi,* XLII-XLIII); and (c) in opposition to Jefferson's belief that "the earth belongs to the living," the perversion of the Bank of England creating money out of nothing ("By great wisdom sodomy and usury were seen coupled together," *Selected Prose,* page 235; *265*—hence the line "the buggering bank...."). Pound attempts a similar summary in LXXXVIII (580-1).
ὑπὸ χθονὸς: *upo chthonos,* under the earth.
the forms of men rose out of γέα: Cadmus and the dragon's teeth—see

glossary to XXVII (132). **γέα:** *gea*, earth.
"Missing the bull's eye . . . . precise definition": these lines are taken from Confucius, respectively *Analects*, XV, 6 and *The Unwobbling Pivot*, XIV, 5 and XXII (*Confucius*, pages 264, 127 and 173).

469: **so that you cd/ . . . Dublin pilot:** " 'She was so fine and she was so healthy that you could have cracked a flea on either of her breasts,' said the old sea captain bragging about the loves of his youth. It seems a shame that the only man who could have made any real use of that glorious phrase in literature, is dead." (Ezra Pound, "John Synge and the Habits of Criticism," *The Egoist*, 2 February 1914.)
bel seno . . . vide sopra: (I) beautiful breasts (in rare rhymes, see above).

470: **Δημήτηρ:** *Demeter*, goddess of the corn; mother of Persephone.

471: **καὶ "Ιδα, θέα:** *kai Ida, thea*, and Ida, goddess.

472: **"Un curé déguisé . . . déguisé."** (F) "A disguised priest . . ./Seems to me like a disguised priest." At the door/"(I) don't know, Sir, he seems like a disguised priest to me."

473: **Roi je ne suis . . . deigne:** (F) I am not the King, I do not condescend to be the prince. (From the motto of the House of Rohan: *Roi ne puis, prince ne daigne, Rohan suis.*).

474: **Shah Nameh:** Persian epic (Book of Kings) written by Firdausi ('Firdush') *c*. 1010 A.D. **Basil:** the English poet, Basil Bunting.

475: **Sorella, . . . zecchin':** (I) Sister, my sister,/who danced on a golden coin.

LXXVIII

477: **ter flebiliter: Ityn:** see glossary to IV (13).
"and the economic . . . . Mussolini": what was said by the brother of the financier Sir Alfred Mond, at the time of Sanctions (*Selected Prose*, page 283; *313*).

478: **inaltre:** (I) also.
"alla terra abandonata": (I) to the abandoned earth.
"alla" . . . Verona: In the manifesto of the Fascist Republican Party (Salò, October 1943) Mussolini made a distinction between the right *to* ("*alla*") and the rights *of* ("*della*") property.
to dream the Republic: Mussolini was said to have been reading Plato's *Republic* at the time he was setting up his final, doomed government at Salò.
Goedel's sleek head . . . . gekommen!: These lines present incidents from Pound's journey out of Rome (September 1943) to his daughter in the Italian Tyrol (see Mary de Rachewiltz, *Discretions*, pages 184 ff.).
minestra: (I) soup; **il zaino:** knapsack; **branda:** hammock; **"Tatile is gekommen!":** (G) "Daddy is come!"
Roma profugens . . . terras: fleeing Rome to the country of the Sabines.
and belt the citye . . . name . . . "Ere he his goddis brocht in Latio": from Gavin Douglas's translation of the *Aeneid* 1.

479: **Δίκη:** *Dike*, Justice.
"wherein is no responsible . . . duty": quotations from Mussolini. He said, "Liberty not a right but a duty."

Put down the slave trade...: When the Italians invaded Abyssinia (1936) they abolished the slave trade.

480: **nothing worse than a fixed charge:** "A sane and decent tax system .... could have the following characteristics: 1. Aiming at feasible justice it could, as Mencius said it should, consist in a share of available products. Mencius used very considerable lucidity in demanding a share, not a fixed charge, which latter might not be available in a poor year, or produce in a rich year a reserve against famine or future contingency." (*Selected Prose*, page 323; *353*.)

o-hon dit...de tout: (F) it's often said in the village/that a helmet has no use/none/it's good only to give courage/to those who have none at all (echoes XXXIX, 143).

481: **So we sat there by the arena:** see glossary to IV (16).

Two with him...that god-damned amendment: the fight against Prohibition.

METATHEMENON: see glossary to LIII (273).

481-2: **No longer necessary...what is used or worn out/a la Wörgl.:** for a detailed exposition of the ideas of these lines, see *A.B.C. of Economics* (*Selected Prose*). **Wörgl:** see glossary to LXXIV (441).

482: : "The process. Footprints and the foot carrying the head; the head conducting the feet, an orderly movement under lead of the intelligence." (*Confucius*, page 22.) Usually glossed 'the way'—this is the 'tao' of Taoism, though in fact it is a concept which pervades all Chinese thought, moral, political and metaphysical. (J.C.)

videt et urbes πολύμητις: (L and Gk; *polumetis*) [many men] he saw and cities, of many counsels (Odysseus).

Ce rusé personnage: (F) that crafty personage (Odysseus).

483: **No hay amor....:** (S) There is no love without jealousy/Without secrecy there is no love. (Lope de Vega).

Tre donne intorno...mente: (I) three women around my mind (adapted from Dante, Canzone XX).

"The Spring and Autumn": The *Ch'un Ch'iu*, the last of the five Confucian classics.

LXXIX

484: **battistero:** (I) baptistry.

Del Cossa: see glossary to XXIV (114).

485: **Greek rascality...Cicones:** "for the attack of the Ciconian town there was no excuse handy, it is pure devilment, and Ulysses and Co. deserved all they got thereafter..." (*Literary Essays*, page 212). **Hagoromo:** see glossary to XXXVI (178) and LXXX (534).

e poi basta: (I) and then stop!

aulentissima rosa fresca: (I) sweetly smelling fresh red rose (Alcamo, c. 1170, *Dialogue*, the first recorded Italian poem).

486: ἦθος: *ethos*, custom, moral climate.
γλαύξ: *glaux*, little owl (see glossary to LXXIV, 438).
487: **chiacchierona:** (I) babbler.

The ideograms in the margin are (a) **huang²:** yellow (b) **niao³:** bird (c) **chih³:** comes to rest. The characters are quoted from *The Great Digest*, Comment III, 2. They are, in turn, quoted from *The Odes* as part of a comment on the phrase "coming to rest in perfect goodness." (Pound translates this as 'rectitude' or 'equity'. Cf. *Confucius*, page 39, along with page 29 and 45.) (J.C.)

si come avesse...gran dispitto: (I) as if he held hell in great scorn (*Inferno*, X, 36). The heretic, Farinata degli Uberti, remains defiant even in Hell—Pound here connects him with Capaneus, who defied Zeus and was killed by a thunderbolt.

488: **Manitou:** Algonquin Indian name for the natural power which permeates all things—hence his connection here with Dionysus—see commentary on II.
ἐνὶ Τροίῃ: *eni Troië*, in Troy. From the Sirens' song to Odysseus, "We know all the labours that the Greeks and Trojans endured on the plains of Troy."
Eos: the dawn; **Hesperus:** the evening star.

489: **Maelids:** nymphs of apple trees.
Ἴακχος...Κύθηρα: *Iacchos...Kuthera, Io!*, Iacchos is a mystic name for Dionysus. **Io!:** Hail!
ἐλέησον **Kyrie eleison:** Have mercy, Lord have mercy (from the Greek Orthodox liturgy and the Roman Mass).

490: Χαῖρε: *Kaire*, Hail.
Κόρη: Koré (Persephone).
Pomona: Roman goddess of apple trees (Ovid, *Metamorphoses*, XIV, 623 ff.).
γλαυκῶπις: *glaukopis*, with gleaming eyes (see glossary to LXXIV, 438).

491: ἰχώρ: *ichor*, juice which flows in the veins of gods.
Melagrana: (I) pomegranate.

492: Ἥλιος: Helios (the sun god).
δεινὰ εἶ, Κύθηρα: *Deina ei, Kuthera*, You are terrible, Cythera (Venus).
Κόρη καὶ Δήλια καὶ Μαῖα: Koré and Delia and Maia.
aram/nemus/vult: see glossary to LXXIV (446).
Cimbica: Puma, "...friend to man, the most loyal of the wild cats." (*Selected Prose*, page 401; *431*).

LXXX

493: θέμις: *themis*, justice.
senesco/sed amo: (L) I grow old/but I love.
"Come pan, niño!": (S) eat bread, boy!

494: ἀγλαὸς 'αλάου πόρνη Περσεφόνεια: *aglaos alaou porne Persephoneia.*
Jumbled Greek of uncertain meaning, but based from memory on the
lines from the *Odyssey* quoted XXXIX (194) which Pound translated
at the opening of XLVII.

494: **simplex munditiis:** (L) plain in her neatness (Horace, *Odes*, I, 5).

495: **a dark forest:** "Turgenev said that the heart of another is a dark forest"
(*Guide to Kulchur*, page 200).

497: **luz:** (S) light.

498: **croce di Malta, figura del sol:** (I) Maltese Cross, image of the sun.
何 The ideograms in the margin are: **ho²:** how? **yüan:** far. They
are quoted from *Analects* IX, 30 and also appear with a
paraphrase at LXXVII (465). (J.C.)
遠

499: **temporis acti:** (L) past days (Horace, *Ars Poetica*, 173).
ΟΥ ΤΙΣ/'ἄχρονος: *ou tis/achronos*, No man/without time, timeless.
犬 The ideogram **chuan³:** man and dog. Pound must be seeing
the dot as a 'dog' beyond and to the right of the man—this
is purely fanciful—just a joke? (J.C.)
"But for Kuan Chung...tother way on": Prime Minister of the State
of Chi (684-645 B.C.). This way of buttoning was considered characteristic of neighboring barbarian tribes. (J.C.)
cosi discesi per l'aer maligno: (I) Thus I descended through the evil
air (*Inferno*, V, 1 and 86).
on doit le temps... vient: (F) one must take the weather as it comes.

500: **"a S. Bartolomeo mi vidi.....piatosa sembianza:** (I) at S. Bartolomeo
I found myself with a little boy/nailed to the ground with his arms
spread,/as on the cross, groaning./He said: I am the moon./With his
feet on the silver scythe,/he appeared pitiful to me. (No source has
been found for these lines, so they are probably written by Pound.)
semina motuum: (L) seeds of motion (Pound glosses the phrase, "the
inner impulses of the tree," *Confucius*, page 59).
hagoromo: feather-mantle of a Tennin (aerial spirit). In the Noh play
Hagoromo, a fisherman finds it hanging on a bough. The Tennin demands its return. The fisherman "argues with her, and finally promises
to return it, if she will teach him her dance or part of it. She accepts
the offer." (*Translations*, page 308.) She says she cannot "do the dance
rightly without" the mantle, but the fisherman hesitates, as he is not
certain she will keep her word, saying, "how do I know you'll not be
off to your palace without even beginning your dance, not even a
measure?," to which she replies, "Doubt is of mortals; with us there is
no deceit." He is ashamed, and gives her the mantle. Her dance is
symbolical of the daily changes of the moon: "The jewelled axe takes
up the eternal renewing, the palace of the moon-god is being renewed
with the jewelled axe, and this is always recurring."
At Ephesus she had compassion....: Artemis, the moon-goddess, is
seen here in a more benevolent aspect than in IV and XXX. One of
her most famous shrines was at Ephesus.

501: **Monte Gioiosa:** on the north coast of Sicily; **Allegre:** Haute-Loire, France.
olim de Malatestis: see glossary to XI (50).
wan: (C) precise knowledge, culture (?).

504: **"Les moeurs passent...baladines.":** (F) Customs pass, sorrow remains/"in pink crystal helmets the mountebanks."

506: **Quand vous serez bien vieille:** (F) "When you are old and grey"— (Ronsard)—I've used Yeats's version.

510: **de mis soledades vengan:** (S) out of my solitudes let them come (Lope de Vega).

511: **Les hommes...beauté:** (F) Men have I don't know such strange fear of beauty.
Arthur: Arthur Symons (1865-1945), English poet.
βροδοδάκτυλος 'Ηώς: *Brododaktulos Eos*, Rosy-fingered dawn.
Κύθηρα δεινὰ: *Kuthera deina*, terrible Cythera.

512: **πάντα ῾ρεῖ:** *panta rei*, All flows (Heracleitos, *c.* 500 B.C.).
ὑπὲρ μόρον: *uper moron*, beyond destiny.
Favonus, vento benigno: (L) West wind, gentle wind.

513: **when the raft broke...over me:** a reference to the passage in the *Odyssey* (V, 313 ff.) when Odysseus is nearly drowned after he has left Kalypso's island on his raft.
Immaculata, Introibo: (L) Immaculate, I shall enter (from the Preparation of the Roman Mass).
Perpetua, Agatha, Anastasia: St. Perpetua, d. 203, a Carthaginian martyr; Agatha, a 3rd century virgin martyred by Decius; Anastasia, a 4th century noblewoman, martyred by Diocletian. All three are recalled in the Mass.
saeculorum: (L) immemorial, timeless (the Mass).
repos donnez a cils: (OF) give rest to those (Villon, *Le Testament*, 195).
senza termine funge: (I) "there is no end to its action" (*Confucius*, page 187). Pound is quoting from the end of his Italian translation of Confucius's *Chung Yung*, which he completed during the war.
Les larmes...Tristesse: (F) The tears I have cried flood over me/Late, very late, I know you, Sadness.
Nadasky, Duett....: these names, and most of the others in the next 7 lines, are inmates of the D.T.C. The same applies, over the page, to Zupp, Bufford and Bohon.
(no fortune and with a name to come): Elpenor (I, 4).

516: **Si tuit li dolh...marrimen:** (Pr) "If all the grief and woe and bitterness," first line of Bertrans de Born's *Planh for the Young English King* (*Personae*, page 36).
Tudor indeed is gone....FRANCE: see FitzGerald's *Rubàiyàt of Omar Khayyàm*, "Iram indeed is gone and all his rose."
grand couturier: (F) great dress-maker, pattern-cutter.

517: **Hay aqui mucho....reliHion:** (S) Here is much Catholicism and very little religion.

518: **"Te cavero...corata a te":** (I) "I'll cut your guts out" "And I yours."
ʼΙυγξ...ἐμὸν ποτὶ δῶμα τὸν ᾿άνδρα: *Iugx...emon poti dōma ton andra,* Little wheel...man to my house (Theocritus II). The girl is casting a spell with a magic wheel to bring back her man.

519: **at my grates no Althea:** "And my divine Althea brings/To whisper at the grates" (Lovelace, *To Althea from Prison*).
Lawes: Henry (1596-1662), English composer; **Jenkins:** John (1592-1678), musician to Charles I and II.
Dolmetsch: Arnold (1858-1940), French musician and instrument maker. See Pound's essay on him (*Literary Essays*, pages 431-440).

520: **Dowland:** John (1563-1626), English composer.
Your eyen two...susteyne: from Chaucer's *Merciles Beauté.*
Ed ascoltando...mormorio: (I) and listening to the light murmur (Pound's Italian).
hypostasis: substance; personal existence.
diastasis: separation (literally, separation of bones without fracture). Here perhaps, aloof.
Εἰδὼς: *Eidōs,* Knowing.

521: **Elysium:** Paradise; the land of the blessed dead.
Paquin: Parisian dress designer. Echoes the last line of LXXX (516).
Rathe: quick (archaic).

522: **Blunt:** Wilfred Scawen (1840-1922), English poet and political thinker. He opposed British Imperialism, supporting the ideas of Mazzini. Pound wrote of him in 1912, "the grandest of old men, the last of the great Victorians...." (*Poetry,* January 1913).

LXXXII

523: **Dirce:** see glossary to L (249).
ΕΜΟΣ ΠΟΣΙΣ...ΧΕΡΟΣ: *emos posis....cheros,* my husband...hand (Aeschylus, *Agamemnon,* 1404-5). See glossary to LVIII (323).

525: **res non verba:** (L) things not words.
ideogram jen: "*Humanitas,* humanity, in the full sense of the word, 'manhood.' The man and his full contents." (*Confucius,* page 22.) It may also be glossed 'benevolence,' 'altruism,' even 'Love' (as that which extends beyond the members of one's own tribe). This is the primary Confucian virtue, the first of "THE FOUR TUAN/ or foundations" (LXXXV, 545). (J.C.)
Tereus!: see commentary on IV.

526: **"O troubled reflection...heart":** from Whitman, *Out of the Cradle Endlessly Rocking.* Like Canto LXXXIII, its theme is death.
GEA TERRA: (L & Gk) the Earth.

fu Nicolo...del Po: (I) was Nicolo d'Este/and on this side and the other of the Po. See commentary and glossary to XXIV.

ἐμὸν τὸν ἄνδρα: see glossary to preceding canto.

connubium terrae: (L) marriage with the earth.

ἔφατα πόσις ἐμός: *ephata posis emos,* she said my husband.

ΧΘΟΝΟΣ...ΧΘΟΝΙΟΣ: *chthonos...chthonios,* of the earth...beneath the earth, or, sprung from the earth.

'ΙΧΩΡ: *ichor,* juice that flows in the veins of gods.

527:    δακρύων/ἐντεῦθεν: *dakruon/enteuthen,* tears/thence.

periplum: see glossary to LIX (324).

LXXXIII

528:    **HUDOR et Pax:** (Gk & L) Water and Peace.

Gemisto: see glossary to VIII (31).

lux enim...accidens: (L) for light is an attribute of fire (Grosseteste?).

omnia quae sunt, lumina sunt: (L) all things that are, are lights (Erigena, see glossary to XXXVI, 179).

529:    **consiros:** (Pr) with grief (See Yeats, *Down by the Sally Gardens*). Uncle William is Yeats.

soll deine Liebe sein: (G) is to be your love.

Olim de Malatestis: (L) see glossary to XI (50).

πάντα ῥει: see glossary to LXXX (512).

530:    Δρυάς: *Dryas,* Dryad (wood nymph).

Plura diafana: (L) many translucent forms (see glossary to XXXVI, 177).

532:    The ideograms are **wu⁴**: do not; **chu⁴**: help; **chang³**: to grow.

Kung-Sun Chow: 2nd book of the *Works of Mencius* where there is a story about a man from Sung, who against the natural life force, tried to make his crops grow better by pulling at them—they withered— hence the words "do not help to grow."

Ca': (Italian, from *casa*) house [of].

DAKRUON: (Gk) tears.

La Vespa: (I) The [female] wasp.

533:    **The infant has descended:** Pound imagines the infant wasp re-enacting, in miniature, Odysseus's journey to the shades.

OI ΧΘΟΝΙΟΙ: (Gk) those of the underworld.

εἰς χθονίους: *eis chthonious,* to those (or the gods) of the underworld.
Περσεφόνεια: *Persephoneia.*
Cristo Re, Dio Sole: (I) Christ King, Sun God.

534: **aere perennius:** (L) more enduring than bronze (Horace, *Odes* III, 30).

535: **The eyes, this time my world,... pool, sky, sea:** Pound has become one with the "new subtlety of eyes" that came into his tent in LXXXI. "They have chang'd eyes," to quote Prospero's words in *The Tempest* (I, ii, 444).
Mir Sagen... Greis: (G) The ladies say to me you are an old man.

LXXXIV

537: **Si tuit.......τέθνηκε:** (Pr & Gk) If all the grief and tears/ *tethneke:* He is dead/all the worth, all the good (the Provençal is by Bertrans de Born, see glossary to LXXX, 516). **J.P. Angold** (1909-43), English poet, killed in World War II.

539: **Wei, Chi and Pikan:** Confucius wrote, about the decline of the Yin dynasty in the 12th century B.C., "The Viscount of Wei retired. The Viscount of Chi became a slave. Pi-kan protested and died.... Yin had three men..." (*Analects,* XVIII, 1).
Xaire: (Gk) Hail. **Alessandro:** probably A. Pavolini; **Fernando:** probably F. Mezzasoma. Both senior ministers of Mussolini's Salò Republic. After his assassination, they were shot and hung up by the heels with him in Milan.
il Capo: Mussolini; **Pierre:** P. Laval; **Vidkun:** V. Quisling.
quand vos venetz... l'escalina: (Pr) when you reach the top of the stairs (adapted from Dante, *Purgatorio,* XXVI, 146).
ἦθος: *ethos,* see glossary to LXXIX (486).

明 ideogram **ming²:** "The sun and moon, the total light process, the radiation, reception and reflection of light; hence the intelligence. Bright, brightness, shining. Refer to Scotus Erigena, Grosseteste and the notes on light in my *Cavalcanti.*" (*Confucius,* page 20.)

540: 中 ideogram **chung¹;** pivot, point of balance. See fuller glossary LXX (413).

Kumrad Koba: Stalin.
e poi dissi.... uguale: (I) and then I said to the sister/of the little shepherdess of the pigs:/and these Americans?/Do they behave well?/ and she: not very well/And I: better than the Germans?/and she: the same.

SECTION: ROCK-DRILL

Pound was flown to Washington in November, 1945, a sick man from the treatment he had received at Pisa. It was not long before he was found mentally unfit to stand trial. In December he had been transferred to Howard Hall, St. Elizabeth's Hospital—a barred, windowless ward, reserved for criminal lunatics. A letter he wrote to his lawyer from there on Sunday, at the end of January, reads, as Hugh Kenner has said, like a coda to *The Pisan Cantos:*

<pre>
end of   Dungeon
Jan.   Domenica
mental torture
constitution a religion
a world lost
grey mist barrier impassible
    ignorance absolute
                    anonyme
futility of 'might have been'
coherent areas
        constantly
                invaded
    aiuto¹
        Pound
</pre>

He remained in "the hell hole," as he called it, for just over a year, until the hospital decided to move him to another ward, where he had a room of his own. His health gradually improved and he resumed writing. At first he concentrated on translations: *The Confucian Analects* (1949), Sophokles, *Women of Trachis* (1953) and *The Classic Anthology Defined by Confucius* (1954). It was probably not until 1953 or 1954 that he started working on the *Cantos* again.

Rock-Drill is divided into two parts: LXXXV-LXXXIX are historical, didactic; XC-XCV is an extended lyric, "above civic order, l'AMOR" (634), showing a

---

¹help

89

kind of beauty that has rarely been present in English since mediaeval times, and was only there in flashes then. The two parts animate each other— LXXXV-LXXXIX provide an historical basis for XC-XCV. They form different sides of the same reality.

Cantos LXXXV-LXXXIX are a condensation and restatement of the main historical and economic ideas of the poem. It was essential for Pound to do this, so that he could re-orient himself to continue the *Cantos*. He had described the way history is presented here as early as 1911, "the method of luminous detail . . . certain facts give one a sudden insight into circumjacent conditions, into their causes, their effects, into sequence and law" (*Selected Prose*, pages 21 and 22).

Rock-Drill deals with the "two forces in history: one that divides, shatters, and kills, and one that contemplates the unity of the mystery. . . . There is the force that falsifies, the force that destroys every clearly delineated symbol, dragging man into a maze of abstract arguments, destroying not one but every religion. But the images of the gods, or Byzantine mosaics, move the soul to contemplation and preserve the tradition of the undivided light." (*Selected Prose*, pages 276–7; *306–7*.) This conflict is best summed up by the last line of LXXXVI and the beginning of LXXXVII: "Bellum cano perenne . . . ./ . . . . between the usurer and any man who/wants to do a good job" (568–69).

Canto LXXXV goes back to the beginnings of the Confucian tradition by presenting radiant ideograms from the *Shu King* (Book of History), the oldest complete Chinese classic, which covers seventeen hundred years, from 2357 to 631 B.C. Thus, taking up themes from the previous summary of Chinese history (LIII-LXI), the roots of Confucianism are embodied in *Rock-Drill*, just as the late (eighteenth century) Confucianism of Kang Hi and Iong Ching will be presented in *Thrones*—a final manifestation of a tradition persisting for over 4,000 years. The ideograms act as an important means of creating the general effect of radiance which pervades *Rock-Drill*—the beauty of the lay-out of the words on the page is more marked here than anywhere else in the poem.

Canto LXXXVI juxtaposes more Chinese from the *Shu King* against facets of nineteenth and twentieth century European confusion; many of the lines indicate the seeds of the two world wars, driving home, with an almost bumpy rhythm, perceptions radical to the *Cantos*—"luminous details"—from the time of Alexander the Great to the present. "Pine seed splitting cliff's edge" (572)—it is not for nothing that "This section is labelled Rock-Drill" (601).

In LXXXVIII and LXXXIX, American history is presented in detail for the last time, with new heroes (Thomas Hart Benton and Randolph of Roanoake) who fought for the same values as Adams, Jefferson and Van Buren.

Canto LXXXVIII opens with an account (from Benton's *Thirty Years View*) of the duel between Randolph and Henry Clay, which is followed by a summary of events in the perennial war between the usurers and the creators of real wealth. The reader who knows the middle cantos should be able to follow the gist of the argument easily. LXXXVIII closes with a summary of Benton's speech against the renewal of the U.S. Bank Charter. This continues the "Bank War" theme, which was introduced in XXXVII, and clarifies that section of the poem.

Canto LXXXIX continues with Benton, Randolph, money and history: "Without historic blackout/they cannot maintain perpetual wars" (595). John Frémont, the American explorer, is introduced, and his journey, with his guide Kit Carson, "3 days with no food but rosebuds" (598) across the snow-covered mountains into California, rhymes with other journeys of exploration: Hanno (XL) and the expedition of Joseph Rock to the Na-Khi people (*Thrones* and *Drafts and Fragments*). Frémont's climbing, "I want Frémont looking at mountains" (604) is a fitting introduction to the paradisal ascent which is to follow.

Cantos XC-XCV are to some extent an attempt to write the "Paradise" Pound had planned in 1940, which the war prevented; but it is important not to oversimplify, as paradise has flashed through the poem from the beginning;—some words he wrote as early as 1913 provide as good a commentary as any on this section of *Rock-Drill*:

> Richard of St. Victor who was half a neo-Platonist, tells us that by naming over all the beautiful things we can think of, we may draw back upon our minds some vestige of the unrememberable beauties of paradise. If we are not given to mystical devotions we may suspect that the function of poetry is, in part, to draw back upon our mind a paradise, if you like, or equally, one's less detestable hours and the outrageous hopes of one's youth.
>
> ("The Approach to Paris VI," *New Age,* 9 October 1913)

T.S. Eliot, in his essay on Dante, said that we have lost the habit of seeing things in a visionary way. XC-XCV attempt to restore this "lost kind of experience" (617).

These six cantos, by interaction between what is living in the classical and mediaeval worlds, cohere in a way which earlier portions of the poem intentionally did not, because they grow out of the highest use of the intellect, "contemplation" as defined by the twelfth century theologian, Richard of St. Victor. Pound summarised Richard's definitions as follows: "There are three modes of thought, cogitation, meditation, and contemplation. In the first the mind flits aimlessly about the object, in the second it circles about it in a methodical manner, in the third it is unified with the object." (*Guide to Kulchur,* page 77.)

Beginning with XC we are in what Pound called "the radiant world where one thought cuts through another with clean edge, a world of moving energies...magnetisms that take form, that are seen, or that border the visible, the matter of Dante's *Paradiso,* the glass under water, the form that seems a form seen in a mirror, these realities perceptible to the sense, interacting..." (*Literary Essays,* page 154). To use the words of Richard of St. Victor, "contemplation, guided by a ray of vision, sheds light over numberless things."

Thus innumerable images are here formed in the mind, "to remain there, resurgent" (LXXIV, 446): the fountain of Castalia; the moonlight, "always there"; the great concourse of beasts before the altar in XC, recalling Dionysus, "and where was nothing/now is furry assemblage" (the heaviness of the word "assemblage" brings them physically before us); the beasts have come to be present at the raising of the spirits of the dead, "free now, ascending," with incense and myrrh, not, as in Canto I, "by ditch digging and sheep's guts" (638); the sea caves out of whose green depths rise the eyes of Aphrodite, "manifest and not abstract," which are the same colour as the holly leaf that

91

Saint Hilary may have looked at; Queen Elizabeth, Drake and the Armada; first the crystal river, and then the deep sapphire over which the Princess Ra-Set voyages, which recalls the colour of the blue serpent that "glides from the rock-pool"; Brut's invocation to Diana (compare XXX); the place where the light was "almost solid"; the Egyptian king, Kati, who said "A man's paradise is his good nature"; Odysseus/Pound who is saved from drowning and reaches Phaeakia by the aid of Leucothea's veil; and who moves through XCIV, in the form of Apollonius of Tyana, who "made his peace with the animals";—these are some of the images and themes that, taking light from each other, build a paradise, and, by the recurrence of the birth of Venus, "Dea Libertatis" (681): "crystal waves weaving together toward the great healing"[1] help to give form, which, to quote Kenner, is "both orderly and free," to the whole poem.

These cantos are packed, and their patterns of thought, complex; the constant variation of speed and tone, the sense of a live man talking, prevents boredom. Pound has here evolved a form ideally suited to writing a long poem. One canto will range from humorous aphorism, "ten to charge a nest of machine guns/for one who will put his name in a chit" (628), to the sustained lyricism, with its slow rhythm, of the prayer beginning, "The autumn leaves blow from my hand" (628), to the magical, "Au bois dormant,/not yet... Not yet!/do not awaken." There is no incongruity, and worlds of experience are contained in each line, or half line. To quote Keats, Pound never "lets go an isolated verisimilitude caught from the Penetralium of the Mystery"—as he says in XCIII, "There must be incognita" (631).

"The essence of religion is the *present* tense" (*Selected Prose*, page 72; *70*). Pound's paradise is moving because it is of the moment—real, but fragile as a moth's wing, "Beloved, do not fall apart in my hands" (631).

---

[1]Also an image of Drake's victory.

LXXXV

543: **LING**[2]		Rationality, spirituality; Pound uses the equivalent, 'sensibility', which works in context. It is the quality which distinguishes men from animals, a gift of 'Heaven.' (J.C.)
I Yin:		18th century B.C. minister to Emperor Tching Tang (LIII, 264-65); the two characters to the right stand for his name.

Wellington's peace...: a victory for usury; see L.
chih[3]: see glossary to LII (261).

92

hsien²: virtuous, worthy; also virtuous ministers.

544: **turbae:** (L) tumult; the masses.

jen²: see glossary to LXXXII (525).

chih⁴: wisdom; the bottom element is a "sun under it all."

chèu: beginnings, as in "things have scopes and beginnings" (LXXVII, 465).

i li: equity (Pound's usual equivalent) or righteousness, and propriety, or the rites. Two of the virtues which form with 'jen' and 'chih' (above) the 'Four Foundations.' (J.C.)

chung¹⁻⁴: inner nature; the heart instilled with the above virtues. (J.C.)

wei heou: precisely the sovereign (where the virtues are most effectively instilled). (J.C.)

Σοφία: *Sophia,* Wisdom.

545: **THE FOUR TUAN:** the fundamental Confucian virtues, 'jen', 'chih', 'i', and 'li' which have been named on the opposite page: Love; wisdom; righteousness and the rites.

 The ideogram is 'tuan,' foundation. (J.C.)

bachi: (I) cocoon, silk worms. "The peasant women carrying silk co-coons to Church carefully hidden in their clasped hands . . ." (*Selected Prose,* page 71). This is introduced here as an example of a living rite which Pound had seen in Rapallo.

Ygdrasail: ash tree in Nordic mythology whose roots and branches join heaven, earth and hell.

shih²: time, season.

ch'ên²: sincere.

i moua pou gning: and all were well (said, in the context, of the spirits of mountains and rivers).

Perspicax qui excolit se ipsum: (L) perceptive the man who cultivates his talents.

546: : The first ideogram, 'tê,' usually translated 'virtue,' is a key Confucian word corresponding in some of its original usages with Latin *virtus* (also of interest to Pound). In *Confucius* (page 21) it is glossed: "What results, i.e., the action resultant from this straight gaze into the heart. The 'know thyself' carried into action. Said action also serving to clarify the self-knowledge."

Τέχνη: *Techne,* skill, art.

σεαυτόν: *seauton,* oneself.

CONTEMPLATIO: (L) contemplation; a term from Richard of St. Victor, who defined it as the highest form of thought where the mind is unified with the object of contemplation.

"in T'oung loco palatium": (L) in T'oung the place of palaces. T'ung was where Ch'eng T'ang (cf. LIII, 264-65) was buried and where his heir mourned him, until . . .

ko tchoung iun te: in the end he became sincerely virtuous.

szu':   sacrifices, sacrifices to the dead (the apostrophe is probably a misprint for a '4' tone mark).

547:   **i jênn iuên . . . chên:**

These characters go together and are extracted from two clauses in the *Book of History* which may be translated (using Pound's words where appropriate): ". . . The One Man (or ruler) is particularly virtuous; whereby, ('in the long run') all the people will follow suit." 'I jen' is the One Man; the first ideogram on this page corresponds to 'whereby'; and 'chên', the second character, is the virtue or purity inspired in the people. (J.C.) This character is noted in Pound's *Confucius* (page 268, comment on *Analects* XV, xxxvi): "The proper man has a shell and a direction. . . . This *chên* is a key word, technical, from the 'Changes' it is more than the atoraxia of the stoics . . . it implies going somewhere."

reddidit gubernium imperatori: (L) he returned the rule to the Emperor.

ch'ên chiai: he sent out admonitions.

陳
戒

I Yin advises the heir of Ch'eng T'ang, Tài Chia, after returning the rule to the young Emperor.

quam simplex animus Imperatoris: (L) how pure (simple) the spirit of the Emperor.

: The 7 characters at the bottom of the page are quoted in a somewhat scrambled form (unless Pound is trying to manipulate the old Chinese) from the section of the *Book of History* (in Couvreur's translation) cited by Pound. I set them here in the order in which they appear in the above book. I have put a dash where the character 'not' is missing from the graphs as they appear in the *Cantos*.

As well as stressing the interdependence of sovereign and people, the passage affirms their absolute right to self-fulfillment. The following is James Legge's translation: "If ordinary men and women do not find the opportunity to give full development to their virtue the people's lord will be without the proper aids to complete his merit." (J.C.)

548: **P'an Keng:**   17th king of the Shang dynasty. He reigned in the 14th century B.C. The first character on this page is *P'an*, part of his name. (J.C.)

:P'an Keng was responsible for moving the dynastic capital. The next 5 ideograms are part of an exhortation to engage in this enterprise and "Seek every one long continuance in this (new city), which is to be our abode;..." (Legge's translation). (J.C.) The passage connects with the next gloss, i.e., do not "pawn your castles."

Baros metetz en gatge: (Pr) Barons pawn your castles!
549: **prezzo giusto:** (I) just price.
UBI JUS VAGUM: (L) where law is undefined (vague). See glossary to LXVIII (396).
Alexander paid ... soldiery: a frequently repeated line in *Rock-Drill*.

He, like Tching Tang (who opened the copper mine, LIII, 264), understood "the distributive function of money."
cymba et remis: (L) a boat with oars.
Praecognita bonum...moveas: (L) Have foreknowledge of the good
in order to act.
550: **"Fatigare in sacris...revereri":** (L) Officiousness in sacrifice is ir-
reverence.
Fou iue: First minister to Kao Tsoung.
chung wang hsien: Pound's "Up to then, I just hadn't
caught on" is as good a translation as
any. The character, *hsien*, means, in this
context: 'to be clear (about), to be enlightened'. It first appeared in LXXIV (429). (J.C.)
Sicut vinum ac mustum: (L) just as wine and must. Kao Tsung is
asking Fu Yüeh to be his ferment, to activate and ultimately refine his
will. (J.C.)
tchéu: the will; the direction of the will. (See glossary to LXXVII, 467.)
tao tsi: the way (of virtue) will accumulate (in you). Part of Fu Yüeh's
reply. (J.C.)
551: **Nisi cum sapientibus...regit:** (L) Unless he does not rule with the
wise. Compare, "When the prince has gathered about him/All the
savants..." (XIII, 59).
abire decere: (L) It's time to go.
Ad Meng vadum: (L) To Meng ford. Where the founder of the Chou
dynasty rallied his supporters, preparing to undertake the 'Mandate
of Heaven.' (J.C.)
Les moeurs...fleurit: (F) Customs were reformed/virtue flourished.
552: **"ch'e' ditta dentro":** (I) what is dictated within (Dante, *Purgatorio*,
XXIV, 54).
demittit aerumnas: (L) sends down suffering.
Ts'oung　　intelligent,

Tàn　　sincere

ming　　perspicacious: the qualities enabling one to...

tso iuên heóu: become a great sovereign. For the third ideogram, *ming*,
see glossary to LXXXIV (539). (J.C.)
Wu:　　First ruler of the Chou dynasty, Wu Wang (LIII, 266).

"e canta la gallina,: (I) "and the hen crows." "The Chinese have a
very old saying, that it is an ill omen if the hen crows" (*Radio Speeches*,
page 286).

553: **nai tcheu t'si:** then stop and adjust your ranks; a reference to Wu Wang's good military practice. The characters cover the last two words.

quasi silvam convenit: (L) met like a forest.
jo lin: like a forest; the character is clearly a pictogram for forest.

These three characters, in the middle of the page, below the trees, mean respectively, 'perfection,' 'blood' and 'bias.' The first refers to the perfection of the ruler's virtue, the second is either the blood spilt in the battle for Chou supremacy, or a mistake for the word 'without' as in the quality of being 'without bias' (in appointments etc.) which is part of the ruler's perfection. (All this is based on the context of the *Book of History* from which the characters are taken.) (J.C.)

T'oung kouan nài chenn: make (the people's) hardships your own. Another exhortation, this time Wu Wang to a vassal. (The last character of this group is the first over the page.)

554: **min kién:** people (as) mirror. (The first character is a mistake—'min' is the corrected reading.) "Let not men look into water; let them look into the glass of other people" (Legge's translation, *Shu King*, V, xi, 2). (J.C.)

97

土
中
旦
日
配
皇

: These 6 characters form a group. They are **t'u chung:** in the earth's centre; **Tan yüeh:** Tan said; **pei houâng:** would become the companion of august (Heaven). This is part of a speech by Tan, the Duke of Chou, to the young second Emperor of that dynasty concerning the benefits of the new capital at Lo which was considered to be the 'centre of the earth.' When the Emperor was able to reside there, it would make him 'the companion of Heaven.' This Duke was one of Confucius's heroes, the model of a cultivated, accomplished and virtuous statesman. His given name is the word for 'dawn' in Chinese and Pound almost certainly felt that this was significant. The relevant character, 'tan,' occurs in a number of places throughout the later Cantos; (cf. especially XCI, 615). (J.C.)

554-5: k'i p'eng . . . . tcho: (indulge) partiality . . . . burning fire.

其
朋
火

555:

This is part of a warning, again by the Duke of Chou, against partiality, which, if it is not held in check, will develop into a conflagration. The characters at the bottom of 554 are literally 'his companions' (hence the Odysseus allusion); the one over the page is the 'fire'; and 'tcho' refers to another word describing its burning and increasing destructiveness. (J.C.)

敬

ching[4]: reverence. In the relevant part of the *Book of History*, it is used to describe an attentiveness to self, particularly appropriate to a ruler. Pound elsewhere saw it as 'respect,' "respect for the kind of intelligence that enables grass seed to grow grass; the cherry stone to make cherries" (*Confucius*, page 193). It is last used in the *Cantos* in connection with prayer (CX, 781).
Praetantissimos regere: (L) the most outstanding men to rule.

甸

tien[4]: to rule.

nullus non splendidas . . . . benefaceret: (L) no one failed to do splendid deeds/so that he could benefit.

556:

丕

p'i: This is in fact the 'great' of the 'great sensibility' (see glossary to LXXXV, 543). While putting down a rebellion, King Ch'eng, the second of the Chou dynasty, affirmed "Our dynasty came in because of a great sensibility" (*Book of History*, Couvreur's, IV, xiv, 13), and "In this business we have followed no double aims" (*ibidem* IV, xiv, 15). This second affirmation is the explanation of *pou éul cheu* (*pu erh*[4] is simply part of the Wade-Giles for this phrase: pu erh shih) which corresponds to 'follow no double aims.' (J.C.)

 pou éul cheu:
pu erh[4]   Follow no double aims.

"O nombreux officiers: (F) O numerous officers.
          : City.

Imperator....dico: (L) The Emperor said. Again I say.
cognovit aerumnas: (L) he has known suffering.

557:   **invicem docentes:** (L) teaching each other.
Sagetrieb: (German coined by Pound) oral tradition; *Sage:* speak; *trieb:* life force, instinct.
The large ideogram next to *Sagetrieb* means to teach. In the *Book of History* the Duke of Chou tells us that, of old, ministers were used to teaching each other. (J.C.)

chêu:
          it depends on us.

ngò

Diuturna cogites: (L) thinking of the distant future.

558:   **Hio kòu jou kouàn:** study antiquity before entering into your offices.
touán: determination, decisiveness. Pound here makes a reference to the *Ta Seu* which he called the *Ta Hsio* or *Great Digest.* See *Confucius,* page 77, where 'tuan' is "cut the cackle (ideogram of the axe and documents of the archives tied up in silk)."

pei[4]: all (complete); the 'all things complete from/in one man,' of the line above.

yung[2]: 'tolerance' corresponding to 'charity' in the line below; it is the 'ioung' of

iou ioung te nai ta: have forbearance and your virtue will be great (Legge's translation—*Shu King,* V, xxi, 3).

chong
          to be born good (of mankind)

heów

che funge: (I) which acts.

559: **"One of those days...heaven.":** "There speaks the supreme sense of human values. There speaks WORK unbartered. That is the voice of humanity in its highest possible manifestation." (*Selected Prose*, page 253; *283*.)

οὐ ταῦτα...κακοῖσι δειλίαν: *ou tauta kakoisi deilian*, isn't that adding cowardice to our ills (Sophokles, *Elektra*, 351).

as the hand grips the wheat:

The ideogram next to this line means (i) to grasp (ii) a handful of grain. The hand ![hand] may be seen gripping the wheat ![wheat]

The various Chinese references on this page take us back to the *Book of History* (IV, xvi, 12-14 in the Couvreur edition) and in particular to a passage relating to the transmission of virtue and wisdom from the sage King Owen (Wên) to his people and down the ages. The 'Prince of Kouo' et al. were the men of talent required to spread this virtue; 'Sagetrieb' was necessary in order that they instruct themselves and others; the 'grip' was the tenacity required to maintain the virtue; and the final character on this page ![char]

describes how this virtue is 'carried forward' into the future, often only by the taking of 'risks' or even through '(blind) presumption' which are further implications of this particular character. In the case of King Wên this strategy succeeded and his fame "reached the ears of God..." (J.C.)

aperiens tibi animum: (L) opening the spirit to you:

LXXXVI

560: ![ideogram hsu] The first ideogram is **hsü**: pity, sympathy. Pound's 'solicitude' translates it: the concern for the people of a virtuous ruler.

turbationem: (L) confusion.

"Dummheit, nicht Bosheit": (G) idiocy, not wickedness.

"Sono tutti eretici...cattivi": (I) "They are all heretics, Holy Father, but not evil."

je peux commencer....fiiniiiir: (F) I can begin a thing (a sculpture) every day, but/to finish.... Pound wrote a small book about the great Romanian sculptor, Brancusi (1876-1957), who he considered to be in "some dimension a saint" (*Guide to Kulchur*, page 105). His sculpture of a bird becomes an important image in *Drafts & Fragments:* "The marble form in the pine wood" (CX, 781).

![ideogram hsiang] **hsiang²:** particulars, details and, as an adverb, carefully: the way things should be observed; for the next character, *Ling²*, see glossary to LXXXV, 543.

tien: statutes; in the context from which Pound takes it in the *Book of History*, it means 'to serve' (the spirits of heaven).

561:

chiao: to teach (cf. glossary to LXXXV, 557).

'to select.' Both these characters are used of the co-founder of the Chou dynasty, Wu Wang, who was 'taught' and 'selected' by Heaven. (J.C.)

 jóung touan: 'and thus engaged'...the verbal part of this phrase is covered by the character, the 'tuan' of THE FOUR TUAN (see glossary to LXXXV, 545). Here it is a verb and refers to Kings Wen and Wu undertaking the 'mandate of Heaven.' (J.C.)

Edictorum: (L) of Edicts.

t'i iao: the body, the human frames, the essentials. In context, the substance combined with concision to be expected of written work and Edicts in particular. (J.C.)

ta seu...tá hiún: In the first of these two short lines Pound seems to be comparing the "ta hsün" found in the relevant paragraph of the *Book of History* with the *Ta Hsio,* or *Great Digest.* 'tê' is virtue and 'i' is equity or righteousness. The appropriate passage translates: "....virtue, and righteousness!—these are the great lessons" (Legge). (J.C.)

Quis erudiet...documenta?: (L) Who learns without examples?

Non periturum: (L) imperishable.

kiue sin: The first character corresponds to the 'chi' quoted later and means 'since,' though here it is used verbally for 'to exert,' or 'follow through with.' The second character is that for 'heart' and 'mind' which are not dissociated in Chinese. The words are taken from a bit of the *Book of History:* "...do not say, 'I am unequal to this'; but exert your mind/heart to the utmost" (Legge). As Pound notes, this is "leading to" Mencius I, i, VII, 10-11, where another monarch is similarly admonished for falsely claiming that he is unable (rather than unwilling) to exercise 'true kingship.' (J C.)

562:

tou: sincerely.

 tchoung: loyal.

101

tchen: virtuous (see glossary for LXXXV, 547).

These are King Mou's words of praise for the ancestors of one of his ministers, 'Kiun Ia,' in the hope that Kiun will carry on the tradition. (J.C.)

'constitution'—'the regular laws of duty' (Legge) in the exercise of government.

Part of the name of the Marquis of Lü who, as Minister of Justice under King Mou, gives his name to one of the chapters of the *Book of History* which is concerned with law.

etiam habitus inspiciendus: (L) even the appearance (or dress) should be examined (see next entry). (J.C.)

563:   **mao⁴:** appearance, bearing (dress). From a passage on the administration of justice which suggests that in making a judgement these things must be taken into account. These characters are translated by "It may depend on one man" and are taken from the last words of the *Book of History:* "The decline and fall of a state may arise from one man. The glory and tranquility of a state may also arise from the goodness of one man." (Legge.) (J.C.)

Edwardus: Edward VIII, "& the three years peace we owe Windsor/'36-'39" (XCV, 645).

i⁴: equity, or righteousness, associated with peace because, as in "The Spring and Autumn," "there/are/no/righteous/wars" (LXXVIII, 483). (J.C.)

564: **Geschäft:** (G) business.

For the ideogram on this page, which corresponds to 'trust', see glossary to XXXIV (171).

"Alla non della": see glossary to LXXVII (478).

οὐ ταῦτα...κακοῖσι: see glossary to LXXXV (559).

OBIT apud Babylonios: (L & G) He (Alexander) died with the Babylonians (323 B.C.).

565: **HE:** F.D. Roosevelt.

"What" (Cato speaking)...murder?": see glossary to XCVI (664).

566: **"Vous voullez.....trop rosse":** (F) "you wish to lay me/but I won't lay you/because I'm too canny."

litigantium dona: (L) gifts of litigation.

 féi: are not precious.

pào: acquisitions (treasure).

From a passage from the *History* where it is said that goods or money acquired in the form of bribes while judging a litigation are not precious but 'an accumulation of guilt.' Connects with a central passage of the *Great Digest:* "...a country does not profit by making profits, its equity is its profit," although this is at the national level (*Confucius,* pp. 87, 91).

non coelum non in medio: (L) it is not that heaven is not neutral.

La donna che volgo: (I) the lady who turns (Cavalcanti). "Fortune goodnight,/Smile once more, turne thy wheele" (*Lear,* II, 3).

CHÊN: 震 to shake; excite; to quicken; thunder (cf. XCI, 613).

567: **in angustiis me defendisti:** (L) you have defended me in my difficulties.
ne inutile quiescas: (L) be not uselessly at ease.

568: **Eleven literates...Morrow:** This was Senator Cutting's reply, when Pound asked him in the thirties how many intelligent senators there were.
hysteric...'39: probably Hitler. "Adolphe is, an almost, pathetic hysteric;" (Pound writing in *The New English Weekly,* 24 May 1934).
Bellum cano perenne: (L) I sing perpetual war.....

LXXXVII

569: **without regard to production...credit:** Pound's definition of usury.
"Why do you want...order?": Mussolini asked Pound this.
Roanoake: John Randolph (1773-1833), American statesman who figures prominently in LXXXVIII-LXXXIX.
paideuma: (Gk) "...the active element in the era, the complex of ideas which is in a given time germinal, reaching into the next epoch, but conditioning all the thought and action of its own time" (*Selected Prose,* page 254; *284*). Pound took the word from the writings of Leo Frobenius.
Infantilism increasing...issue: the problem of the control and issue of money.

570: **Χρεία:** *Chreia,* Need.
"Cogitatio, meditatio, contemplatio": For definitions of Richard of St. Victor's terms see my general commentary on *Rock-Drill.*
centrum circuli: (L) the centre of a circle. "'I am the centre of a circle which possesseth all parts of its circumference equally, but thou not so,' says the Angel appearing to Dante ('Vita Nuova,' XII)" (*Selected Prose,* page 29).
διάβορον...κακοῖσι: *diaboron....edeston ex autou phthinei pros kakoisi.* "Seemed to corrode of itself. Ate itself up..." (Sophokles, *Women of Trachis,* page 48). Daianeira is telling what happened to the wad of sheep's wool she used to daub the shirt of Nessus.

quia impossibile est: see glossary to LXXIV (442).
Ver novum: see glossary to XXXIX (193).
hic est medium: (L) here is the centre.
571: **chih:** see glossary to LII (261).
Ἀθάνα: *Athana,* Doric form of Athene. When Orestes was judged and the jurors couldn't agree, he was acquitted by her casting vote (Aeschylus, *Eumenides*). The beginnings of jury trial.
Ocellus: Pythagorean philosopher.
jih hsin: see glossary to LIII (265).
The play: *Women of Trachis;* **φλογιζόμενον:** *phlogizomenon,* flame, blazing.
gospoda: (Romanian) lady of the house, **Δηάνειρα** (the wife of Herakles). **λαμπρὰ συμβαίνει:** *lampra sumbainei,* cohere in radiance. See *Women of Trachis,* "...what/SPLENDOUR,/IT ALL COHERES" (Page 66).
572: **chih⁴:** "direction of the will..." (*Confucius,* page 22).
gros légumes: (F) bigwigs (see *Selected Prose,* page 406; *436*).
in pochi: (I) in the few. Machiavelli said, "The life of the race is concentrated in a few individuals" (*Selected Prose,* page 38).
causa motuum: (L) cause of movement.
Bib Bin: Laurence Binyon (1869-1943), English poet, writer on oriental art, and translator of Dante.
San Ku: Three ministers in ancient China who were appointed by the emperor, "to diffuse widely all the transforming influences; they with reverence display brightly the powers of heaven and earth" (*Shu King,* page 202, translated by James Legge). The ideograms mean, literally, "...of heaven and earth."
573: **The tower wherein...shadow:** Tour Maubergeon, Palais de Justice, Poitiers.
Jacques de Molay: the last Grand Master of the Templars; he was burnt in the 14th century. "King and Pope met to suppress that order in Poitiers" (Kenner, *The Pound Era,* page 330, where there is an excellent commentary on these lines).
"We have", said Mencius...John Heydon: "...the intelligence working in nature and requiring no particular theories to keep it alive: a respect that is reborn in a series of sages, from Confucius, through Dante, to Agassiz" (*Edge,* 6 January 1957). **John Heydon:** 17th century English neoplatonic visionary and astrologer; author of *Holy Guide,* a treatise on magic, herbs and metals. "Mencius said, 'All who speak about the natures (of things), have in fact only their phenomena (to reason from)...'" Legge's translation (*Mencius* IV, ii, xxv, 1).
Σελλοί: *Selloi,* ancient inhabitants of Dodona, guardians of the Oracle of Zeus (*Iliad,* XVI, 235); "...breathed out at the Selloi's oak—/Those fellows rough it,/sleep on the ground, up in the hills there" (*Women of Trachis,* page 66).
hsin: the heart or mind (see glossary to LXXXVI, 561).
Butchers of lesser cattle...grain god: Pound divided primitive men into four categories: "1. Hunters. 2. Killers of Bulls. 3. Killers of lesser

104

cattle. 4. Agriculturalists. Ethics begins with agriculture. I.e. enough honesty to let him who plants reap. Plenty of religion in hunters, magic, etc. with reverent apology to ancestor of beast killed." (Letter to the author.)

574: **Mont Ségur:** see glossary to XXIII (109).
nel botro: (I) in the deep gully.
Tê: Awareness; virtue.
"Nowt better than share ... fixed charge": see glossary to LXXVIII (480).

575: **T'ang Wan Kung:** The Duke Wen of T'ang, the title of this section (III, i) of the *Works of Mencius* just mentioned in the previous line.

上 'shang' meaning 'up' or 'upper' here simply refers to part one of the 'T'ang Wan Kung' section. For *pu erh*, which corresponds to *No dichotomy*, see glossary to LXXXV (556).

利 : profit. (Mencius, I, i, I, 3 (and c), the opening chapter.) "Why must say profit. . ." is a literal version of four characters which appear at LXXXIX (630) with the ironic comment, "This quotation is not from Mr. Webster." Pound published his own version of the first four chapters of Mencius in the *New Iconograph* (N.Y., Vol. I, I [Fall 1947], 19-21), where the words in question are somewhat expanded: "Mencius replied, with due politeness in the tone of his voice: What forces your Majesty to use that word 'profit'? I have my humanity and my sense of equity (honesty) and that's all."

智 The 3rd character on this page is *chih*, 'wisdom', which has a 'sun' as its lower element (see glossary to LXXXV, 544). (J.C.)

Henry: Henry James.

576: **Sikandar:** Indian name for Alexander the Great.

LXXXVIII

577: **It was Saturday .... Mrs. Clay's blood-relation?:** Randolph of Roanoake asked Thomas Hart Benton if he would be his second in the duel to which Henry Clay had challenged him—Benton had to refuse because he was related to Clay's wife (*A Thirty Years View*).
Vague report ... Salazar's letter: The reason for Clay's challenge was that he had heard that Randolph had said that "a letter from General Salazar, the Mexican Minister at Washington ... bore the ear-mark of having been ... forged by the Secretary of State [Henry Clay], and denounced the administration as a corrupt coalition between the puritan [John Quincy Adams] and the 'blackleg' [Clay]." Clay thought that Randolph had accused him of "having forged .... a paper connected with the Panama mission," trying to involve the U.S.A. in Mexican politics. "Adams and Clay were for entanglement" (577). But, apart from this, Randolph and Clay were on opposite sides over the question

of the renewal of the U.S. Bank Charter which Randolph and Benton opposed; this, though it did not cause the duel, is the real subject of LXXXVIII.

579: **The place was a thick forest...basis:** No one was hurt in the duel; after three shots, it ended with both parties shaking hands.

Bellum perenne: (L) perennial war.

1694: on what it creates out of nothing: The foundation of the Bank of England. See XLVI.

1750: shut down on colonial paper./Lexington;: "In 1750 the paper currency of the Colony of Pennsylvania was suppressed. This meant that this confederacy of gombeen-men, not content with their sixty per cent, namely the interest on the moneys they created out of nothing, had, in the fifty-six intervening years, become powerful enough to induce the British government to suppress, *illegally,* a form of competition which had, through a sane monetary system, brought prosperity to the colony. Twenty-six years later, in 1776, the American colonies rebelled against England." (*Selected Prose,* page 308; *338.*)

'64 "greatest blessing" said Lincoln: Very shortly before his assassination, Lincoln said, "...and gave to the people of this Republic THE GREATEST BLESSING THEY EVER HAD—THEIR OWN PAPER TO PAY THEIR OWN DEBTS" (*Selected Prose,* page 129; *159*).

1878: in circulation as currency: Pound's grandfather, T.C. Pound (see XXII), suggested to his fellow congressmen that "some of the non-interest-bearing national debt" should be used in circulation as currency."

sangue, fatica: (I) blood and hard labour.

580: **T'ang:** see glossary to LIII (264).

581: **Dai Gaku:** Japanese form of Confucius's *Ta Hsio* (Great Digest).

"Captans annonam...plebe sit!": (L) Hoggers of harvest, cursed among the people! (St. Ambrose).

Dum ad Ambrosiam...nemori: (L) While he climbed to Ambrosia, in the sacred grove. (?)

altro che tacita: (I) the other who is silent.

ἀφρήτωρ...ἀνέστιος: *aphretor, athemistos, anestios,* without society, without right, without hearth (*Iliad,* IX, 63).

ching⁴: prayer; reverence. See glossary to LXXXV (555).

582: **Pere Henri Jacques:** see glossary to IV (16).

583: **OBEUNT 1826, July 4:** records the deaths, on the same day, of Adams and Jefferson.

584: Γᾶν ἄφθιτον...: *Gan aphthiton akamatan apotrueti.* Wears the immortal, unwearied earth. (Sophokles, *Antigone,* 339).

LXXXIX

590:

The ideograms stand for the *Shu King* (Book of History) which formed the basis of LXXXV.

Hao: good, excellent.
Chi crescerà: (I) who will increase—"Ecco chi crescerà li nostri amori," Here comes one who will increase our loves (Dante, *Paradiso*, V, 105).

591:　　王　**wang:** king.

While this is not a direct quote from any of Pound's immediate Chinese sources it is probably based on *Analects*, XII, xi, where the word 'prince' *is* however different from the 'king' Pound speaks of. When asked about the primary requirement for good government, Confucius replied, in Pound's word for word translation: "Prince to be prince; minister, minister, father, father; son, son" (*Confucius*, page 246). (J.C.)

595:　**i:** equity (see glossary to LXXXV, 544 & 545 and LXXXVI, 563).

何　**ho²:** "Why must say profit?" (See glossary to LXXXVII, 575).

必　**pi⁴⁻⁵**

曰　**yüeh⁴⁻⁵**

利　**li⁴**

596:　**masnatosque liberavit:** (L) and he liberated his slaves. Links Randolph of Roanoake with Cunizza (VI, XXIX etc.), as she did the same.
POPULUM AEDIFICAVIT: (L) He built the nation. The rhyme with Sigismundo is because he built the Tempio.

598:　Τὴν τῶν ... ἀρχήν: *Ten tōn olōn archen,* universal authority, or origins of everything (Sophokles, *Ajax,* 1105-6).
Quam parva sapientia regitur: (L) such small wisdom is hidebound.

易　**i⁴:** to change, as an adverb: easily.

599:　**Mang**　　**tzu:** Mencius; the character corresponds to 'Mang,' the philosopher's name.

caliginem vespertinem: (L) evening darkness.

πύρωσιν... θαλάττης: *pyrosin kai tis thalattis,* and he set fire to the sea.

600: **i jin:** the One Man (see glossary to LXXXVI, 563).

δἀνθρώπων ἴδεν: see glossary to XII (54).

601: **"Neither by force... should be:** Pound's definition of law; one of the central ethical principles of the poem. These lines anticipate CVII-CIX, which deal with Sir Edward Coke, and also link back to John Adams.

Ἀθήνη: *Athene* swung the hung jury: see glossary to LXXXVII (571).

tuan: see glossary to LXXXV (545).

chen: see glossary to LXXXV (547); **ataraxia:** (Gk) impassivity.

602: **Agamemnon killed that stag... rites:** he angered Artemis, unlike Brut, who had no need to fear her because he had not killed "save by the hunting rite" (XCI, 612).

603: **"κατὰ σφαγάς":** *kata sphagas,* by slaughter (?).

semina motuum: (L) "inner impulses of the tree" (*Confucius,* page 59).

chi[1] also means the above—connecting with Dionysus; see commentary on II.

XC

605: **Animus humanus... procedit:** (L) The human spirit is not love, but love flows from it, and it cannot therefore delight in itself, but only in the love flowing from it (Richard of St. Victor).

Ygdrasail: see glossary to LXXXV (545).

Baucis, Philemon: a poor, old country couple who lived in Phrygia. When Zeus and Hermes visited the earth in disguise and were turned away by the rich, they entertained them hospitably. As a result, they were saved from a flood, and their home was transformed into a temple, of which they were made priest and priestess. Zeus granted their request to die at the same time, and they were turned into trees whose boughs intertwined. (Ovid, *Metamorphoses,* VIII, 618 ff.) See Pound's early poem, "The Tree."

Castalia: spring, sacred to Apollo and the Muses, N.E. of Delphi.

Templum aedificans: (L) building the temple.

"Amphion": in Greek mythology; he raised the walls of Thebes with the magical music of his lyre.

San Ku: see glossary to LXXXVII (572).

Sagetrieb: see glossary to LXXXV (557).

Jacques de Molay: see glossary to LXXXVII (573).

Erigena: see glossary to XXXVI (179).

606: **Kuthera δεινά:** see glossary to LXXVI (456).

sempiterna: (L) everlasting.

Ubi amor, ibi oculus: (L) Where love, there the eye [is].

Vae qui cogitatis.... imago: (L) Woe to you who think without direction (uselessly)/[The good things of will] Through which an image of the divine likeness will be found in us. (See *Selected Prose,* page 73:*71,* for Pound's selections from Richard of St. Victor.)

ἠγάπησεν πολύ: *egapesen polu,* loved much.
liberavit masnatos: Randolph, like Cunizza, freed slaves.
Evita: probably Evita Peron.
m'elevasti: (I) raise me (Dante, *Paradiso,* I, 75).
Isis: Egyptian fertility goddess, who was also, with Osiris, queen of the dead. Her mysteries were akin to those of Demeter and Persephone. She is here joined with the Chinese goddess of mercy, Kuanon.
607: **And they take lights...outward:** see glossary to XLVII (236).
"De fondo": (S) from the deep (Juan Ramon Jimenez).
rilievi: (I) reliefs (in sculpture).
608: **ac ferae,/cervi:** (L) and wild beasts,/deer.
ἐπὶ χθονί: *epi chthoni,* upon the earth.
οἱ χθόνιοι: see glossary to LXXXIII (533).
pineta: (L) pine wood.
χελιδών, χελιδών: *chelidōn,* swallow, swallow.
Tyro, Alcmene: see commentary on II and glossary LXXIV (443).
e i cavalieri: (I) and the knights (Dante, *Inferno,* V, 71 & *Purgatorio,* IV, 19).
609: Ἠλέκτρα: *Elektra* (see Sophokles play of that name).
ex animo: (L) from the spirit.

XCI

610: **ab lo dolchor...vai:** (Pr) with the sweetness that goes to my heart. "ab lo dolchor" is by Guillaume de Poitiers (see glossary to VI); "qual cor mi vai" is adapted from Bernart de Ventadour's *Can vi la lauzeter mover* (when I see the lark fly). The melody written in mediaeval notation over the words is partly Pound's, and also based on Bernart's notation for his poem about the rising lark.
Reina: (I) Queen.
qui laborat, orat: (L) who labours, prays.
Circeo: see glossary to XXXIX (195).
Apollonius: neo-Pythagorean sage, born at Tyana, near the beginning of the Christian era. A wandering teacher, possessed of miraculous powers, he travelled extensively over the known world including India. He reformed and restored the rituals of Greek religion and fought against blood sacrifices. Most of XCIV will be devoted to him.
Helen of Tyre: there is a legend that she was freed from a brothel in Tyre by Simon Magus. "There would seem to be in the legend of Simon Magus and Helen of Tyre a clearer prototype of 'chivalric love' than in anything hereinafter discussed" (*The Spirit of Romance,* page 91n).
et libidinis expers: (L) and without lust (LIX, 324 and LXXVI, 457).
611: **Justinian:** (A.D. 527-65) Roman Emperor of Byzantium, who was crowned jointly with his wife Theodora. His greatest achievements were (a) the building of Santa Sophia in Byzantium and (b) the codification of Roman law.

The **GREAT CRYSTAL**: see glossary to LXXVI (459).

pensar di lieis m'es repaus: (Pr) it rests me to think of her (Arnaut Daniel).

compenetrans: (L) pervading and permeating.

The Princess Ra-Set: an Egyptian goddess, invented by Pound, from **Ra**: the sun god and **Set**: the evil male deity.

convien che si mova/la mente, amando: (I) should move the mind, in love (Dante, *Paradiso,* reference given by Pound).

khan: (A) building, inn.

612: **The golden sun boat . . . sail**: In "the Book of the Underworld dating back to the New Kingdom . . . we find a description of the nightly progress of the sun through the underworld, along with various magic formulae by which humans may attain immortality. Although not visible in the drawing [see pictograph of the boat below] the crew of the sun-boat is made up of persons enumerated in the 'First Hour' of the Egyptian text: the Lady of the Boat (i.e. Isis), Horus the Supplicant, the Bull of Truth, The Prudent One, Will, and the Oarsman, all being personifications of the qualities required for undertaking the voyage . . . . The symbolic oar signifies that the voyage is a carefully charted one that will not rely on the fortuity of the winds. . . . The motif of the sun-boat achieves full significance only when it is seen as forming a thematic rhyme with a much earlier voyage to the underworld recorded in Canto XXIII: 'With the sun in a golden cup/and going toward the low fords of ocean' " (Boris de Rachewiltz, "Pagan and Magic Elements," *New Approaches to Ezra Pound.*)

παρὰ βώμιον: *para bōmion,* translated in next line.

"Tamuz!": see glossary to XLVII (236) and LXXXV (545).

hsien: see glossary to LXXIV (429).

'Ελέναυς: HELENAUS, destroyer of ships (Elizabeth I, recalling Helen from II).

The Egyptian hieroglyph is that of the sun god Ra.

ne quaesaris: (L) ask not (Horace, *Odes,* I, xi).

He asked not . . . sanctus.: Brut, great grandson of Aeneas, and legendary founder of Britain which bears his name, voyaged from Greece and landed on an island which was full of deer, but otherwise empty, the inhabitants having been driven out or killed by outlaws. Here he found a temple to Diana. He prayed to her, asking that she might lead him to a pleasant land. He then slept, and, in a dream, she told him to voyage beyond France, to find Britain, "mid the narrow sea." (Layamon's *Brut.*)

Leafdi Diana . . . londe: (ME) Lady Diana, beloved Diana, help me in my need. Make me to know through your skill, where I may go to a pleasant land. (Layamon's *Brut,* 601-4.)

613: **Now Lear in Janus' . . . laid**: Layamon says he was buried there, in Leicester. The ideogram **chên**: shake, terrify, is often used in connection with thunder.

Constance: legendary king of ancient Britain—he gave up his monk's hood to become king.

Merlin's fader: Merlin was conceived by a spirit who visited his mother, clothed in gold—connects with Danae (IV and V, 16, 20).

Lord, thaet scop the dayes lihte: (ME) Lord, who made the day's light.

Aurelie: brother of Constance. He became king, was poisoned, and buried at the "east end of Stonehenge" at his request.

Athelstan: see glossary XLVIII (242).

614:   **a dung flow from 1913:** This was the year President Wilson signed the Federal Reserve Act, which, in Pound's view, resulted in Congress giving up its sovereignty over the control and issue of money to a private bank, against the principles of Adams, Jefferson, Van Buren, Benton and Randolph—an abdication by the government of its responsibility, as laid down in the Constitution: "Congress shall have power to coin money and regulate the value thereof; and of foreign coin" (Article 1, Section 8, paragraph 5).

615:   **Rhea:** Cybele, wife of Saturn, mother of Zeus. "Generally represented as flanked by lions, or bearing one in her lap" (*Oxford Classical Dictionary*).

  Musonius: born A.D.30. Stoic, banished by Nero and Vespasian.

tan: The dawn ideogram is, of course, central to the *Cantos*. It appears first in the opaque transcriptions of Canto XLIX (245). The Roman capitals record a Japanese pronunciation of the ideogram, but it looks the same romanised: 'TAN'. "They who are skilled in fire" will see the sunrise figured in the character, with the bottom line representing the horizon, and this is the usual etymology. Recent investigation of the earliest forms of the script reveal another possible derivation which Pound cannot have known about but which would have made this word even more of a focus for him. The bottom line may well represent a 'templum', or sacred clearing over which the sun and other heavenly bodies were observed to rise and from which they were 'contemplated.' (J.C.)

  KADMOU THUGATER: Daughter of Cadmus (*Odyssey*, V, 333). The sea nymph Leucothoe, who saves Odysseus from drowning, after he has left Kalypso's island on his raft.

  "get rid of paraphernalia": She tells him to get rid of his heavy clothes and leave his raft—she gives him her veil ("my bikini is worth your raft," 616) which protects him until he reaches Phaeakia.

  TLEMOUSUNE: (Gk) endurance, misery.

616:   ἄλλοτε ... διώκειν: *allote d'aut' euros zephyrō eixaske diōkein*, and sometimes Euros with Zephyros drove on (*Odyssey*, V, 332); the preceding passage is translated at the close of *Rock-Drill*, "That the wave crashed . . . thistle-down" (XCV, 647).

  Νυκτὸς ... πυρός: *Nuktos d'aut' aether te kai emera Zenos pyros*, and of night, aether, and day, of Zeus's fire.

  natrix: (L) water snake.

  NUTT: Egyptian sky goddess.

  "mand'io a la Pinella...": (I) "I send Pinella a river in full flood" (Cavalcanti, Sonnet XVII, *Translations*, page 58).

617:   **"Et Jehanne":** Joan of Arc (Villon, *Le Testament*, 42).

ch'l terzo ciel movete: (I) who move the third heaven [that of Venus] (Dante, *Convivio*, II, "Canzone Prima").

XCII

618: **And from this mount . . .:** the earthly paradise at the top of the Mount of Purgatory; seeds blow from "la divina foresta" here, causing the diverse plants to sprout spontaneously on the earth (Dante, *Purgatorio*, XXVIII).
Fitzgerald: the Desmond Fitzgerald of VII, "The live man out of lands and prisons" (27).
Signori, . . . sentinella: (I) was I or was I not the sentinel? (echoes Fitzgerald's remark, "I was").
Gran dispitto: (I) in great despite (see glossary to LXXIX, 487).
"A chi stima . . . assai": (I) Nothing is impossible to him who holds honor in sufficient esteem. (See *Confucius*, page 188.)
Ra-Set: see glossary to XCI (611).
619: **e piove d'amor/in nui:** (I) and rain of love/in us.
Ecbatan: see glossary to IV (16) and LXXIV (425).
Anubis: dog-headed Egyptian god. He conducts the spirits of the dead to the region of immortal life—the Greeks identified him with Hermes.
Mont Ségur: see glossary to XXIII (109).
cellula: (L) small cell—"the chief's cell" that recurs CI (725).
ex aquis nata: (L) born from water (Aphrodite).
τά ἐκ τῶν . . . γενόμενα: *ta ek tōn udatōn genomena*, and things born from water.
"in questa lumera appresso": (I) in that light near [me] (Dante, *Paradiso*, IX, 112-13).
Folquet, nel terzo cielo: (I) Folquet, in the third heaven. Folquet de Marseille, Provençal troubadour (*c.* 1160-1231) whom Dante places in the heaven of Venus.
"And if I see . . . thought.": a translation of lines by Bernart de Ventadour given in the original in XX, lines 2-3.
the sphere of crystal: see glossary to LXXVI (459).
farfalla: (I) butterfly.
Nymphalidae . . . erynnis: names of different types of butterfly.
620: **And from far . . . marina:** "si che di lontano/conobbi il tremolar della marina," so that, from far, I recognized the trembling of the sea (Dante, *Purgatorio*, I, 116-17).
"fui chiamat'/e qui refulgo": Cunizza I was called and here I shine (*Paradiso*, IX, 32). For notes on Cunizza see commentary on VI.
Hilary: probably St. Hilary of Poitiers (*c.* 315-*c.* 367).
improvisatore: (I) improviser.
Omniformis: see glossary to V (17).
621: **Semele:** the mother of Dionysus, by Zeus. At the instigation of Hera, she asked Zeus to visit her in the splendour of a god. When he reluc-

tantly did this, she was consumed by lightning. (Ovid, *Metamorphoses*, III, 261 ff.)

"**Io porto...cecità**": (I) I carry.... blindness. Delcroix was a minister in Mussolini's government and head of the Italian veterans. He had lost both his arms, and was blinded in the First World War.

"**Hans Sachs...poet dazu**": (G) Hans Sachs was a poet and shoemaker as well.

Nein! aber in Wolken: (G) No! but in the clouds.

622: **Apollonius:** see glossary to XCI (610).

Avicenna: Arab philosopher and physician (980-1037).

XCIII

623: **Kati:** Egyptian king (11th dynasty, 2252-2228 B.C.) whose principles were akin to those of Confucius.

panis angelicus: (L) angelic bread (*Vulgate*, Psalms, LXXVII, 25).

Antef: Egyptian king (*c.* 1970-1936 B.C.) who said, "Give bread to the hungry..."

two ½s of a seal: Pound compares Kati and Antef to Shun and Wan (see glossary to LXXVII, 467).

Κάδμου θυγάτηρ: *Kadmou thugater*, see glossary to XCI (615).

Apollonius made...animals: "The mark of courtesy which is artistically owed to the animals" (David Jones, *Epoch and Artist*, page 89).

Filth of the Hyksos...cattle: see glossary to LXXXVII (573).

624: "**non fosse cive**": (I) were he not a citizen (Carlo Martello asks Dante [*Paradiso*, VIII, 115-16]) "...would it be worse for man on earth were he no citizen?"

Some sense of civility: civility here carries its original meaning: citizenship.

"**dragons' spleens**": *King John*, II, i, 68; "**pelting farm**": *Richard II*, II, i, 60. The passages from which these phrases come express the chaos wrought by people who are not citizens and have no responsibility to any order in society.

corrent' attrativa: (I) current which draws.

Peitz trai pena...bionda: (Pr) I endured worse pain of love/Than Tristan the great lover/who suffered much sorrow/for the blond Yseult (Bernart de Ventadour lamenting the departure of Eleanor of Aquitaine for England).

625: **dove siede Peschiera:** (I) where sits Peschiera (Dante, *Inferno*, XX, 70).

Cortesia, onestade: (I) Courtesy, honesty (Dante, *Convivio*, etc.).

chih: see glossary to LII (261).

Agassiz: Louis A. (1807-1873), naturalist, born in Switzerland. Appointed Chair of Natural History at Harvard, 1846. He believed that the universe is informed by a "Creative Mind...independent of the influence of a material world." "The connection of all known features of nature into one system exhibits thought, the most comprehensive

113

thought, in limits transcending the highest wonted powers of man" (*Gists from Agassiz*, pages 92 and 91). With Linnaeus, Agassiz is at the root of the way nature is embodied in *Rock-Drill*, *Thrones* and *Drafts and Fragments*. His work shows, to quote Pound, "respect for the kind of intelligence that enables grass seed to grow grass; the cherry-stone to make cherries" (*Confucius*, page 193). Or, as Kung said, "observe the phenomena of nature as one in whom the ancestral voices speak...." (*Analects*, V, xi).

"quest'unire...ama": (I) "this union/takes place inside the spirit/seeing outside what it loves" (Dante, *Convivio*, III, ii, 9).

Risplende: (I) shines (Dante, *Paradiso*, I, 2, etc.).

degli occhi: (I) of the eyes.

626: **che Pitagora si chiamò:** (I) who was called Pythagoras (*Convivio*, III, 11).

"non sempre": (I) not always.

l'amor che ti fa bella: (I) love makes you beautiful.

("ut facias"—Goddeschalk—"pulchram"): (L) that you may make her beautiful (from the *Sequaire* of Godeschalk, see *Spirit of Romance*, page 98).

beltà,/cioè moralitade: (I) beauty,/that is morality.

"e solo...diletta...prode": (I) "and only in sincerity makes oneself delight...and hearing...of courage" (*Convivio* IV, Canzone III, 131 and 135).

"compagnevole animale": (I) Man is a sociable animal (*Convivio*, IV, 4).

"Perche....Pel mio poema.": see glossary LXXXVII (569).

belezza...pargoletta: (I) beautiful....child.

onestade risplende: (I) honesty shines (*Convivio*, IV, viii).

Dio, la prima bontade: (I) God, the first good.

627: **i (four):** equity. See glossary to LXXXV (544) and LXXXVI (563).

"cui adorna esta bontade": (I) which this goodness adorns.

e farlo sparire: (I) and cause to disappear. The "brochure" was Pound's pamphlet *Oro e Lavoro* (*Selected Prose*, pages 306-321; *336-351*).

Zaharoff: see glossary to XVIII (80).

628: **Ub:** Admiral Ubaldo degli Uberti who helped Pound in his journey north from Rome in 1943 (see commentary on *The Pisan Cantos*).

agitante calescimus: (L) his stirring warms us. See Ovid, *Fasti*, VI, 5: "est Deus in nobis; agitante calescimus illo": There is a god within us, when he stirs us we grow warm.

Lux in diafana...oro: (L) Light in translucent forms/She who creates/I pray. (See glossary to XXXVI, 177.)

per dilettevole ore: (I) translated in the preceding phrase.

J'ai eu pitié....Pas assez!: see glossary to LXXVI (460).

628-9: 力 li⁴

行 hsing²

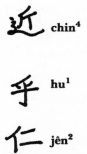 chin⁴

乎 hu¹

仁 jên²

These five characters correspond to "holding that energy is near to benevolence." The quotation comes from *The Unwobbling Pivot* (X, 10)—see *Confucius*, pages 153–55.

Au bois dormant: (F) to the sleeping wood. "La belle au bois dormant"—The beauty in the sleeping wood.

"mai tardi....l'ignoto": (I) never too late [to attempt] the unknown. "Non e mai tardi per tentar l'ignoto" (Gabriele d'Annunzio, *La Nave*, episode 3; the full phrase quoted in *Selected Prose*, page 25).

jih hsin: see glossary to LIII (265).

見 **chien⁴:** to see or perceive.

630: **Amphion:** see glossary to XC (605).
"pone metum...laedit: see glossary to XXV (117-18).
volucres delphinasque ad auditum: (L) birds and dolphins to the ear. (Pound's Latin?)
hsien: see glossary to LXXIV (429).
nuova vita: (I) new life (title of Dante's first book).
e ti fiameggio: (I) and I [Beatrice] glow for you (*Paradiso*, V, 1).

631: **e la bella Ciprigna:** (I) and the beautiful Cyprian (Venus).
alcun vestigio: (I) any vestige? (*Paradiso*, V, 11).
un lume pien' di spiriti: (I) a light full of spirits.
E "chi crescera": see glossary to LXXXIX (590).

632: **e Monna Vanna:** "Primavera" (LXXVI, 452)—a girl loved by Cavalcanti.
tu mi fai rimembrar: (I) you make me remember (*Purgatorio*, XXVIII, 49–51).

XCIV

633: **"Brederode":** Henri, Count of (1531-68), one of the leaders of the Netherlands in their revolt against Philip II.

Tai Wu Tzu: Wu, first ruler of the Chou Dynasty (1122-255 B.C.). These characters are connected with "the city of Dioce"—an ideal city—"the SUGGESTION of Dioce/Tai wu Tze, a POSSIBILITY" (*D.K./Some Letters of Ezra Pound*, page 54).

634: **(Pandects I. 8 out of Gaius):** Justinian's *Pandects* or *Digest*, a collection of excerpts from the surviving juristic literature of the classical period. **Gaius:** (2nd century A.D.) a Roman jurist. His *Institutes* were used by Justinian as a basis for his own law codes.
divini et humani juris communicatio: (L) a communication of divine and human justice (Justinian's law codes). These lines on justice anticipate a major theme of *Thrones*.
Ius Italicum (Digest Fifty, XV): (L) Italian Law.

635: **Agassiz:** see glossary to XCIII (625).
Gestalt: (G) form; character, hence seeds of thought.
From the hawk king ... Abydos: These 9 lines present the most ancient material to be incorporated in the *Cantos*, apart from the timeless mythologies, and the legendary beginnings of Chinese history in LII (262). The hieroglyph of the hawk forms a parallel, from remote antiquity, with Frederick II of Sicily's treatise on falcons (XCVII, 682); it is pre-Egyptian pictographic writing. The source for this, and for the names in these lines, and those where further hieroglyphics recur (XCVII, 679, 681, and 682), is L.A. Waddell's *Egyptian Civilization, Its Sumerian Origins*. Waddell probably erroneously considered the legendary Sumerian king Sargon the Great ("the hawk king") to have been the father of Menes, founder of the Egyptian dynasties. Agade was Sargon's capital. "Goth", Waddell states, belonged to his dynastic line. "Prabbu" is a misprint for "Prabhu" which Waddell "considered a form of Sumerian title 'Par,' corresponding to 'Pharoah'" (Boris de Rachewiltz in *New Approaches to Ezra Pound*, pages 187–88). As B. de Rachewiltz relates, Waddell took an Egyptian cartouche, surmounted by a falcon, which had been discovered by Sir Flinders Petrie at Abydos, "to be the seal of Sargon, and the fringe forming the upper part of the cartouche to be a three-column façade of a temple." When Pound discovered from Boris de Rachewiltz that Waddell had arbitrarily attributed the falcon hieroglyph to Sargon of Agade, he asked his publisher, James Laughlin, to delete it.[1] "Nor sin by misnaming" (C, 720). As Mary de Rachewiltz put it in a letter to me concerning these lines, and those surrounding the hieroglyphs in XCVII, "one has to think of *sound* associations, 'Agada, Ganna...' just as 'Tyanu, Tyana...' and the 'lion head' and the 'falcon' have *visual* associations leading to Alexander, Federico II, etc.... kings committed to equity and quiddity—'gestalt seeds'."

116

caligine: (I) fog.

Agada, Gana...: see glossary to LXXIV (427).

636: **Swans came to the meadow:** This line introduces Apollonius of Tyana, the main subject of XCIV. (See glossary to XCI, 610.) "For just as the hour of his birth was approaching, his mother was warned in a dream to walk out into the meadow and pluck the flowers; and...she came there and her maids attended to the flowers, while she fell asleep lying on the grass. Thereupon the swans who fed in the meadow set up a dance around her as she slept, and lifting their wings...cried out...all at once, for there was somewhat of a breeze blowing in the meadow. She then leaped up at the sound of their song and bore her child...." (Philostratus, *Life of Apollonius*, I, 5).

πολλοὺς... δὲ ὀλίγοις: *pollous timōn pisteuōn de oligois*, to respect many and trust in few—Apollonius's advice to Vadanes, King of Babylon (I, 37).

For styrax...leopards: the leopards of Armenia "traverse the mountains in search of the...gum of the Styrax tree whenever the wind blows from its quarter and the trees are distilling" (II, 2).

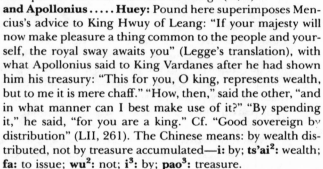

and Apollonius..... Huey: Pound here superimposes Mencius's advice to King Hwuy of Leang: "If your majesty will now make pleasure a thing common to the people and yourself, the royal sway awaits you" (Legge's translation), with what Apollonius said to King Vardanes after he had shown him his treasury: "This for you, O king, represents wealth, but to me it is mere chaff." "How, then," said the other, "and in what manner can I best make use of it?" "By spending it," he said, "for you are a king." Cf. "Good sovereign by distribution" (LII, 261). The Chinese means: by wealth distributed, not by treasure accumulated—**i:** by; **ts'ai²:** wealth; **fa:** to issue; **wu²:** not; **i³:** by; **pao³:** treasure.

rhymed in Taxila: King Phraotes of Taxila rhymes because he told Apollonius, "I regard most things as belonging to my own friends" (II, 26). (A metaphorical parallel.)

636-7: **νυμφόληπτοι...ξυνίστησιν:** *nympholeptoi...bakkhoi tou nephein/*

117

umnon emeran/zōon...ton kosmon...gar zōogonei panta/erōta ischei..kai xunistesin, rapt by nymphs....bacchantic revellers in sobriety (II, 37) hymns to the sun every day (III, 14) living...is the universe...for it engenders all living things...possessed by love...which knits together....

637: **F.C. Conybeare:** translator of Philostratus's *Life of Apollonius* (Loeb edition). I have mostly used his version in this glossary and all the reference numbers are to this.

Ἰάρχας: *Iarchas*, leader of the Brahmin sages who teach Apollonius that "the universe is alive."

προπεμπτηρίους... ἄδειν: *propempterious humnous autō adein*: sings funeral strains for itself (III, 49).

ἐρωτά ἴσχει: *erōta ischei*, possessed by love (III, 34).

ὑμᾶς δεδώκατε... ἔρρωσθε: *umas dedōkate ten thalattan errōsthe*, you presented me with the sea....farewell (Apollonius's parting words to Iarchas, III, 58).

παρὰ τοῖς... τιμῶσιν: *para tois tēn sophian timōsin*, among the lovers of wisdom (III, 58).

καὶ ἐρασθῆναι ἀλλήλων: *kai erasthenai allēlōn*, and to love one another (IV, 1).

638: πολλαῖς ἰδέαις: *pollais ideais*, under many shapes (IV, 7). Apollonius said to the Smyrneans, "...men who visit all regions of the earth may well be compared with the Homeric Zeus, who is presented by Homer under many shapes, and is a more wonderful creation than the image made of ivory [Pound's "set stone"]; for the latter is only to be seen upon earth, but the former is a presence imagined everywhere in heaven" (IV, 7).

πράττειν δύναται: *prattein hekaston...hoi ti dunatai*, each man should do what he best can do (IV, 8). As Kung said, "each in his nature" (XIII, 58).

ἐπὶ τὴν ναῦν ἑσπέρας ἤδη: *epi tēn naun hesperas hede*, on board ship for it was already evening (IV, 11). Apollonius visits Troy and spends the night on the "mound of Achilles" while his companions remain behind on board ship. He raises the spirit of Achilles, not as in Canto I, "by ditch digging and sheep's guts," because we are now, as Pound reminds us in the following lines, "walking here under the larches of Paradise." Apollonius and Achilles talk long in the night and the latter tells Apollonius to set the statue of the hero Palamedes up again in its place "in Aeolis close to Methymna," which Apollonius is later to do, building a shrine round it. The ghost of Achilles "vanished with a flash of Summer lightning, for indeed the cocks were already beginning their chant" (IV, 16).

γὰρ βάσανος...: *gar basanos*, for a touchstone. When, because of their fear of Nero, most of Apollonius's followers forsake him, he is undismayed, saying that "chance has thrown in my way a touchstone to test these young men..." (IV, 37).

καθαρὸν....θνητοῦ: *katharon kai ap' oudenos thnētou*, pure....made from no dead matter (IV, 40). Apollonius's reply to a consul who asks what clothes he is wearing.

"Hic sunt leones": (L) Here are lions.

δὲ τοῖς ὅσια πράττουσι: *de tois hosia prattousi ... gen men pasan asphale,* the whole earth affords secure ground for the doers of holiness (V, 17).

639: **Five, twenty two:** in this chapter, Apollonius speaks to a rich, uneducated young man, who says people should be valued more for their wealth than for themselves. Pound juxtaposes the ideograms, **fa$^{1-5}$:** to issue; **ts'ai^2:** wealth, which leads to chapter 29, where Apollonius says, "I was never the slave of wealth ... even in my youth." This wisdom is set beside the *yung chung* (*Unwobbling Pivot*) of Confucius. For *chung,* see glossary to LXX (413).

VESPASIAN: Emperor A.D. 69-70. Apollonius suggests he should take the throne.

Antoninus: see glossary to XLII (209).

Daughter of a sun priest ... Tyana: The Roman Empress, Julia Domna, commissioned Philostratus to write the life.

τῶν ἑαυτοῦ ... θεοῖς: *tōn eautou paidōn upo tois theois,* of his own children .... governed by the Gods (V, 35). Apollonius says here that if Vespasian "accepts the throne, he will have the devoted service of his own children ..." and he adds later, "For myself I care little about constitutions, seeing that my life is governed by the Gods."

ἐπὶ νοῦν ... ᾽ώκεις: *epi noun elthon eiresetai/ei ten psychen ten emen ōkeis,* it is enough that he says what he really thinks/if you were a tenant of my breast ... (In the first line, Apollonius is telling Vespasian what is "enough for a man ... of philosophic habit." In the second, Vespasian says that Apollonius has expressed his own "inmost thoughts.").

640: The ideograms: **wang:** king (see glossary to LXXXIX, 591).

ἑλληνίζοντας μὲν Ἑλληνικῶν: *hellenizontas men hellenikon,* over the Hellenes should be set men who can speak Greek.

Euphrates: an adviser of Vespasian who was jealous of Apollonius.

and sent the lion ... Amasis: In Egypt Apollonius met a man who had a tame lion on a leash. He spoke to it (XCI, 616) and it told him that it contained the soul of Amasis, the Egyptian pharoah. At Apollonius's suggestion, the priests send the lion "up country" to Leontopolis, to be "dedicated to the temple there."

ἐπ' αὐτῶ ᾽άδοντες: *ep auto adontes,* singing about him.

"μὴ ὀβολὸς ὀβολὸν τέκη": *me obolos obolon teke,* penny not make a penny. In Ethiopia, Apollonius contrasts the simplicity of the Egyptian and Ethiopian method of conducting trade by direct exchange of goods, with Greek avarice.

Ἠῷω Μέμνονι: *Eōō Memnoni.* Memnon was a son of Eos, the Dawn. Apollonius visited a statue (reputed to be of him) in Ethiopia (VI, 4).

ψυχὴ ἀθάνατος ἥ ... τιμητέον: *psyche athanatos e ti meta zōoisin eon timeteon,* The soul is immortal ... so why, as long as thou art among living beings [do you explore these mysteries] (VIII, 31).

本 The ideogram is **Pen^3:** Root, origin, basis. (The character shows a tree with a line marking its roots.)

That is of thrones ... Justice: These lines serve to introduce the next section, *Thrones,* and the principle, for which Sir Edward Coke fought in Parliament (641), that the law should be above the king, which remains to this day the foundation of democratic liberty—CVII-CIX deal with Coke.

641:    **with an Eleanor . . .:** Eleanor of Castile, wife of Edward I. These lines present events in the latter's reign, closing with his taking the Stone of Scone to Westminster in 1297.

Be Traist: Be Faithful.

και κελαδοῦνος ἀκοῦσαι: *kai keladounos akousai,* and the roar of its waterfalls. After visiting the naked Egyptian sages, Apollonius intends to go up to the source of the Nile.

Φαντασία σοφωτέρα μιμήσεως: *Phantasia sophotera mimeseōs,* Imagination wiser than imitation. Apollonius is referring to Greek sculpture, portraying images of the gods, and goes on, "imitation is often baffled by terror, but imagination by nothing" (VI, 20).

μὴ ἐνομιλούντων: *mē enomilountōn,* not mingling. Apollonius is praising Sparta for keeping her institutions "in their original purity by preventing outsiders from mingling in her life" (VI, 20).

642:    **jih hsin:** see glossary to LIII (265).

---

[1] I am indebted to Barbara Eastman for this information.

XCV

643:    **"Consonantium demonstratrix" . . . . nimbus:** (L) "Demonstrator of harmonies," said Bede [ἔφατ': *ephat,* said]/God is the spirit of the world,/a being best and everlasting./Time is everywhere,/unmoving/in the evenings of the world./To be awakened in the bedroom/mist weighs down the wild thyme plants. All these phrases are taken, and at times altered, from different places in Migne's *Patrologia Latina,* Volume 90, the first of six volumes which cover the Venerable Bede (A.D. 673-735). The lines thus constitute, in a sense, an original Latin poem by Pound.

Adams to Rush: see glossary to LXXI (416).

campagnevole animale: see glossary to XCIII (643).

πόλις, πολιτική: *polis, politiké,* city, citizens.

reproducteur,/contribuable. Paradis peint: (F) reproductive,/taxpayer. Painted paradise. The last two words are from Villon's *Prayer for his Mother.* See XLV (229).

πολύγλωσσος: *poluglōssos,* many tongued. The vocal, oracular wood at Dodona.

644:    **Κάδμου θυγάτηρ:** *Kadmou thugater,* daughter of Cadmus (see glossary to XCI, 615).

per diafana: (L) through translucent forms (see glossary to XXXVI, 177).

λευκὸς Λευκόθοε: *leukos Leucothoe,* shining Leucothoe.

chin[4] hu[1] jên[2]: to approach benevolence—repeated from XCIII (629).

YAO: see glossary to LIII (262).

The ideograms at the bottom of the page are **i jin:** one man. (See glossary to LXXXVI, 563.)

645: **Elder Lightfoot ... downhearted:** a black American religious preacher.
"Are ... daughters of Memory": Yeats said this of the Muses.

646: **a hand without face cards:** "(1) The intimate essence of the universe is *not* of the same nature as our own consciousness. (2) Our own consciousness is incapable of having produced the universe. (3) God, therefore, exists. That is to say, there is no reason for not applying the term God, *Theos,* to the intimate essence.... (5) Concerning the intimate essence of the universe we are utterly ignorant. We have no proof that this God, Theos, is one, or is many, or is divisible or indivisible, or is an ordered hierarchy culminating, or not culminating, in a unity.... (7) Dogma is bluff based upon ignorance." (*Selected Prose,* page 49.)

647: **dicto millesimo:** (I) in the said year.
(vine leaf? San Denys ... Dionisio ...: Pound puns Dionysus with Dionysius the Areopagite, who was converted by St. Paul and is said to have been the first bishop of Athens where he was martyred *c.* A.D. 95. "There is a tradition that he visited Paris, and an attempt has been made to identify him with St. Denis (cent. iii), the patron saint of France. In the Middle Ages he was universally credited with the authorship of works ... which now bear the name Pseudo-Dionysius and are admitted to be the productions of a Neo-Platonist or of Platonists of centuries v or vi. The work, *Celestial Hierarchy* was translated into Latin in cent. ix by Johannes Erigena, and became the mediaeval textbook on angelic lore." (*Dante Dictionary* by Paget Toynbee, page 228.) Dante places Dionysius among the great theologians in the heaven of the sun (*Paradiso,* X, 115-17).
Eleutherio: another title of Dionysus; also, probably connected with "ἐλευθερία": freedom—see glossary to II (9).
Calvin: "Calvin's god and the god of all writers leading to and descending from Calvin is a maniac sadist, one would prefer other qualities in one's immediate parenthood" (*Selected Prose,* page 72; *70*).
That the wave crashed ..... sea-god: adapted from *Odyssey,* V, 313-338. Ino, daughter of Cadmus, was changed into the sea nymph, Leucothoe.
νόστου/γαίης Φαιήκων ...: *nostou/gaies Phaiekon,* return/to the land of the Phaeakians ... (*Odyssey,* V, 344-45). "The vocation of the poet is homecoming" (Heidegger).

Thrones

Thrones

Pound explained his aim in writing XCVI-CIX in his *Paris Review* interview (see Item Q, page xxi). Some words he wrote in 1942 also help in the understanding of this section: "History is recorded in monuments, *that* is why they get destroyed" (*Selected Prose*, page 292; *322*). *Thrones* is one of the most solid historical achievements of the *Cantos*. While illuminating earlier parts, it is a coherent structure in itself, resting upon three "monuments" to justice and good government: (1) the *Eparchikon Biblion*, the Byzantine Eparch's Edict (XCVI); (2) Iong Ching's commentary on his father's *Sheng U* (*The Sacred Edict*) (XCVIII-XCIX); and (3) the *Institutes* of Sir Edward Coke (CVII-CIX).

Canto XCVI opens with the shipwrecked Odysseus—who has been saved from drowning by Leucothoe's veil which is to enable him to reach Phaeakia as recounted at the end of *Rock-Drill*—seeing her disappear in the waves: "and the wave concealed her/dark mass of great water" (651). He is then borne "thru these diafana" into a catalogue of late Roman, and Byzantine emperors, reminiscent of the Chinese history cantos, which is based (a) on the works of a Lombard historian, Paulus the Deacon (*c.* 725-*c.* 799), who was patronised by Charlemagne, and (b) on the writing of Landulph, both to be found in Migne's *Patrologia Latina*. This section closes with the war which Justinian II waged against Abdel Melik for striking and issuing "gold coins without the Imperial stamp or authority" (Alexander Del Mar, *History of Monetary Crimes*, page 5), which illustrates a major theme of *Thrones*, that the nature of sovereignty and kingship inheres in the prerogative over coinage. The catalogue of Emperors serves as a prologue to the real subject of XCVI, Byzantine civilization as manifested in the Eparch's Edict of Leo the Wise (866-912), Roman Emperor in the East.

The Edict consists of ordinances addressed by Leo to the Eparch of Byzantium, who was a kind of mayor, responsible for the order of the city.

The Greek scholar Philip Sherrard has kindly provided me with the following notes on the nature of the Edict itself:

> The ordinances were intended to regulate the operations of the various trade and other guilds (drapers, spicers, wax-chandlers, soapmakers,

saddlers, butchers, fishmongers, bakers, innkeepers, contractors, advocates etc.) to estáblish price controls and legislation against hoarding and profiteering ... to lay down rules affecting artisans generally and disputes between employers and employed (it sets up a kind of court of arbitration, to be invoked by either party), and to make observations about currency and scales, weights and measures. In other words, it was intended to regulate the social and economic sphere of life in the manner in which God regulated the cosmos, so that no one should overstep the measure of justice.

This is the first time that Byzantium figures prominently in the poem—"'Constantinople' said Wyndham, 'our star'" (661). XCVI is, in Pound's paradise, a sort of map for the possibility of an ideal city. Its poetic strength stems from its accumulation of realistic detail.

The first half of XCVII is based largely on the work of the nineteenth century American historian Alexander Del Mar, and deals with the ratio between gold and silver in Imperial Rome and the Orient. The details are hard to follow, unless the reader consults Pound's source (Del Mar's *History of Monetary Systems*), but the main import of the canto is clearly conveyed by the memorable line, "When kings quit, the bankers began again" (672). Pound started reading Del Mar in the fifties; his books were a momentous discovery for him as they confirmed and documented many of the conclusions Pound had drawn from his own historical research:

> The Emperors of Rome controlled the emissions of European money for thirteen centuries, and the kings and dukes for nearly four centuries afterwards; whilst the usurers have held it, to the present time, for about two centuries. It is not too much to say that during these two centuries greater monetary changes have been made and more losses have been occasioned to the industrial classes of the European world than were made by all the degradations and debasements of the Imperial and regal periods put together. Monetary systems have been changed from gold to silver, from silver to gold, and from both silver and gold to paper; tens of thousands of worthless banks have been erected, thousands of millions of worthless notes have been issued, and the entire products of industry have been seized and perverted to the enrichment of a class who only know how to scheme to undermine and to appropriate the earnings of mankind ..."The control of money," says an eloquent author on the subject, "is the ground upon which an international or cosmopolitan combination 'finances' the world and 'farms' humanity."
> (Del Mar, *History of the Netherlands Monetary Systems*)

Pound did much to promote the reprinting of Del Mar's works. (One function of the *Cantos* has been to rescue vital literature from oblivion. Del Mar is a fine writer and a meticulous and perceptive historian—his books are worth reading in their own right, not merely as sources for the *Cantos*.)

The second half of XCVII, from "New fronds ..." (675) is in lyric form, moving the mind through clear colours, lights, and fine discriminations drawn from the definitions of words. Subtlety of intonation is exactly conveyed, "'As THAT!' said Ungaro,/'It is just as hard as that'/(jabbing a steel cube with his pencil butt/and speaking of mind as resistant)" (680). In the late cantos, Pound has found a form that weaves the lyrical, factual, anecdotal and didactic into a single texture, so there are none of the dry stretches that we get in some of the middle sections of the poem.

Canto XCVIII leads us, via a passage radiant with the energies of the gods,

" 'Are Gods by hilaritas'; and their speed in communication" (685), to "the next pass" through these mountains, *The Sacred Edict*. The rest of XCVIII, and all of XCIX, are devoted to this. The tone of these two cantos is one of "hilaritas" which is particularly marked in the word-play of XCVIII.

The Manchu Emperor, Kang Hi (generally known as Kang Hsi), who reigned from 1662 to 1722 (see LIX-LX), wishing to revive Confucianism, just as Coke renewed the ancient liberties of England (CVII-CIX), composed an *Edict* restating the main principles of Kung's work, which he caused to be displayed widely throughout the Empire in 1670. His son, Iong Ching (LXI), then redid it as a book, adding a long commentary. This was published in 1724. Soon after this, the Salt Commissioner of Shensi, Iu-p'uh, "taking the sense down to the people" (688), rewrote the Edict in colloquial language. Pound used a bi-lingual edition of this popular version which was produced by an American missionary, F.W. Baller.

Canto XCIX presents eighteenth century neo-Confucianism, rhyming with LXXXV which dealt with the origins of Kung's teaching taking shape in Chinese history long before he was born. Taken with this, and LII-LXI, which close with Iong Ching, it demonstrates the persistence of the Confucian tradition. The least difficult part of *Thrones,* it has a beauty that is comparable to the serenity, "That his ray came to point in this quiet," of *The Classic Anthology,* and a simplicity akin to XIII (where Kung first entered the poem), "Hills and streams colour the air,/vigour, tranquillity, not one set of rules./Vigour, quietude, are of place" (699).

In C, amid nuggets of nineteenth and twentieth century history etc., Odysseus/Pound lands on Phaeakia and drops Leucothoe's magic veil "in the tide rips/... that it should float back to the sea" (716-17).

In CI a new, and final, landscape enters the *Cantos:* that of the Na-khi people who live in the Li-Chiang district of Southwest China, and this place, and their religious rites, are the source of many of the paradisal images in the latter half of *Thrones,* and in *Drafts and Fragments.*

Pound's source for the Na-khi material is *The Ancient Na-khi Kingdom of Southwest China* by Joseph Rock. As Moelwyn Merchant has written, "It is a matter of constant wonder that Pound's work ... assimilates immediately a new intellectual source to the material previously deployed. . . ." The Na-khi religion stems from ancient Tibet; it is one of the oldest in the world, and is a form of nature worship. As Jamila Ismail has put it, "The Na-khi scene returns us to the China and Greece that form the core of the *Cantos'* stillness, the perspectiveless luminosity that locates *kosmos* not in a transcendant otherness ... but within itself" (" 'News of the Universe': [2]Muan [1]Bpo and the *Cantos*"[1]). In CI and elsewhere, Pound splices images of Li-Chiang landscape with that of the Provence of the Albigensians, as the Na-khi have suffered a similar religious persecution.

Interlaced with these natural images, the political and economic argument continues in C-CV, presenting a welter of "luminous details" and sudden insights from history, philosophy and theology, each line ramming home a point related to the pattern of the *Cantos* as a whole, often obscure, because of the extreme concision, but always honouring human intelligence: "via mind is the nearest you'll get to it" (CV, 747).

Canto CVI returns to the Eleusinian mysteries and the world of the spirit. In passages such as these, Pound makes us "see again" (CXV, 796) a beauty that has always been there; that the world has forgotten it does not make it any less real. In this context it is worth recalling what he wrote in 1938: "Sober minds have agreed that the arcanum is the arcanum. No man can provide his neighbour with a Cook's ticket thereto." (*Guide to Kulchur*, page 292.)

Cantos CVII-CIX are centred around English history, and in particular the *Institutes* of Sir Edward Coke (1552-1634): "hospitality ... of the ancient ornaments and/commandations of England" (758). Coke said, "the king hath no prerogative but that which the law of the land allows him." The conception of law as a safeguard against tyranny adds an element that is missing from the Chinese principles of good government expressed in XCIX, while Coke, in his commentary on, and collection of, the centuries of English law preceding him, is in some ways a Confucian. It is fitting, also, that he should come into the poem at this point because he was an important part of Adams's heritage— Coke first appears in the Adams cantos.

Coke, in his fight against King James, is a heroic figure. His function in CVII-CIX can be defined by a phrase from *Rock-Drill*, "thrones,/and above them: Justice" (XCIV, 640). He wrote, in his commentary on the Magna Charta, "all monopolies are against this great charter, because they are against the liberty of the subject, and the law of the land." He also said that Edward I's law against usury was "worthy to be written in letters of gold." He thus represents the principle "Law's aim is against coercion" (XCVI, 657), and is the third, and probably the most essential element, to the foundations of good government that are laid down in *Thrones*.

Behind the rage and fragmentation of much of XCVI-CIX, there is a stillness and peace, underlying the surface activity of the verse: the inkling of a permanent world beyond the merely temporal facts of all the emperors and kings, "stone to stone, as a river descending/the sound a gemmed light,/form is from the lute's neck" (C, 716). And images, defining with a precision unequalled even by Wordsworth, the delicacy of nature, flash through the historical or monetary material, so that the *place* where the reader's mind remains is paradise, even though he is simultaneously following, or trying to follow, a political or economic argument: "For thirty years nothing of interest occurred in that country/but the Burgomeister's Schwager/mistrusted Fetzen Papier/ Where deer's feet make dust in shadow/at wood's edge" (CIV, 745).

---

[1]*Agenda*, vol IX, nos. 2-3.

XCVI

651:   Κρήδεμνον: Kredemnon, [Leucothoe's] veil (*Odyssey*, V, 351).
      & on the hearth ... juniper: recalls Odysseus' seven years on the island of Ogygia with the goddess Kalypso. She burns these woods on her hearth (*Odyssey*, V, 59–60).

diafana: see glossary to XXXVI (177).

Aether pluit... cadavera... thure: (L) The air rains money/The earth vomits corpses... Tuscans who by incense.

lumina mundi, ἐπικόμβια... τὸν λαόν: (L & Gk) *epikombia... ton laon,* lights of the world, money to the people.

652: **Migne 95, 620:** Paulus the Deacon's work appears in Migne's *Patrologia,* Vol. 95.

653: **verbo et actu corruscans:** (L) shining in word and deed. The Chinese ideogram to the right means 'resplendent'—the surname of a Chinese friend of Pound's.

654: **ΕΠΑΡΧΙΚΟΝ ΒΙΒΛΙΟΝ:** *Eparchikon Biblion,* Eparch's book.

θῖνα θαλάσσης: *thina thalasses,* the sea shore.

655: **the Chinese ideogram is fa:** to issue; it refers to the line, "TIBERIUS.../ by his spending." See also glossary to XCIV (636) and LIV (290).

656: **pervanche:** (I) periwinkle, hence blue. Applied to Fortuna again XCVIII (676).

CHEN: see glossary to LXXXVI (566).

e che permutasse: (I) and who changes. Dante (*Inferno*, VII, 78) is describing the goddess, Fortuna, who rules the earth, "all under the moon." She is central to the late cantos.

With castled ships... Dei Matris: Heraclius comes to Byzantium to become Emperor with ships bearing images of the Madonna. The next 36 lines deal mainly with his actions: in particular his wars against the Persian King Chosroes II which were eventually successful. Heraclius is one of the minor heroes of the poem.

imperator simul et sponsus: (L) Heraclius was Emperor and bridegroom at the same time, when he was crowned in 602.

Chosroes... sun: Chosroes was a sun-worshipper. The ideogram is **jih⁴:** the sun.

εἰκόνος: *eikonos,* the ikons.

657: **Χρυσολόχας:** *chrysolochas.* Chosroes called his army the Golden Spears.

Fu Lin: (C) This refers to Byzantium against which Chosroes was marshalling all these races.

Turcos quos... vocant: (L) Turks who are called Cazars.

God's Mother... magnitudinis: These lines concern the defeat of Chosroes. Heraclius' men enter Persia where they have feasts (*epulantes*), and in Chosroes' palace they find astonishingly huge tigers (*tigrides mirae magnitudinis*).

sed susciperent: (L) but that they should accept.

658: **Anno sexto... columnae:** (L) In the 6th year of his reign, Justinian II foolishly dissolved peace which he had kept with Habdimelech, and irrationally wanted the whole of the people of Cyprus to migrate: and when he looked again at the imprint on the coin that had been sent from Habdimelech, he did not accept it.... And, hearing this, Habdimelech, urged on by the devil, asked that the peace should not be dissolved, but that they should accept (*sed susciperent*) his coinage, since the Arabs would not accept the Roman imprint on his coins. Indeed, giving the weight of the gold, he said: "There will not be any loss to the Romans if the Arabs are allowed to mint new . . ." Thus it was done, and Habdimelech sent to build Muchan temple, and he wished to transport some columns.

PANTA 'REI: (Gk) All things flow (Heracleitos).

Hyacinthinis: (L) Purplish blue (like the flower).

μεγαλοζήλων: *megalozelōn*, means the same.

659: **δέκα νομισμάτων:** *deka nomismaton*, of ten coins. **Nicole:** Dr. Jules Nicole, professor at the University of Geneva, who discovered the Eparch's book in 1891. **purpureas vestes:** (L) purple clothes.

τὰ βλαττία: *ta blattia*, means the same.

ἀναιδῶς: *anaidos*, whenever they please, slapdash.

μὴ αὐξάνοντες . . . . τιμήν: *me auxanontes e elattountes ten timen*, not to raise or lower the price.

ἀλογίστους: *alogistous*, careless, negligent.

καπηλεύων: *kapeleuōn*, retailer.

στομύλος: *stomulos*, huckster.

ἀγοραῖος: *agoraios*, forensic.

λάλος: *lalos*, smooth talker, babbler.

 The 4 ideograms mean (approximately): Purple spoils red (a true colour), which idea links with the previous page, "fake purple," *Hyacinthinis*, **μεγαλοζήλων.** A passage from Confucius explains what Pound is getting at here, viz, distinctions: "I hate the way purple spoils vermilion, I hate the way the Chang sonority confuses the music of the Elegantiae, I hate sharp mouths (the clever yawp, mouths set on profits) that overturn states and families." (*Analects*, XVII, xviii.)

ταραχώδης: *tarakhōdes*, confused, quarrelsome. Pun on Tarascon, opposite **Beaucaire** on the Rhône.

Ducange: Charles du Fresne Du Cange (1610-1688), scholar who produced dictionaries of medieval Greek and Latin. He was also a student of Byzantine history. **στατήρ:** *stater*, coin.

660: **ἥ καὶ . . . ξέει:** *e kai nomismata xeei*, and who files the coinage.

aureus: (L) gold coin.

vel pactum . . . augens: (L) or raises the agreed price.

καιρὸν . . . . ἀποθησαυρίζη: *kairon endeias apothesaurize*, hoard for a time of need.

XOIREMPERS: pork butchers.

ad pretium empti: (L) to the selling price of grain.

κατὰ τὴν . . . ἑνὸσ: *kata ten exonesin nomismatos henos*, the selling price of grain, one gold coin.

bankers: misprint for bakers!

μηδεμιᾷ λειτουργίᾳ: *medemia leitourgia*, no public service (bakers are exempt from this—a pun on "liturgy)."

ὀικονομία...πιπράσκεσθαι: *oikonomia...opos...pipraskesthai*, the mode...whereby...they sell.

analogous ezonesis: parallel selling (uniform prices).

Stathmos: a cask containing 30 litres.

661: ΒΟΘΡΩΝ: *bothrōn*, assessors of animals (at the market).

662: ΛΕΠΤΟΥΡΓΩΝ: *leptourgōn:* craftsmen.

αὔξει...λόγων: *auxei tous misthous skaioteti tōn logōn*, raise their wages...clumsy use of words.

στομυλία: *stomulia*, see glossary to 659.

ἀπληστία...κακουργία: *aplestia...kakourgia*, avarice....malice.

663: ἐγκύκλιος παίδευσις: *egkuklios paideusis*, encyclopaedic education.

12% says Nicole, illegal: Pound believed that low interest rates caused the Byzantine state to endure for so long, "And Byzance lasted longer than Manchu/because of an interest rate" (XCVIII, 690).

κατὰ....ζώων: *kata ten poiotita/(tōn zōōn)*, for the quality/(of the animals).

Χαιρε ὁ ''Ηλιος....clarore: *Chaire o Helios*, Hail O Helios (the sun god)...Hail brightness.

664: **iustitiae...antiquius:** (L) justice...nothing more ancient (Cicero, *De Officiis*).

"Honest feathers": "onesta piume" (*Purgatorio*, I, 42, where Dante meets the honest Cato, looking like a noble bird).

"What about murder?": see Cicero, *De Officiis*, 2, 89 where Cato the elder is asked "What about usury?" and he replies, "How about murder?" ("Quid occidere?").

humiles non omnes improbi: (L) all humble people are not dishonest (*De Officiis*, 2, 71).

"An ater, an albus": Catullus, in *Carmina* XCIII, says of Caesar that he doesn't care whether he is black or white.

πολιτικῶν σωματείων: *politikōn sōmateiōn*, political bodies.

Βασιλεῦσι Λέων: *Basileusi Leōn*, King Leo.

666: θυμίαμα...Κυρίου: *thumiama enopion Kyriou*, incense before the Lord.

667: 'Ο δόλον....'ασήμιον: *O dolon poion eis asemion*, the person who corrupts silver.

Καταλλάκτης < > κεκομμένον: *Katallaktes <* > *kekomnenon*, coin measurers...counterfeits.

"pacem": (L) peace.

XCVII

668: **Melik and Edward:** In A.D. 692 Abd-el-Melik, "the Arabian caliph ...determined to assert his independence of Rome...struck gold coins with his own effigy, holding a drawn sword, as afterwards did Edward III..." (Alexander Del Mar, *Roman and Moslem Moneys*, page 89).

Emir-el-Moumenin: the title which Melik took means "Commander of the Faithful."

six and ½ to one: "The ratio between silver and gold was that oriental valuation of 6½ for 1, which marked for several centuries the line of separation between the Moslem and Christian States of Europe.... This ratio may have been due to the fact that in all western countries conquered by the Moslem, silver was chiefly in the hands of the people, whilst gold was in those of the rulers." (*Ibidem*, page 90.) (I give the above three examples of the way Pound uses Del Mar in the first half of XCVII; for reasons of space, it is impossible to continue. The cryptic way he presents his source may be intended to stir the reader to go to Del Mar directly.)

669: **"not for coining".... Royal.":** adapted from *King Lear*, "No they cannot touch me for coining. I am the King himself" (Act IV, Scene v).

670: **"That most powerful engine" says Del Mar:** He wrote, "Money is perhaps the mightiest engine to which man can lend an intelligent guidance. Unheard, unfelt, unseen, it has the power to so distribute the burdens, gratifications, and opportunities of life that each individual shall enjoy that share of them to which his merits or good fortune may fairly entitle him, or, contrariwise, to dispense them with so partial a hand as to violate every principle of justice, and perpetuate a succession of social slaveries to the end of time." (*Roman and Moslem Moneys*, page 2.)

Athelstan: see glossary to XLVIII (242).

671: πρόσοδος φόρων ... μεταθεμένων: *prosodos phorōn e epeteios...metathemenōn*, the regular income of taxes...altered. (See glossary to LII, 273.)

"Senna": see XXXVIII (187).

Captn. Wadsworth: see glossary to CIX (773).

672: **Mons of Jute...name in the record:** Christian II of Denmark, with Troll, the Roman archbishop of Uppsala, murdered many Lutherans (1620) with the result that, "It was not merely Norway and Sweden that rose up to throw off the shackles of Rome, it was all Scandinavia ....Jutland...transmitted to the tyrant of Denmark a demand of deposition which was read to him by a single unarmed man, the chief magistrate of the Jutes, whose act should never be permitted to fall into oblivion. This hero's name was Mons, and it deserves to be written over the gateway of every oppressor. The unlooked-for result of Mons's brave act was the abdication and flight of the cowardly Christian." (Del Mar, *History of Monetary Systems*, pages 278–79.)

and "limitation is the essence of good nomisma": Del Mar wrote, "These principles of money—namely, that Money is a Measure, and must be of necessity an Institute of Law, that the Unit of money is All Money within a given legal jurisdiction, that the practical Essence of money is Limitation...." (*Ibidem*, page 8).

673: **as I have seen them by shovels full/lit by gas flares:** Pound here recalls his childhood—his father was an assayer at the U.S. mint in Philadelphia.

674: **18, CHARLES SECOND c. 5:** "an act that bargained away the Measure of Value...the State practically lost its control of money. In 1816 the

Crown was persuaded to suspend the exercise of its power over the ratio. In this manner was silver demonetized. By the... Mint act of 1870... the last remnant of a prerogative whose exercise is essential to the autonomy of the State was innocently surrendered to private hands. Practically, since 1816 the Measure of Value for the vast transactions of the British Empire has not been Money, which may be limited by law and counted by tale, but Metal, which cannot be thus regulated, and which therefore has been resigned practically to the control of a class whose chief interest in the State has been to render it subservient to their own private advantage...." (*Ibidem*, pages 388–89.)

Goldsmiths not aiming at i: The ideogram means equity. See also glossary to LXXXVII (563).

Sophia ... πίστις: wisdom, ... *pistis*, faith. Del Mar relates how Charles gave up his prerogative over coinage to the goldsmiths.

"Portcullis" struck by the Crown, but Charles/let the East Indies do it: Del Mar tells us that these were coins minted for the Crown by the East India Company for use in India. In 1666 Charles signed an act which authorized the Company to issue private coinage and in 1677 "East India Company authorised by the British Crown to coin gold, silver, copper, or lead, with its own devices ...." (*Ibidem*, pages 395 ff.)

675: **"The signal was given by Mr. Marble":** "In 1868, one of the two great national parties having declared itself favourable to the retention of the greenback in circulation, it was suddenly deserted by its leaders on the eve of the Presidential election, and, as a consequence, defeated at the polls. The Chairman of the National Committee of this party was August Belmont, who was the agent in New York of the great European house of Rothschild. The sign of desertion, known as 'The Betrayal,' was given by Manton Marble, editor of *The New York World*, the trusted organ of the party." (*Ibidem*, page 420.)

The first ideogram is **hsin¹:** make new (LIII, 265).

ch'in; tan⁴: near to dawn.

οἶνοσ αἰθίοψ: *oinos aithiops*, wine; red-brown, burnt.
ἀλιπόρφυρος: *aliporphyros*, sea-purple (*Odyssey*).
orixalxo, les xaladines: (Gk) gold-bronze, copper.
Ling: see glossary to LXXXV (543).
Kuanon: see glossary to LXXIV (428).
διïπετέος: *diïpeteos*, flowing from heaven ("the celestial Nile," V, 17).
ἀίσσουσιν: *aissousin*, rushing.
Bernice, late for a constellation...: Berenice, wife of Ptolemy III. When her husband left for a campaign in Syria, she placed a lock of her hair in her mother-in-law, Arsinoe's, shrine at Zephyrium (see CVI, 755) for his safe return. The lock disappeared. The court astronomer, Conon, discovered it as a new constellation, *Coma Berenices*. See Yeats, "Her Dream," Callimachus, 110, and Catullus, 65 and 66.

676: **Uncle William...every individual soul...:** Yeats said God has need of every individual soul.

δολιχηρέτμοισι: *dolicheretmoisi,* long-oared (Homeric epithet for the Phaeakians).

 The 6 ideograms mean (roughly): "does not treasure jewels and such wealth, counting his manhood and the love of his relatives the true treasure" (*Confucius,* page 75).

splendor' mondan': (I) worldly splendours (Dante, *Inferno,* VII, 77).

beata gode: (I) enjoys [her] blessedness. "She is in bliss, and hears it not: with the other Primal creatures joyful, she wheels her sphere, and enjoys her blessedness." Virgil here describes Fortuna to Dante (*Inferno,* VII, 94–96).

hoc signo: (L) by this sign; **chen⁴:** see glossary to LXXXV (547).

pervanche: see glossary to XCVI (656).

677: **tan:** see glossary to XCI (615).

forsitan: (L) perhaps.

sempre biasmata,/gode: (I) always blamed,/she [Fortuna] rejoices. "Mortal blame has no sound in her ears" (C, 720).

678: πανουργία: *panourgia,* villainy.

plenilune: full moon.

679: **From Sargon of Agade:** legendary Sumerian king. For a note on the pictographic writing in this canto see glossary to XCIV (635).

a thousand years before Tang: Tching Tang—see glossary to LIII (264).

680: μετά τὰ φυσικά: *meta ta physica,* after the physics.

"Buckie": R. Buckminster Fuller, American architect and inventor.

681: **PAUL, the Deacon...33 years:** These lines return us to the source of the first part of XCVI: Paulus's *History of the Lombards.* The Lombards originated in Sweden; Agelmund was their earliest king. Fricco was one of their gods. "He was often represented by an enormous phallic or priapic figure [**ingenti Priapo**]. His wife was Frea, for whom Friday or Freitag was named, which corresponds with the name *venerdi,* or Venus-day, in Roman countries. The "frei" root of her name is as-

131

sociated with freedom. . . ." (J. Wilhelm, *The Later Cantos,* page 104.) Hence **Dea Libertatis, Venus:** Goddess of Liberty, Venus.

PUER APULIUS/"Fresca Rosa": (L & I) the boy from Apulia (Frederick II of Sicily)/"Fresh Rose." See glossary to XCVIII (689) and CVII (757).

682:    **That he wrote the book of the Falcon:** Frederick II wrote a treatise on falcons.

Mirabile brevitate correxit: (L) [Justinian] corrected with marvellous brevity.

The two ideograms are **Cheng⁴ Ming²:** right name (LI, 252).

ἀρσενικὰ: *arsenika,* masculine.

ἀνδρικὰ: *andrika,* male.

θηλυκά: *thelyka,* feminine.

Deorum Manium, Flamen Dialis . . . : (L) of Gods, of Shades, Priest of Zeus . . .

Pomona: see glossary to LXXXIX (490).

aethera terrenaeque: (L) heaven and the lands of the earth.

Manes Di: (L) Shades, Gods.

ἐν νέμει . . . δαίμων: *en nemei skierō/epi te lin embale daimōn,* in the shady grove, the god sent a lion.

683:    **Flamen Portualis:** (L) priest of Portumnus. (Portualis is a misprint for Portunalis.) Portumnus, a sea god, with jurisdiction over harbours, was the son of Ino (Leucothoe). See Ovid, *Fasti,* VI, 547.

inter mortua jam et verba sepulta: (L) now among dead and buried words—"dead words out of fashion" (CII, 730).

 pe: 'elder' or 'paternal uncle.'

馬 Ma   These two characters are probably the name of a goddess of the sea—a link with Portumnus. "Of gods of the sea, the most effective (spiritually) is Ma Tsu who anciently was one of the divine imperial concubines of Heaven. She will invariably respond to the prayers of any ocean-going vessel in distress. A mandate of the time of K'ang Hsi elevated her to the position of Queen of Heaven." (From a Chinese dictionary.) (J.C.)

祖 Tsu

kadzu, arachidi, acero: (J & I) ground ivy, peanuts, maple trees.

無   The two characters which close this Canto mean, 'without weariness' and correspond to 'not lie down'. Compare LXXVI (454) "and in government not to lie down on it." Both are taken from *Analects,* XII, XIV: "Tze-chang asked about government. He said: Not to lie down on it; to act from the middle of the heart." (*Confucius,* page 246.) (J.C.)

倦

XCVIII

684: **The boat of Ra-Set:** see glossary to XCI (611-12).

Agada, Ganna, Faasa: see glossary to LXXIV (427).

hsin[1]: make new (LIII, 265).

Τὰ ἐξ... φάρμακα: *ta ex aigyptou pharmaka*, drugs out of Egypt.

Χρόνος... σοφίας: *Chronos/pneuma theōn/kai erōs sophias*, Time/breath of gods/and love of wisdom.

ne quaesaris: see glossary to XCI (612).

ius Italicum, more Sabello: (L) Italian justice, according to Sabellan customs. "Sabelli" is the Roman name of speakers of the Oscan language, the inhabitants of Campania, southern Italy, who migrated north.

"Ut facias pulchram": see glossary to XCIII (684).

θῖνα θαλάσσης: *thina thalasses*, the sea shore.

685: **The Manchu at 36 legal, their Edict:** This line introduces the main subject of this, and the following canto. For details, see general commentary on *Thrones*.

Anselm: see glossary to CV (746).

"The body is inside": Plotinus said, "The body is inside the soul" (*Enneads*, IV, 3, 22, where he quotes Plato to this effect). See also glossary to XIV (66).

Gemisto: see glossary to VIII (31).

and their speed in communication: Compare David Jones, "But if unsullied light and therefore infinite agility are part of our image of celestial beings, a seraphic exactitude would seem to be part of that image too" (*The Dying Gaul*, page 195).

et in nebulas simiglianza: (L & I) and their likeness in clouds.

καθ' ὁμοίωσιν Deorum: *kath omoiōsin*, according to the likeness of gods.

must fight for law as for walls: "The people must fight for its laws as for its walls" (Heracleitos, fragment 100—Bywater's edition). This line anticipates the Coke cantos (CVII-CIX).

And that Leucothoe rose...Apollo: not the same person as the sea nymph who saved Odysseus, *this* Leucothoe was a daughter of Orchamus, who was loved by Apollo. Her father, angered, buried her in the earth and the sun god transformed her into "an incense bush" (Ovid, *Metamorphoses*, IV, 190 ff.).

Est deus in nobis: (L) a god is within us—see glossary to XCIII (628).

Χρήδεμνον: *Kredemnon*, [Leucothoe's] veil.

不 **pu[4.5]:** not, a negative. For an elucidation of "had no ground beneath 'em" see glossary to LXXXV (556) and compare the forms of the two ideograms. (J.C.)

Orage: see glossary to XLVI (232).

Per ragione vale: (I) precious through reason (Cavalcanti, *Donna mi priegha*).

686: **"Noi altri borghesi...piazza":** (I) "We bourgeois people..."

ψεῦδος....πεπνύμενος: *pseudos d'ouk ereei/ ...gar pepnumenos*, doesn't

133

tell a lie ... knowing (*Odyssey*, III, 20). The line refers to Nestor and is translated by Pound, XCIX, "too intelligent to prevaricate" (697).

ich bin am Zuge: (G) I'm on the move. Refers to the previous line, "Patience, I will come to the Commissioner of the Salt Works/in due course" (685), and is a humorous way of telling the reader that Pound is soon to start on the real subject of XCVIII & XCIX: the Salt Commissioner Iu-p'uh's popular version of Iong Ching's commentary on his father's *Sacred Edict!*

ἀρχή: *arche*, origin.

volgar' eloquio: (I) common speech (Dante).

 The two characters beside this phrase stand for the Salt Commissioner, Iu-p'uh. The second one also means 'sincere'; especially that sincerity which is the quality of things which are plain, simple and unadorned. (J.C.)

Sagetrieb: see glossary to LXXXV (557).

 pen yeh: one's original calling or profession (for *pen* see glossary to XCIV, 640). Pound glosses it "a developed skill from persistence" (XCIX, 698). In *The Sacred Edict*, this word is used in two senses: (i) the 'fundamental' or 'primary' occupation, i.e., agriculture; and (ii) the sense outlined above. (J.C.)

687: τέχνη: *techne*, see glossary to LXXXV (546).

καθόλου: *katholou*, generalities—see LXXIV (441).

"and that Buddha abandoned such splendours ... likely!": Buddha "hid himself in the heights of a snowy mountain to practise asceticism. Parents, children and wife he alike neglected: is it likely he will concern himself about all you people and expound his tenets to you?" (F.W. Baller, *The Sacred Edict*, pages 72 ff.).

feng-ko: palace; literally 'phoenix mansions', abode of royalty—one of the splendours the Buddha *ch'i'd* and *shed*.

 chi: These two characters form a compound, meaning 'to abandon.' (J.C.)

 she

688: **ma:** interrogative particle, made up, as Pound says, of "a horse and mouth"—a pun on "from the horse's mouth"!

hsiao jin: petty man

689: i⁴: equity (see glossary to LXXXVI, 563).

 shên: deep, profound.

 li³⁻⁴: within, corresponding to 'contains.'

 yüan²: originally (as Pound notes, the etymology suggests a 'spring').

 t'ai⁴: Great.

 p'ing²: Peace.

'T'ai p'ing' is the Chinese phrase for the ideal state of the Empire. (J.C.)

tso fengg **tso feng suh:** Baller translates 'Feng suh' "good manners and customs." The character in the midst of the romanisations is *feng*, usually meaning breath, wind and traditionally extended to mean the influence which inclines the people (as wind inclines the grass) to goodness.

en¹ grace, mercy, kindness.

ch'ing²: affections. The character is composed of 'heart' and 'the colour of nature' (green, blue and the black of darkness).

And as Ford... words: "Pestered [by Pound]... as to what a young writer ought to read, Ford [Madox Ford] groaned: "Let him get a DICTIONARY and learn the meaning of words" (*Pavannes and Divagations,* page 155).

"Aulentissima... L'estate": (I) "sweetly smelling... singing the Summer." **Alcamo:** the earliest recorded Italian poet (fl. *c.* 1170). See glossary to CVII (757).

cassia: (L) a tree with aromatic bark; the wild cinnamon.

690: i⁴: equity (see glossary to LXXXVII, 563).

ch'i⁴: breath, wind, energy, pneuma.

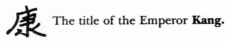 The title of the Emperor **Kang.**

 Hi

From Kati to Kang Hi: Approximately 4,000 years separate Kati (see glossary to XCIII, 623) from Kang Hi (who produced the first version of *The Sacred Edict*)—Pound here compares them to Shun and Wan (see glossary to LXXVII, 467).

"De libro Chi-king ... incitaque: see glossary to LIX (324).

Plotinus: see glossary to XIV (66).

Gemisto: see glossary to VIII (31).

Anselm: see glossaries to CV—this Canto is mostly concerned with St. Anselm.

Thus the gods appointed john barleycorn Je tzu: Pound puns Jesus with Hou Tsi, linking him with John Barleycorn—see *Classic Anthology*, Ode 245. **Je tzu:** (C) he who incites. See glossary to CV (747).

691:    **Without ²muan ¹bpo ... anticipate:** anticipates the religious rites of the Na-khi people which will be presented in CI, CIV, CX, CXII etc.

τò καλόν: *to kalon,* the beautiful.

order   孝   Hsiao: 'order' as in XIII (59).

It is usually translated 'filial piety'—earlier in XCVIII it has been recognized as "a filiality that binds things together" (686). (J.C.)

cheng   正   right (see glossary to LI, 252 & LXXIII, 352).

king   經   classics; the Confucian Classics.

These characters correspond, surprisingly, to the 'gentleman' of the line before (a direct quotation from Baller, page 5). We are asked to consider the meaning *cheng king.* The image is of correctly aligned warp threads; here the warp of tradition and orthodoxy. 'Ching' also refers to 'The Confucian Classics'—the 'warp' of literary tradition.

From Kung's porch   門   mên³: gateway, or porch i.e., entrance to knowledge. 'Schools' in China, as in the 'Confucian School', were called this, from which a master was used to hold forth.

692:    **II. Ten thousand years say men .... who lie in a law-court!":** the numbered lines on pages 691–693 are alternative titles for the various corresponding sections of *The Sacred Edict*, or selected passages in them, using a variety of tricks of translation, selection and interpretation. (J.C.)

136

ut supra: (L) as above.

ne ultra crepidam: (L) perhaps based on the proverb, "Let the cobbler stick to his last"—i.e., persist in your own trade or skill.

693: 毌 These two characters correspond to "unblurred" in the line beside them (**wu:** un-, **hu:** blurred).

忽、

顯 **hsien** These words, like most of the rest in this canto, both Chinese and English, are taken from Iong Ching's preface to his version of the *Edict.* They mean **ming** 'clear and enlightening' and Pound compares this usage to that quoted in *The Unwobbling Pivot,* XVI, 4: "Intangible and abstruse/the bright silk of the sunlight/pours down in manifest splendour" (*Confucius,* page 33). See also glossary to LXXXV (550).

明

Pitagora: Dante's name for Pythagoras.

non si disuna: (I) does not disunify ("che quella via luce che si mea/dal suo lucente, che non si disuna/da lui, ne dall amor che a lor s'intre" (Dante, *Paradiso,* XIII, 55-7).

Sheng 聖 These are the characters for *The Sacred Edict.*

The Edict 諭

XCIX

695: **KOINE ENNOIA:** (Gk) ideas in common, common language.

cognome, indirizzo: (I) surname, address ("Wherein is no reponsible person/having a front name, a hind name and an address," LXXVIII, 479—Mussolini said this).

697: **Nestor too intelligent to prevaricate:** see *Odyssey,* III, 20. Nestor was king of Pylos.

698: **se non fosse cive:** see glossary to XCIII (624).

699: **water, earth and biceps, fa$^{3-5}$lu:**

This is Pound's fanciful analysis of the character to the right, which means law. On 'law' as 'not outside their natural colour' see glossary to XCVIII (689).

fromm: (G) holy, reverent.

kuang^1 ming^2: light, radiance. Repeated 702.

tuan^1: foundations—see glossary to LXXXV (545).

cheng^4: correct; see also glossary to LI (252) and LXIII (352).

137

700: **Plotinus:** see glossary to XV (66) and XCVIII (685).

701: **pu k'o hsin:** do not believe them (Baller, page 85).

hsin¹ shu⁴⁻⁵: devices of the mind (or heart) which...

hai⁴: harm (men. i.e. heretical sects which undermine the people's orthodoxy—Baller, page 86). (J.C.)

cheng⁴: see glossary above.

702: **huo⁴⁻⁵ fu²⁻⁵:** 佛 living Buddhas, here referring to one's parents whose "incarnation" obviates any necessity to worship idols. The ideogram is **fu:** Buddha.

Kuang Kuang...tien t'ang² hsin¹ li³⁻⁵: This "doubled kuang¹ ming²" or enlightened radiance, has already been invoked on page 699, and associated with Khati's "A man's paradise is his good nature" (XCIII, 623). Here Pound has rearranged a sentence which Baller translates: "the mind enlightened is heaven" (page 87) so that it reads literally, "heaven (is) heart-within." This saying comes paired with its complement in *The Sacred Edict:* "the mind in darkness is hell."

But their First Classic...aim: Buddhist Heart Classic.

706: **PANURGIA? SOPHIA:** (Gk) Villainy? Wisdom.

709: **nung/sang:** to farm mulberry.

710: **en¹:** see glossary to XCVIII (689).

711: **jen, i, li, chih:** the four TUAN, or foundations (see glossary to LXXXV, 545). Pound must have appreciated the statement that the foundations are from nature, which comes from the end of the sixth section of the *Edict* (Baller, page 71). (J.C.)

712: **fu jen:** wise man (can also mean everyman)—the sentence Pound is paraphrasing comes from the *Edict* as expanded by Iong Ching (not the salt commissioner's version) and may be translated: "Man receives (his place) between Heaven and Earth and thereby flourishes." (J.C.)

C

713: **Eu ZoOn:** (Gk) well living.

Not that never should...liberties: Not that the President should never exceed his powers...

714: **John Law:** (1671-1729) Scottish financier. The bank he set up in France (1716) soon became the Royal Bank, with power to issue paper currency as legal tender. He believed that the state has credit in the same way as a bank, and his ideas were in many ways ahead of his time. After his "Mississippi scheme" failed, presumably because of the avarice of speculators, he had to flee to Venice in 1720 where he died in poverty nine years later. He was buried in San Moise.

SUMBAINAI: (Gk) coheres (Sophokles, *Women of Trachis*, "What/ SPLENDOUR/IT ALL COHERES").

Grevitch: an inmate of St. Elizabeth's Hospital.

715: **"In locis desertis/laetamur....viventia.":** (L) "In desert places/we rejoice, in the middle of the woods./are sheared, you kill, they are

138

milked/by which you till the land./You shed their blood/their flesh fills you inside/you thus become a living sepulchre of dead bodies." The source of these lines is a translation, possibly made by St. Ambrose, of a Greek account of Alexander the Great's conversation with the Brahmins of India (*De Moribus Brachmanorum*). They explain to him their simple way of life, which was totally opposed to Greek and Western values. In particular they attack the raising of cows for slaughter, and thus the mentality of "the butchers of lesser cattle" (LXXVII, 573; XCIII, 623). They, like Apollonius, have "made peace with the animals" not to exploit them—as Pound put it later, "Ambrose:/'First treason: shepherd to flock'" (CV, 750).

716: **Letizia:** Joy (Dante, *Paradiso*, XVIII, 42).
Buona da sè voluntà: (I) Will, good itself (*Paradiso*, XIX, 86).
Lume non è, ... sereno: No light but from the serene (*Paradiso*, XIX, 64).
stone to stone ... descending: from *Paradiso*, XX, 19-20.
gemmed light: *Paradiso*, XX, 17; **form ... from the lute's neck:** *Paradiso*, XX, 22-23.

717: **DEXATO XERSI:** (Gk) she [Leucothoe] received it in her hands (*Odyssey*, V, 462).
AGERTHE: gathered back (*Odyssey*, V, 458).
CODE: Justinian's law code.

718: **Nel mezzo:** (I) In the middle (*Inferno*, I, 1).
fu$^{2-5}$: Buddhists.

719: **Kuan Ming:** 光 明   see glossary to XCIX (699 and 702). 'Kuan' here is a mistake for 'Kuang.'

Durch das Bankhaus Pacelli kompromittiert: (G) Pacelli (Pope Pius XII) compromised through the bank.

720: **Peregrinus:** (A.D. 100-65) Cynic philosopher who committed suicide by throwing himself on the flames at the Olympic Games.
Coelum tecto ... largitur: (L) Sky [my] roof, nor does God sell; Earth [my] couch, but He confers [wisdom]. Spoken by the Brahmins to Alexander the Great (St. Ambrose, *De Moribus Brachmanorum*).
Cherbury: Lord Herbert of C. (1583-1648), philosopher, poet and diplomat. His most important work, *De Veritate*, is the first purely metaphysical work by an Englishman. He belonged to the neo-Platonist tradition—hence his connection here with Erigena and Psellos.
Rémusat: Comtesse de R. (1780-1821), lady in waiting to the Empress Josephine. Her *Mémoires* will be used in CI. Her husband, Augustin, was an adviser of Napoleon. Her son, Charles, wrote books on Lord Herbert of Cherbury, Saint Anselm, and Thiers. Perhaps it is he, rather than his mother, who is referred to here.

721: **Neque aurum deligunt:** (L) Nor did any choose gold.

Gardner, A.G.....specific: He wrote, "If we crush Germany and make Russia dictator of Europe and Asia it will be the greatest disaster that has ever befallen Western Europe" (*London Daily News*, 1 August 1914).

EX OUSIAS...HYPOSTASIN...EROTAS: (Gk) an existent, projec-tion or generation from the essence...On love. The phrases come from Plotinus, *Enneads*, III, 5, 3, *PERI EROTOS* (On Love)—"We ought not to disbelieve that Love is a reality and a substance, less than that which made it, but all the same substantially existent" (*Plotinus*, translated by A.H. Armstrong, Loeb Classical Library).

hieron: (Gk) temple, sacred place.

722:    **nous to ariston autou:** (Gk) intellect its best (?). Compare "and via mind is the nearest you'll get to it" (CV, 747).

pathema/ouk aphistatai: (Gk) emotion does not separate from it (?). Compare R.R. Collingwood, "The intellect has its own emotions" (*Principles of Art*).

per plura diafana: see glossary to XXXVI (177).

aloof: this, and the Greek above, perhaps echoes "there came new subtlety of eyes into my tent...hypostasis...diastasis...." (LXXXI, 520).

CI

723:    **Monsieur de Rémusat:** Augustin de R., adviser to Napoleon. His wife's *Mémoires* are the main source for the Napoleonic material here.

(junipers, south side): approaching the Na-khi landscape in the Li-chiang district of Southwest China in summer, the hills "are blue-green with juniper" (725).

Chalais, Aubeterre: "The association of Na-khi and Albigensian in Cantos CI and CX indicates their common fate—the endurance of religious-political oppression" (Jamila Ismail, "News of the Universe", *Agenda*, Vol. IX, Nos. 2-3).

Kublai: "*En passant* through Na-khi territory in the mid-13th century, Kublai Khan lay with the chieftain's daughter; their child, so the legend goes, became the ancestor of the Na-khi kings" (*Ibidem*).

Timur: Tamburlaine, who also came to Li-chiang as a conqueror. A subject-rhyme with Napoleon's conquests which faded even more rapidly.

A-tun-tzu: the last frontier town in Northwest Yunnan, at the head of the valley.

4 letters patent...chair-coolies, horses: In 1406 the 8th generation Na-khi king received the Imperial reward for having urged the wild tribes to pay tribute to the Ming court. In 1853 the Na-khi were given provisions and animals to fight Moslem rebels.

724:    **(Del Pelo Pardi...cunicoli):** This Italian archaeologist discovered an-cient underground canals (*cunicoli*) near Rome—a prehistoric irriga-tion system of great sophistication which does not fit with established chronology.

725: **Obit 1933,...Honour:** Tsung-Kuan is honoured for putting an end to banditry in the Li-chiang region.
Kuanon: see glossary to LXXIV (428).
Sengper ga-mu: Tibetan mountain god. The Na-khi fled from Tibet to Li-chiang taking their gods with them.
Achilöos: Greek river, and also, here, its god, "symbol of the power of damp and darkness, triform as water, cloud and rain" (*Women of Trachis*, page 25).

726: **KALON KAGATHON:** (Gk) good and beautiful.
Marengo: Napoleon's victory against the Austrians—"That day was right with the victor/mass weight against wrong" (L, 247).
EN THEORIA 'ON NOUS EXEI: (Gk) in contemplation the intellect holds him (?).
"Should," said H.J....."...existence": Henry James said that if his characters didn't exist, then we ought to pretend "for humanity's credit" that they did!
With the sun and moon...: the remaining lines deal mainly with Na-khi religious rituals, anticipating CX and CXII.
Rossoni: "cosi lo stato...": a minister in Mussolini's government. Referring to Silvio Gesell's idea of *stampscript* (a direct tax on the medium of exchange itself—see glossary to LXXIV, 441), Pound said, "That's where the state gets its cut, because Gesell, as a merchant, was thinking about nothing but a quick turnover. Rossoni saw the stamp on the stampscript as a tax." ("A B.B.C. Interview," *New Directions* 17.)
Delcroix: see glossary to XCII (621)."...when he first heard of stampscript, he beat on his head with his little wooden artificial arms and said "che magnifica idea"—what a magnificent idea. He saw where it led to and he grabbed a telephone and telephoned to somebody to come over and hear about it." (*Ibidem.*)
The green spur...peace: "during the 7th Moon 'when all is green and the plants have not yet turned yellow,' Earth is worshipped and thanked" (J. Ismail, *op. cit.*).

CII

728: **This I had from Kalupso...Hermes:** Hermes has told the nymph Kalypso that she must release Odysseus so that he can make his way home to Ithaka (*Odyssey*, V, 97 ff.).
"A cargo of Iron": Athene pretends to be Mentes, a friend of Odysseus, when she visits Telemachus telling him to seek news of his father—she lies that she has a ship, whose cargo is iron (*Odyssey*, I, 184).
keinas...e Orgei: [Odysseus] never wronged any man—which is "why Penelope waited" (*Odyssey*, IV, 693—"639" is a misprint).
The ideogram: pu$^{4.5}$: not, a negative. I.e., "*no* ground to stand on" (see glossary to XCVIII, 685).
OIOS TELESAI ERGON...EROS TE: (Gk) such as to complete the

141

task...and love. Based on *Odyssey*, II, 272, "What a man to go to the
end of his acts and words." Pound has changed ἔπος, word, to EROS,
love.

729: **Barley is the marrow of man:** see *Odyssey*, II, 290.

"50 more years on the Changes": Confucius said, "If many years were
added to me, I would give fifty to the study of The Book of Changes,
and might thereby manage to avoid great mistakes" (*Analects*, VII, xvi).

Took the Z for the tail...teacher: "The oral tradition, surviving rites,
and also the practical import of archaeological findings, are all part of
his [Frobenius's] total perception. He saw nothing ridiculous in a child's
wanting to know if the last letter of the word *Katz* stood for the cat's
tail and the first one for its head. But to the schoolteacher, who cared
little for intelligence, or lively curiosity, the child just seemed stupid."
(*Selected Prose*, page 298; *328*.) **Dummheit:** (G) Stupidity.

"pseudos d'ouk...ei gar pepneumenos": see glossary to XCVIII
(686).

730: **Atalant:** Atalanta (?), fast runner and huntress in Greek mythology.
Here, perhaps, she represents speed: "Green yellow the sunlight, more
rapid" (CIX, 773) and also, possibly, the Greek word ἀτάλαντος, balance, may be intended.

aithiops...oinops...haliporphuros...AISSOUSIN: see glossary to
XCVII (675).

KAI ALOGA: (Gk) and things without reason.

APHANASTON: (Gk) of invisible things (?).

OU THELEI...KOSMOU: (Gk) you do not want to come into the
world.

amnis herbidas ripas: (L) fast flowing stream [through] grassy banks.

731: **Julian:** "the Apostate," Roman Emperor (A.D. 361-63). He tried to
restore the Greek religion, attacking Christianity, but not persecuting
the Christians. He fought high prices, "Built granaries," and reformed
the coinage. He died in a war against Persia.

Marcellinus: historian; officer under Julian.

Assyrios fines ingressus: (L) entering Assyrian boundaries.

Quem mihi febricula eripuit: (L) whom a slight fever took away from
me (Julian's cousin, Constantius, died suddenly of a fever just before
their forces were about to engage in battle).

infaustus: (L) unfortunate.

CIII

732: **kolschoz:** (R) collective farm.

"I see its relation...to ten": Tze-Kung says this to Confucius (*Analects*,
V, viii) concerning his favourite disciple.

caelum renovabat: (L) he restored heaven.

cuniculi, canalesque: (I) tunnels and canals (see glossary to CI, 724).

733: **"tranne nella casa del re":** (I) except in the house of the king. Mussolini had not expected to be betrayed there—but it was where a trap was laid for him (Mary de Rachewiltz, *Discretions,* page 184).

734: **Edishu ... Poland:** the Katyn massacre.

735: **cheu i:** one who perceives.

736: **nec Templum ... rem:** (L) nor built the Temple/nor restored anything.

737: **"quae a thure ... sacrificiis:** (L) who with incense/enjoyed sacrifices (echoes XCVI, 651, as do other lines on this page).
Das Leihkapital: (G) loan-capital.
Mensdorf letter: a letter which Count Albert von Mensdorff and Pound drafted jointly and sent to the Carnegie Endowment for Peace, 18 June 1928, suggesting points worth study, "considering the causes of war, which it might be perhaps more useful to go into carefully than to investigate the effects of war.... 1) Intense production and sale of munitions; ... 2) Overproduction and dumping, leading to trade rivalries and irritation..." (*Impact,* page 281.)

CIV

738: **Na Khi made talk ... game:** They are at one with nature so the birds of the forest do not regard them as intruders. Their paradisal way of life is here contrasted with decadence and corruption in the West.
Ling: see glossary to LXXXV (543).
semina: (L) seeds [by ling (sensibility) only].

The second ideogram is **wu$^{1\text{-}2}$**: a medium, or witch. It also suggests the magical rites and dancing to induce the descent of spirits. It is the bottom component of the *Ling* character. Pound relates it to the priestess at Delphi (740) though it is interesting to note that the spiritual communication implied in these two cases runs in complementary directions: the oracle emerges from the earth and the 'voices' of the *ling* ideogram descend from under the cloud (740).

739: **PANURGIA:** (Gk) villainy; **Xreia:** (Gk) need.
^{2}muan ^{1}bpo: the Na-khi rite of Sacrifice to Heaven. "The oldest and most important of the Na-khi ceremonies ... it takes about a week to perform, and consists of more than a dozen rites of purification, confession, thanksgiving, and various offerings of grain, wine, flesh to the gods.... During the ceremony, the following is chanted: 'If ^{2}Muan ^{1}bpo is not performed, all that which we accomplished is not real, if ^{2}Muan ^{1}bpo is not performed, we will not attain perfection like others.' " (Jamila Ismail, "News of the Universe," *Agenda,* Vol. IX, Nos. 2-3.) The various rites of the ceremony will be embodied in *Drafts and Fragments,* CX and CXII.
agitante: see glossary to XCIII (628).

740: **Basinio left Greek ... cadence:** "In the margins of his Latin narrative you can still see the tags of Homer that he was using to keep his melodic sense active" (*A.B.C. of Reading,* page 48).

143

The Pollok was hooked... "**black sea**": Sir Ian Hamilton told the Poles they could expect help via the Black Sea if Germany invaded, which "help" never materialized because the Soviet-Nazi pact had intervened, and you couldn't reach Poland from the Black Sea.

Pitonessa/The small breasts....tripod: the priestess of the oracle at Delphi. "The word 'inspiration' is generally referred to the belief that a spirit took possession of the seer, and spoke through his mouth. Older than that belief, perhaps, was the discovery that the natural vapors of a cave or medicinal spring had an intoxicating power, as in the famous case of the Oracle at Delphi. The seer, in this case a woman, took her stand on a three-legged stool, or tripod, placed over a crack in the floor of a cave, and became literally inspired by the fumes that issued from the earth." (Allen Upward, *The Divine Mystery*, page 15.) The middle component of the *Ling* ideogram is three mouths—the top section is a cloud.

pao³: treasure.

da radice torbida: (I) of turbid root (This, and the ideogram for a wild cat, serve to introduce the lines about Hitler.

741: **maalesh:** painter.
Ambroise Paré: (1517-1590) French medical officer who saved many lives by introducing the tourniquet.
THEMIS: Greek goddess of Justice.
Yo-Yo: an inmate of St. Elizabeth's Hospital.
Light for lasso: see glossary to CV—Charles Suevi—(749).
742: **William's monoceros:** Yeats's, the unicorn.
743: **phyllotaxis:** pattern of leaves on a stem.
744: **PAGGKALA:** (Gk) all beautiful.
pen yeh: see glossary to XCVIII (686).
745: **curet cogitare perennia:** (L) he cares to think about permanent things.

CV

746: **rem salvavit:** (L) he saved the state—Mussolini is here rhymed with Sigismundo who was said to have "Saved the Florentine state" (IX, 35).
semina motuum: see glossary to LXX (534).
Sulmona: the birthplace of Ovid.
(Cesena, Zezena...colonne): see glossary to XI (50).
Anselm "Monologion" scripsit...: This line introduces the main subject of CV, the life and works of St. Anselm (*c.* 1033-1109). *Monologion* was his first philosophical writing. Dante places him in the heaven of the sun (*Paradiso,* XII). He is important in *Thrones* (a) in his respect for reason and precise terminology and (b) because, in his struggle

against William Rufus, he represents an important stage in the evolution of the rights of the individual against arbitrary power which Pound traces from the Anglo-Saxons, via Magna Charta, to Sir Edward Coke's fight for the independence of the judiciary at the time of James I (CVII-CIX). Anselm, as Archbishop of Canterbury, quarrelled with William over the right of the Church to freedom from interference from the king. There are obvious parallels with St. Thomas à Becket.

"non spatio, sed sapientia": This quotation, which Pound translates in the next line, "concerns a definition of God, who exists 'not huge in space, like a certain body' but 'more worthily, as wisdom does'" (James Wilhelm, *The Later Cantos*, page 156).

746-7: **non pares...rerum naturas**: (L) not equal...the natures of things (*Monologion*, adapted by Pound).

747: 稷 **Hou Je...Terrestre**: The first ideogram is **chi²·⁵**: panacled millet; the second is **hou⁴**: king. "Prince Millet" (*The Classic Anthology*, Ode 205). Pound is thus again referring to Hou Tsi and to "Christ in the grain" (LXXX, 513) linking with

后 "John Barleycorn...Je Tzu" (XCVIII, 690) and the story told in XXII (102)—also see, "Luigi...makes his communion with wheat grain..." (XCVII, 679 and CVI, 753).

"L'adoravano"...Santa Lucia": "At Terracina the sacristan showed a little marble barocco angel on the floor of the sacristy, the bishop had had to have it taken out of the church because the peasants insisted on 'worshipping IT as Santa Lucia'" (*Jefferson and/or Mussolini*, pages 30–31).

Bari: "At Bari Anselm made his famous speech against the Greeks, who were trying to tamper with the Trinity by linking the Holy Spirit directly to the Father and thus bypassing the Son, the human Christ element" (J. Wilhelm, *The Later Cantos*, page 208[1]).

anima....vagula, tenula: (L) soul...wandering, tenuous (adapted from Hadrian's dying address to his soul).

"non genitus"..."discendendo": (L) not born....[nor] descending from. *Discendendo* is probably a misprint for *discedendo* which is the word Anselm uses in *Caput* (Chapter) 57, where he says, "Love proceeds from the Highest Nature ineffably, not in separating (*discedendo*) from it, but in existing out of it, perhaps in a way that can only be likened to breathing" (J. Wilhelm's translation, *The Later Cantos*, page 157).

vera imago: (L) true image.

"rationalem": (L) reason; **"intenzione"**: (I) intention. Cavalcanti wrote, "Deeming intention to be reason's peer and mate" (XXXVI, 178).

Ratio: (L) reason; **luna**: moon. This leads to the image of reflection which follows, 748.

748: **Sapor**: (L) savour; **pulchritudo**: (L) beauty.

ne divisibilis intellectu: (L) not to be divided by the intellect.

fertur: (L) he is borne.

alvearia: beehives.

uranici templi...amictus: (L) starry temples (?)/with light as a cloak.

This image leads to the vision of Charles of the Suevi, "looping the light over my shoulder" (751).

Canterbury well...that had caught one: Two incidents in the life of St. Anselm are here alluded to: (1) When he was staying in Liberi, "nine miles approx east of Capua," a monk told him there was a scarcity of water. Anselm told him where to dig and a spring jetted, which became known as "Puteus Cantauriensis" (Well of the Archbishop of Canterbury). (2) When Anselm was ill he said, "I might eat a partridge." After an unsuccessful search by the monks, a stable boy 鬼 found a marten (a kind of weasel—"martin" in text is a misprint) with one in its mouth. Eating the partridge cured Anselm. The Chinese characters are related to both these 諂 incidents—the first is **kuei⁴:** spirits; the second, **ch'an:** to flatter or appeal. I.e., to appeal to the spirits.

consuetudines: (L) customary rights; liberties.

749: **usu terrae:** (L) by custom of the land.

Unitas Charitatis: (L) Unity of Love.

consuetudo diversa: (L) customary right, diverse [in operation].

Khati: see glossary to XCIII (623).

"ordine": (I) order.

33 years after the Bard's death...: Charles I was beheaded.

"en gatje": (Pr) in pawn—see glossary to LXXXV (548).

Charles of the Suevi: Charles of the Swabians (839-888), Emperor from 881 to 887. After seeing a vision of hell, purgatory and paradise, he retired to a monastery giving up all his worldly possessions. Charles described the beginning of his vision in this way, "Suddenly I was seized by a spirit, and that one who took control of me was most shiny, and he held in his hand a solid ball emitting the brightest ray of light, just as comets do when they appear, and he began to unwind it and said to me: 'Take a thread of this brilliant light, and tie and knot it firmly around the thumb of your right hand, because you will be led by this through the labyrinthine punishments of hell.'" When the sinners tried to drag him down into their pits, the spirit guide "threw a thread of light upon my shoulders...and drew me along strongly behind him, so that we thus ascended the highest fiery mountains." (*Patrologia Latina,* Vol. 174, columns 1287-88; James Wilhelm's translation, *The Later Cantos,* page 165.)

Athelstan...Egbert: Pound traces here, and on page 751, the beginnings of English liberties taking shape at the time of the Anglo-Saxon kings.

750: **οὐ θέλει....κόσμον:** see glossary to CII (730).

By sheer grammar: Essentia: Pound is playing on the fact that **Essentia:** the highest essence, which Anselm uses, is feminine in gender.

Immaculata/Immaculabile: (L) immaculate,/unstainable.

Ambrose:/"First treason...flock": see quotations from *De Moribus Brachmanorum* (C, 715).

751: **πανουργία:** *panourgia,* villainy.

Proslogion: St. Anselm's second philosophical work (1077-78).

---

¹See Chapter 12 for a detailed commentary on CV.

CVI

752:   **Demeter:** goddess of the corn and mother of "Dis' bride," Persephone. **Dis:** King of the Dead. **Phlegethon:** the fiery river in Hades. **The strength of men ... the Kuan:** This line is quoted from *The Kuan Tzu*, Economic Dialogues of Ancient China, page 38. The "NINE decrees" are the "Basic Methods of Government" (*The Kuan Tzu*, pages 57–59).

 Kuan: (the philosopher, Kuan—this also refers to the book attributed to him).

 Tzu:

Kuan Chung: Prime Minister of the State of Chi (684-645 B.C.) ὁ θεός: *ho theos*, the gods, or God.
Apeliota: The East Wind.

753:   **nueva lumbre:** (Pr) new reflections (Arnaut Daniel).

Kuan: The ideogram is kuan[1]: a gate, or pass. It is used in an onomatopoeic compound in the famous first line of the first of the *Odes*, where it mimes the sound of a 'fish-hawk'. Pound turned this into " 'Hid! Hid!' the fish-hawk saith" (*Confucian Odes*, page 2); "All gates are holy" (XCIV, 634). The first ode is a nuptial hymn. (J.C.)

Ad posteros urbem donat: (L) He gave a city to posterity—"a city remaineth" (CIX, 772).
XREIA: (Gk) need.
near Enna, at Nyssa: the meadow where Dis "caught up" Persephone (XXI, 100).

754:   **Athene Pronoia:** (Gk) Athene of Providence.
Help me to neede .... Whuder ich maei lidhan: see glossary to XCI (612).
Xoroi: (Gk) choral dance.

755:   **That great acorn of light bulging outward:** "a dense emblem of Pound's *paradiso*. It is akin to the 'great ball of crystal' (CXVI, 795) ... It is also the visionary eye, Emerson's 'transparent eyeball' casting its light outward—'God's eye art'ou, do not surrender perception' (CXIII, 790). There is still another, more Gourmontian meaning here, though, for the acorn (Latin *glans*) is a traditional sexual symbol and thus rejoins the 'spermatozoic' light ('bulging outward') of Pound's 'Postscript' to the *Physique de l'amour* ... The acorn is finally and most literally the seed of the oak; like thought itself .... the repository of potential patterns of energy waiting to be released ..." (Richard Sieburth, *Instigations, Ezra Pound and Remy de Gourmont*, pages 153–54.)

Selena Arsinoe ... into heaven: Arsinoe II, Queen of Egypt, married Ptolemy II (her brother). She was the mother-in-law of Berenice (see glossary to XCVII, 675). Arsinoe II was worshipped as a manifestation of Aphrodite. Her apotheosis is Hellenistic.

Zephyrium: a promontory in lower Egypt, with a temple of Arsinoe-Aphrodite (Kupris) after which the goddess was called Zephyrites.

EUPLOIA: (Gk) of good sailing—a name of Aphrodite.
At Miwo...renewed: see glossary to LXXX, 500 (*Hagoromo*).
HREZEIN: (Gk) do (in a religious sense).

CVII

756: **The azalea...sleep:** echoes "And the rose grown while I slept" (XXXIII, 108) and the sleeping wood of XCIII (629). Perhaps it is partly an image of the slow evolution of liberties which Pound traces, in CVII, from Greece, via the Sicily of Frederick II, to England.
Selinunt': city on the west coast of Sicily. **Akragas:** city in Sicily founded by the Greeks *c.* 580.
Coke. Inst. 2...yeare: In his *Proeme* to the 2nd part of his *Institutes of the Laws of England* Sir Edward Coke says that Edward I decreed by Act of Parliament that great Charters (*Magna Carta, Carta de Foresta* etc.) were thus to be read publicly—a parallel with *The Sacred Edict*.
20. H. 3: In the 20th year of his reign, Henry III confirmed both *Magna Carta* and *Carta de Foresta*.
that is certainty...repose: Coke closes his *Proeme*, "our expositions or commentaries upon Magna Carta...are the resolution of judges in courts of justice...and shall produce certainty, the mother and nurse of repose..."
Milite: Authore Edwardo Coke, Milite, J.C. (title page of the *Institutes*).
"that light...Sigier": "essa e la luce etterna di Sigieri" (Dante, *Paradiso*, X, 136). Siger de Brabant was a 13th century French philosopher who was condemned in 1270 for Aristotelean teaching. Dante places him with the great theologians in the heaven of the sun ("nel Sole"). Richard of St. Victor and St. Anselm are also there.
Eleanor: Queen of Henry III, daughter of Count Berengar of Provence.
quod custod...debent: (L) such custody must not be sold. Someone who holds land on trust must return it to its rightful heirs (Magna Charta, cap. V).
non per color...parvente: showing not by colour but by light (*Paradiso*, X, 42).
Custumier: Norman Law Book, composed, as Pound notes in the margin, in the 14th year of Henry III.
de la foresta: Articles concerning forests were added to *Magna Carta* in Henry II's reign which then came to be called "The Forest Charter."
757: **ancient eit franchies:** (OF) that it have its ancient liberties. **ne injuste vexes:** not unjustly harass. **progressus ostendunt:** progress reveals. Coke cites an old Latin rule of law that "the progress of things reveals much that could not have been foreseen at the beginning."
periplum, assise...: Judges had to travel throughout England to the local assize courts, bringing justice to the people, like Kung.
the root is that charter: Coke said in Parliament (1621), "Magna Charta is called...The Charter of Liberty because it maketh freemen. When

the King says he cannot allow our liberties of right, this strikes at the root. We serve here for thousands and ten thousands." (C.D. Bowen, *The Lion and the Throne*, page 391.) For the ideogram, which means 'root', see glossary to LXCIV (640).

"It appeareth ... (his cart): Glanvil was a chief justicer of Henry II who wrote that fines should not be so severe as to take away a man's livelihood.

hominum de vicineto ... proborum: (L) by the oath of honest men of the area. **laicum tenementum:** lay tenement.

H.2 E.1: Henry II and Edward I were both dedicated to justice, unlike James I, "that slobbering bugger," who believed that the concept of the Divine Right of Kings, and the royal prerogative, put the king above the Common Law. He imprisoned Coke in the Tower for his opposition to these ideas.

Puer Apulius ... ver l'estate: Frederick II (1194-1250), *stupor mundi*, the wonder of the world. He is here put in conjunction again (as in XCVII, 681) with Alcamo, the Sicilian poet, who wrote *Aulentissima Rosa Fresca* in which are the words **ver:** singing ... **l'estate:** the summer. It was at the court of Frederick II that, as Dante says, Italian poetry began. Frederick is also important in the Coke cantos for his creation of the law code which he gave to Sicily in 1231. This has been described as "the fullest and most adequate body of legislation promulgated by any Western ruler since Charlemagne." He thus also rhymes with Justinian in *Thrones*. Frederick "gathered about him/All the savants and artists" (XIII, 59). Scholars and poets, Jewish, Mohammedan and Christian were welcome at his court. He himself knew six languages, and was learned in mathematics, natural history, philosophy, medicine and architecture.

758: **Queen of Akragas:** Athene, goddess of Justice and Wisdom. There was a temple dedicated to her in Akragas, which is referred to in the following line.

Segesta: another city in Sicily, where there was a temple of Artemis.

nec alii boscum: (L) nor [we nor] other [shall take his] wood. Coke states that no officer of the king can take anyone's possessions without his consent.

in Fleta, maeremium/qui utlegatus est: (L) in Fleta, mourning,/who has no legal commission. The *Fleta*, a 13th century treatise on the Common Law, was reputed to have been written in the Fleet Prison.

wave pattern at Excideuil: see glossary to XXIX (145) under Arnaut.

Atque in re ... iura belli: (L) and for the public good the laws of war are to be observed.

butlerage: Import duties used to be paid to the king's butler—hence the term.

759: **paid only ... ad mesure:** These lines concern taxes on trade etc. The duty "on currants" was judged to be against the Common Law. "The common law hath so admeasured (*ad mesure*) the prerogatives of the king, that they should not take away, nor prejudice the inheritance of any" (*Institutes*, II, Cap. 30, page 62).

ex satrapia: (L) from all satrap counties.

sil ne fuit dizein: (OF) if he were not of a group of ten.

quod trithinga teneatur integra: (L) that the trithing be entirely kept— the trithing, now 'riding', was a division between a shire and a hundred.

decemvirale ... religiosis et ...: (L) group of ten ... except to religious institutions and.....

vide Bracton: Bracton, d. 1268, wrote *De Legibus et consuetudinibus Angliae* (on the laws and customs of England), which was one of the main sources of Coke's *Institutes*.

sub colore donationis: (L) under colour of a gift (sale of land not to be made thus).

his testibus: (L) these being witnesses.

That is our PIVOT: the *Magna Carta*. The chief clauses of the Magna Carta were: (i) Freedom of election to the Church—this is what Anselm and Becket had fought for. (ii) Definition of feudal dues. (iii) Grants to King, other than customary feudal dues, only to be levied with consent of the Barons in Council. (iv) Justice to be administered to all. No imprisonment without trial. (v) Freedom of trade for merchants (including "merchant strangers" [759]). (vi) Reforms of the forest laws.

Statute of Merton: (1236) concerned widows' dowers; enclosures of common land, usury etc. The Parliament met at the monastery of the "canons regular" at Merton.

760: **de la plus beale:** (OF) of the most beautiful.

Bede's time: The Venerable Bede, *c.* 673-735.

One thousand ... St. Martin: in 1267, the 8th day after the feast of St. Martin, the *Statutem de Marlebridge* was adopted, which reaffirmed the principles of *Magna Carta*. Peace was restored to the people, "as well high as low."

 Sapiens incipit a fine: (L) A wise man begins at the end. The ideograms are **chung**^{1}: end; **shih**^{3}: beginning—as Kung said, "Thing have ends and beginnings" (LXXVII, 465).

Box hedge ... the short tails: The English gardens that Coke knew from childhood are here juxtaposed with the rising larks Pound saw at Allègre, Haute Loire (LXXX, 501 etc.).

Was new coin 1560: Elizabeth called in all debased coinage, two years after she became queen, and issued a completely new and sound currency—"ad valorem reducta" brought back to true value (CVIII, 768).

761: **de heretico comburendo:** (L) of burning heretics. Bartholomew Legate and Edward Wrightman were burnt in 1612. Coke opposed "the monstrous writ" that the Bishops Court issued ordering this. "A religion is damned, it confesses its own ultimate impotence, the day it burns its first heretic" (*Selected Prose*, page 52).

In a white sheet ... gave sentence: Coke's daughter was fined 500 marks for adultery, and ordered to do public penance in a white sheet.

3 months to habeas: Parliament opposed Charles I for 3 months until he capitulated and granted *habeas corpus*, preventing imprisonment without trial.

B.18: under the British government's 18 B regulations in the Second World War, *habeas corpus* was suspended to allow the imprisonment of those who opposed the war.

μὴ ὄν: *me on*, non being (Marlowe's *Dr. Faustus*, I, v, ii). Pound connects this with Hamlet's, "To be or not to be."

762: **color prediletto:** (I) beloved colour. Echoes XXIV (110).

σῆραγξ: *seragx*, sea cave; cave hollowed out by water.

Σειρήν: *Seiren*, Siren.

hippocampi: sea-horses; **θελκτήριη:** *thelkterie*, mind-bending, spell; enchantment.

Norfolk tumbler: a present from Coke to Robert Cecil who built Hatfield House.

Gondemar: the ambassador of Spain. An apprentice described him as "the devil in a dung cart" when he drove through the London streets.

And Raleigh's head...platter: James I was determined that Raleigh should be executed, partly because of his opposition to the proposed marriage between the Spanish Infanta and Charles.

"That the dead...December eleventh: Coke replied to those who would flatter James by servile petitions against the Spanish alliance, that they should go to *Magna Carta*, the laws of their ancestors, "Best to ask counsel of the dead! For they will not flatter nor fawn to advance themselves, nor bribe nor dissemble" (C.D. Bowen, *The Lion and the Throne*, page 390).

So that Dante's view is quite natural: Dante's heaven of the Sun.

763: **Alan Upward...Sitalkas:** see glossary to LXXXIV (437).

caelator: (L) carver, engraver.

CVIII

764: **COMMINUIT:** (L) it splits, splinters. Compare, "pine seed splitting cliff's edge" (LXXXVII, 572). Another image of the evolution of liberties, like the "azalea" in CVII.

nurse of industry: Edward III's statute says that an Englishman's right to property is this.

BRUM: possibly Latin, **bruma:** winter, the winter solstice, and/or French, **brume:** mist. Also, perhaps an allusion to **Brumaire:** French revolutionary month, October 22-November 20. Broomplants (?).

"alla": see glossary to LXXVIII (478).

pen yeh: see glossary to XCVIII (686).

From the Charter...Petition: The Petition of Right (1628) which Charles I reluctantly accepted (**DROIT FAIT:** should be done) made new the principles of the *Magna Carta*. The chief points were (i) that taxation by Act of Parliament only is legal (ii) that arbitrary imprisonment is illegal.

Statutem Tallagio: an important statute of Edward I which stated that no tax should be levied without the consent of the people.

"all monopolies": Coke wrote, "...all monopolies are against this great charter, because they are against the liberty and freedome of the subject, and against the law of the land" (*Second Institute*, Cap. 29, page 47).

"nor against his will into Ireland": "No man exiled" (*Ibidem*.)

Owse, Wherfe...Tine: concerns an act for the prevention of unseasonable salmon fishing in these rivers.

765: **Post Festum...:** (L) After the feast of St. Hilary. This, and the following 17 lines, concern Edward I's statute forbidding usury, and his expulsion of the Jews at this time. In the latter connection, it should be stressed, as Del Mar makes clear (*Usury and the Jews*), that the Jews had been largely pushed into the role of usurers by the Christian rulers, because they were excluded from other occupations.

mults des mals....prochainement: (OF) many evils and disinheritings [because of usury] ran in the next reign of St. Edward and in the reign of Edward III's father Henry III before him.

ne quis injuriam....conductum: (L) no one suffer injury/safe conduct. (An act forbidding the persecution of Jews on their way out of England.)

Holl...Dunstable: Three ancient historical sources cited by Coke.

Angliae exeuntibus: (L) they left England.

No officer of our...cujus bona: concerns the Statutem Tallagio mentioned on the preceding page. Property must not be taken by the agents of the king without the owner's consent.

Et Forestae: introduces the Charter of Confirmation which re-affirmed the main liberties previously guaranteed by the *Magna Carta*. "*De Libertatibus et Forestae*": concerning Liberties and Forests. Edward I had been trying to tax without authorization and the barons forced him to accept this *Confirmatio Chartarum* on 5 November 1297.

765-6: **Devant eux...a guier:** (OF) Before them in judgement/that is to say/ and in amendment/have to guide.

766: **this nient tenus:** (OF) held for nothing.

mises ne prises: (OF) two kinds of tax no longer authorized, unless "by the common assent." The figures in the margin give the date of Edward's succession to the throne, plus 25 years, to the signing of *Confirmatio Chartarum* in 1297.

Cap. VI...Disraeli: Chapter VI explains that "for no business from henceforth we shall take such manner of aids taxes...but by the common assent..." Coke commented, "every aide and task have two special properties, the one in the creation viz. that it be given by the common consent of the whole realm in parliament; the other in execution, viz. that it be given and imployed for the common benefit of the whole realme, and not for private or other respects." (Disraeli arranged the Suez Canal purchase behind Parliament's back.)

de la maletot...trecenti pellibus: (OF & L) of the fiscal tax/a charge of forty shillings on each sack of wool/our letters patent/Witness Edward our son at London the tenth day of October/half a mark for three hundred pelts. (Edward I had been taxing wool without Parliament's consent to finance his wars. It was in response to this that the Confirmation Charter was enacted.)

aliorum liberorum... in pleno parliamento: (L) [consent] of other freemen/no tax/in full parliament.

et vacua nulla: (L) null and void.

nihil capiatur: (L) nothing shall be taken [like the wool tax].

767:   **Bohun of Hereford; John de Ferraris:** Barons who courageously stood against the king, forcing him to accept the Confirmation Charter.

Articul:...CESTASCAVOUR: (OF) Clause [of Charter]: to his people/THAT'S TO SAY. I.e., the liberties of these charters extend to everyone. A subject rhyme with the *Sheng Yu* (*Sacred Edict*) being taken "down to the people" (XCVIII, 690). The *Edict* was read monthly to the people.

and Charles kept... 1634-'41: Charles I attempted to levy ship money in contravention of the terms of the Charter. Parliament ordered the publication of *The Second Institute,* Coke's commentary on the *Magna Carta,* in 1641.

Felton's knife...: He assassinated Buckingham (1628) who represented arbitrary power unchecked by Parliament.

articuli super Chartas: (L) clauses supplementary to the charters.

Soient esleus... autre avisés: (OF) will be administered by three just/or other knowledgeable [men]. (These aspects of the Charter concern the administration of local justice.)

"Vierge": (OF) verge; area of jurisdiction.

Hastings...Sandwich: the Cinque Ports, vital to the defence of the realm, where the king had special jurisdiction.

 The ideograms are: **chi²:** the royal domains, set apart in ancient times for the Emperor; **pi⁴:** silk, wealth, coin.

768:   **Elfynge/Cler/Domus/Com:** H. Elfynge, the clerk of the House of Commons. He wrote (12 May 1641) that Coke's commentaries on *Magna Carta* should be published.

Be marked with a leopard's head: no silver vessel to leave worker's hand unless so marked, "auxy soit signe teste de leopard" which line recurs (CIX, 774), where it again stresses the king's prerogative over coinage and precious metals, insuring that they are not debased. "No, they cannot touch me for coining. I am the king himself." (*Lear,* Act IV, scene v.)

and of 12 graines... mediae spicae: the weight of a denar (coin) must be 12 grains of wheat, taken from the middle of the stalk.

magnalia coronae: (L) the great things of the crown. I.e, the prerogative over coinage which Elizabeth stood for. "Sovereignty inheres in the power to issue money. The sovereign who does not possess this power is a mere rex sacrificulus, non regnans." (*Selected Prose*, page 322; *352*.)

ELIZABETH/ANGLIAE AMOR/...reducta: (L) love of, and for, the English/[coinage] brought back to true value (part of the inscription on Elizabeth's tomb). In 1560, she called in the old, debased coinage, and issued a new one. "Characters by their coinage" (LXXXVI, 565).

To take wood...fundendam: Coke states that the king has had the right, "time out of memory," to use wood for "burning and melting" of gold and silver for coinage.

769: **& souls of the dead defrauded:** This and the next 15 lines concern the *Statutem de Asportatis Religiosorum* (the exporting of wealth by the clergy). Coke shows how both the "souls of the dead" and the poor are "defrauded" by money being sent out of the kingdom. As a result, the seal of the Abbot was put in the custody of four men, **dignioribus:** more worthy. A cardinal called **Paragots** had received 10,000 marks a year. **Alienigae superiores:** foreign superiors had similarly benefited, and in consequence alms to the poor had been cut.

That grosbois...tithe shall be paid: the hard woods, oak, ash, elm etc. should not be tithed (taxed) because they take years to develop, "but of acorns tithe shall be paid"....."because they renew yeerly," like lambs.

dies solaris...ut pena ad paucos...perveniat: (L) days of the sun/[punishment] to the few will serve as warning to the many. (These phrases, and lines over the page, concern the selling of horses, that the people should not be deceived—the horse must be seen in the sunlight, in an "overt" place.)

caveat emptor: (L) the buyer is warned.

770: **Coke, Iong Ching:** CVIII has traced the way Coke restored the main Statutes of English history, just as Iong Ching made new the ancient principles of Confucius in eighteenth century China. There are many parallels between this canto and *The Sacred Edict* (XCVIII-XCIX).

reparando: (L) repairing.

For every new cottage 4 acres: A statute of Elizabeth against over-crowding.

CIX

771: **Pro Veritate...curtilagia teneant:** (L) For Truth.../[for those who] live in cottages. (This continues Elizabeth's statute which closed the preceding canto.)

EPARXON: The detail of Elizabeth's legislation is here rhymed with that of the Eparch's Edict (XCVI).

Donaison, denizen: (OF) "merchant stranger" (CVII, 759).

No wight could pinch...: Coke quotes Chaucer who says this about the Man of Law (*General Prologue*).

vocabula artis: (L) names of art.

nemo omnia novit: (L) no man renews all things.

772: **le Concord del fine:** (OF) a fine which brings concord, because it cannot omit **ascun chose** (anything). Hence the recurrence of συμβαίναι: *sumbainai,* coheres—see glossary to LXXXVII (571).

solonques le purpot...terre demeure...liver dit: (OF) so long as the purpose holds/CHARTER said to be certain./in which the earth dwells/ (the book says).

"de ses vicines": of the neighbourhood.

tempora non regum: (L) times not of kings.

arundinetum: (L) a thicket, or jungle of reeds.

Si nomen nescis...artifex nascitur: If names are not known, knowledge of things perishes/no man is born an artist.

Tuan: Foundations (see glossary to LXXXV, 545).

et consuetudino: (L) and custom—customary right (in law).

773: **"In grateful resentment...Hartford:** Captain Joseph Wadsworth, an ancestor of Pound's, in the early years of the American struggle for independence, stole the Connecticut State Charter and hid it in an oak. For this he was publicly rewarded in 1715.

afraid he will balk...hospitals: Edward VIII. Pound considered that he had opposed a second European war, "the three years' peace we owe Windsor/'36-'39" (XCV, 645). He is partly in *Thrones* at this point because he was the last English king to have had some influence on events.

774: **auxy soit...leopard:** see glossary to CVIII (768).

form is cut...bowl: see Dante, *Paradiso,* XX, 22-3.

Selloi: see glossary to LXXXVII (573).

INO...Kadmeia: daughter of Cadmus (Leucothoe).

Herbert and Remusat: see glossary to C (720).

καλλϊαστρά´γαλος: *kalliastragalos,* with beautiful ankles.

San Domenica...Cosmedin: Early Christian churches in Rome.

You in the dinghy....there: "O voi che siete in piccioletta barca" (Dante, *Paradiso,* II, 1)—echoes VII (26).

Drafts & Fragments of
Cantos CX–CXVII

Drafts & Fragments

"And that the universe is alive" (XCIV, 637). In these final fragments, Pound returns to the springs of his inspiration. His sense of numinous nature, "of wood alive, of stone alive," which informed his poetry from the beginning, is expressed with a new simplicity. It is a similar quality which makes the world of *The Tempest* so profoundly poetic. As Pound wrote in 1916, "... this ... sort of mind is close on the vital universe, and the strength of the Greek beauty rests in this, that it is ever at the interpretation of this vital universe, by its signs of gods and godly attendants and oreads" (*The Spirit of Romance*, page 93). "The Gods have not returned. 'They have never left us.'/They have not returned./Cloud's processional and the air moves with their living" (CXIII, 787).

In *Drafts & Fragments,* Pound is, to quote Keats, "straining at particles of light in the midst of a great darkness": "But the record/the palimpsest—/a little light/in great darkness—" (CXVI, 795). The light is "always there" even as it is dependent on darkness for its existence. There is a deep sense of affirmation and tragedy behind the words—another link with *The Tempest.* And also of stillness: "But these had thrones,/and in my mind were still, uncontending—/not to possession, in hypostasis/Some hall of mirrors" (CXIV, 793).

Drafts & Fragments make us realise that Pound had probably oversimplified the world in some earlier parts of the poem. With this late realisation of errors, sadness and beauty are here inextricably interwoven. These are fragments of beauty that because of their fragmentation are permeated by pain. The greatest happiness we know comes in moments which are gone before we can grasp what it is we have experienced. It is instants of this kind that these cantos define.

Always a moral poet, Pound here expresses his scale of values with the simplicity of wisdom: "Fear, father of cruelty,/are we to write a genealogy of the demons?" (CXIV, 791). As he said in the interview for *The Paris Review* of 1960 (Item Q, p. xxi): "I must find a verbal formula to combat the rise of brutality—the principle of order versus the split atom." Thus the theme of these fragments is benevolence, "If love be not in the house there is nothing"

156

(CXVI, 796), and closely bound up with this are images of the splendor, delicacy, and mystery of the universe, presented with a fresh reverence and humility—the rage and didacticism have been purged away.

In 1963, three years after early drafts of these cantos had been written, Pound said in an interview in the Italian magazine *Epoca*, "I cannot get to the core of my thoughts any more with words." *Drafts & Fragments* is poetry on the brink of silence. It is deep with a clear depth that is the opposite of obscurity.

It is one of the tasks of poetry to affirm the existence of paradise, even though it can probably only exist in "the wilds of a man's mind." "For nothing can be sole or whole/That has not been rent." As it is impossible to conceive of perfection without its opposite, it is fitting that the closing passages of Pound's Paradise should be composed of fragments. "To make cosmos—/To achieve the possible—" (CXVI, 795).

"Two mice and a moth my guides—" (802). Except perhaps at Pisa, the vision at the heart of the *Cantos* has never been more movingly, nor more vulnerably, expressed: "I have brought the great ball of crystal:/who can lift it?/Can you enter the great acorn of light?" (CXVI, 795).

Cantos CX-CXVII are a cluster of things felt which spark off new relationships with themselves and with the body of the work on each rereading. They make us see, in flashes, all parts of the poem draw to a deeper unity than had once seemed possible. "Felicem cui datum est dispersiones cordis in unum colligere."[1]

---

[1] "Happy who can gather the heart's fragmentations into unity." (Richard of St. Victor, translated by Pound, *Selected Prose*, page 73; *71*.)

CX

777:    **Thy quiet house:** the Byzantine basilica of Torcello in the lagoon of Venice, where there is a mosaic Madonna "over the portal" (CXVI, 795). **The crozier's curve ... wall:** "the toppling crumble of a wave crest."[1] The image echoes "the wave pattern cut in the stone" that Pound saw in Excideuil (XXIX, 145).

Verkehr: (G) human intercourse; traffic.

Hast'ou seen ... sea-wall: echoes Ben Jonson's *Her Triumph* and "Hast'ou seen the rose in the steel dust" (LXXIV, 449).

Toba Sojo: (1052-1140) Japanese painter.

che paion' si al vent': (I) who appear so on the wind. Adapted from Dante, "e paion sì al vento esser leggieri" (*Inferno*, V, 75), where he asks to speak to the lovers, Paolo and Francesca, "who seem so light on the wind." Pound evokes them here, to introduce a tragic Na-khi tribal love story.

[2]**Har-**[2]**la-**[1]**llü** [3]**k'ö:** (Na-khi) wind sway perform. A ceremony in which the demons of suicide are invited, propitiated and exorcised. "The Na-khi believe that it is imperative for someone to be present at the death of a person, for if anyone dies unattended, the soul becomes a

157

roving spirit; such souls become the constant companions of the wind and the wind demons.... It is impossible for such to be escorted to the realm of their ancestors, and they are destined to remain forever restless." (Joseph Rock, *The Romance of* $^2K'a$-$^2mä$-^1gyu-^{3} mi-$^2gkyi.)^2$ The parallel with Paolo and Francesca is clear and moving, as they were condemned to be forever borne on the winds.

The nine fates ... the oak's root: The nine fates stand for a boy; the seven for a girl in Na-khi folk-lore. The story behind these lines is as follows: "Rather than be wife to a man she does not care for, ^{2}Ka-^{2}mä-^{1}gyu-^{3}mi-^{2}gkyi contemplates suicide: but her shepherd lover ... cannot be persuaded to join her. She goes into high alpine territory to try various methods...: by hanging; she twisted a rope ... to the tree ... the black crown of the tree waved, [her] heart was faint, the black tree was born dumb ... the tree did not invite her ... hence she did not commit suicide and again returned.... By drowning; the surface of the water was a deep blue, her eyes were also a deep blue, my heart is faint (she said), she did not wish to die ... and again returned. Unsuccessful, she makes her way ... down to the alpine meadow to await her lover, but he doesn't turn up. She sends him messages via a raven:... The white stag drinks by the salt spring, [the taste] remains in its mouth, hankers for it.... Reviled by her parents-in-law, and convinced by the demons of suicide ... she hangs herself from an oak (*Quercus*) on Mt. Sumeru (778).... Searching in the mountains for an old black cow gone astray, her lover ... comes upon her body ... hanging ... Weeping, he asks, 'If I give her turquoise and coral eyes, will you again be able to see? If I attach the roots of the pine and the oak, will you again be able to walk?'.... Her answer: 'Even if you give me turquoise and coral eyes, I will not be able to see, there is no such precedent: if you add the roots of the pine and oak, I will not again be able to walk.' Her spirit then tells him of the messages she has sent him. He replies...: he couldn't join her in the autumn [the gentian or frost-flower is symbolic of autumn] because the sheep come down from the mountain.... He [eventually] hangs himself from the canebrake (arundinaria)." I've extracted this from Jamila Ismail's "News of the Universe" (*Agenda*), where she quotes from Joseph Rock's translation.

778:   **yüeh$^{4-5}$ ming^2 ... p'eng^2:** The brightness of the moon ... there are no former friends.[3] As no source has been found, perhaps this is an original Chinese poem by Pound.

heaven   earth ... juniper: "... the juniper ... is the most sacred of Na-khi flora ... worshipped in the ^{2}Mùan ^{1}bpö ceremony together with Heaven and Earth.... it is the cosmic tree, the axis, stabilizer, and nourisher of the Universe, supporter of and vital link between Heaven and Earth ... the Na-khi regard the tree somewhat as the central nervous system of the cosmos: hence one must 'lean 'gainst the tree of heaven,/and know Ygdrasail' (LXXXV, 545)." (Jamila Ismail, "News of the Universe".)

artemisia: "Artemisia is callyd moder of herbes and was somtyme

158

halowed ... to the goddesse that hyght Arthemis" (John Trevisa, 1398). The herb is used medicinally in China as a demon-repellent, and is an important element in the Na-khi purification rites, which recur in CXII.

Kuanon: see glossary to LXXIV (428).

Cozzaglio, Dino Martinazzi ... (Gardesana): engineers who built a road (the *Gardesana*) which begins on the western shore of Lake Garda—much of it consists of tunnels blasted through rock.

779: **Savoia, Novara at Veneto:** refers to a cavalry attack by the Italians against the Russians in Ibukerki (in the Ukraine) in 1942.

Un caso .... memoria: (P) a sad case, and worthy of memory (Camoes, *Os Lusiades*, III, 118, on Ignez da Castro)—see III (12) and XXX (147-48).

Uncle G.: see glossary to LXXIV (433).

Bettoni: commanded the cavalry attack at Ibukerki.

Cozzaglio ... tracciolino: (I) Cozzaglio, the road builder.

Oleari: Italian theatre of operations during World War I.

Felix nupsit: (L) he married happily.

Khaty: see glossary to XCIII (623).

Euridice: wife of the pre-Homeric legendary poet, Orpheus. She was a dryad. When running away from Aristaeus, she was bitten by a snake and died. Orpheus visits Hades to try to persuade Dis and Persephone to allow her to return to the world. Persephone relents, but makes the condition that he must not look back on her as they journey from the underworld. Just as they were "within/A kenning of the upper earth, When Orphye did begin/To dowt him lest she followed not .... he his eyes did backward move./Immediately shee slipped backe. He retching out his hands/Desyrous to bee caught and for to ketch her grasping stands./But nothing save the slippry aire (unhappy man) he caught." (Ovid, *Metamorphoses*, X, translated by Arthur Golding.)

Laurel bark ... unrooted?: Daphne, fleeing Apollo, turned into a laurel tree.

Endymion: a shepherd of Latmos who was loved by Selene, the moon.

780: **KALLIASTRAGALOS:** with beautiful ankles.

hsin[1]: renew (see glossary to LII, 265).

Awoi: a court lady, who was possessed by the demon of jealousy—see the Noh play *Awoi No Uye* where the demon is exorcised (*Translations*, pages 323–331).

La Tour, San Carlo ... Voisin: restaurants.

Galla's rest: The tomb of Galla Placidia—see glossary to XXI (98).

Quos ego Persephonae: (L) which I to Persephone (Propertius, VI, 26). See *Homage to Sextus Propertius*, "There will be three books at my obsequies/Which I take, my not unworthy gift, to Persephone" (*Collected Shorter Poems*, page 236; *Personae*, page 219).

Chih[3]: see glossary to LXXXV (543).

781: **and the sun .... new with the day:** Heracleitos said, "The sun is new every day" (*Fragment 32*, Bywater's edition).

Mr. Rock still hopes ...: Joseph F. Rock (1884-1962), botanist and ethnologist. Born Vienna, became U.S. citizen 1913. He first went to Li-chiang to study the Na-khi in 1922. His work was interrupted by the war, "his fragments sunk twenty years."

Lux enim—: Light itself (from Grosseteste)—echoes LXXXIII (528).

The marble form in the pine wood: "Brancusi's bird in the hollow of pine trunks" (Notes for CXVII et seq., 801).

From the roots of sequoias: echoes "Only sequoias are slow enough" (LXXXVII, 572).

ching⁴: reverence. See glossary to LXXXV (555).

Komachi: In the Noh play, *Kayoi Komachi*, the spirits of Komachi and her lover are kept apart, until they are brought together by the piety of a wandering priest (*Translations*, pages 226–31).

---

¹Donald Davie, "Cypress Versus Rock-Slide," *Agenda*, Vol. VIII, Nos. 2-3.
²Bulletin d'Etudes Françaises d'Extrême Orient, Vol. XXXIX, No. 5 (1940).
³See Hugh Kenner, "A Note on CX" (*Paideuma*, 8, 1).

Notes for CXI

782: **Hui:** see glossary to CIII (732).
Wadsworth: see glossary to CIX (773).
Roche-Guyon: Louis Alexandre, Duc de (1743-92). He tried to defend the Monarchy.
Austerlitz: Napoleon's victory of 1805 might have resulted in the unification of Italy.
Wu Hsieh (heart's field) Szu: This is a slightly rearranged version of Confucius' famous summation of the *Odes* (*Analects*, II, ii): "The anthology of 300 poems can be gathered into the one sentence: Have no twisty thoughts" (*Confucius*, page 197). 'Heart's field' is an ostensible analysis of the character translated 'thought' and should, in fact, be associated with the syllable 'Szu.' Pound placed the characters for this saying, in the correct order, as a postscript to his version of the *Odes*. (J.C.)

783: **Quemoy:** island near the southeast coast of China occupied by Chiang Kai-Shek's troops.
Geryon: see glossary to XLVI (235).
Veritas, by anthesis: Truth by full bloom. "Ripeness is all" (*Lear*, V, iii).
come burchiello in su la riva: (I) like a raft above the bank (adapted from *Inferno*, XVII, 19, where Geryon is described).
ex profundis: (L) from the deep.
anima into aura: spirit into gold light—*aura* can mean the emanation of the soul.
Edictum prologo: (L) preface by Rothar, 17th king of the Lombards (636-52), to his Code of Laws, which sought protection for the poor— echoes XCVI (652).

CXII

784: **huo³-hu²:** (C) sorrel horse.
Amṛta: (Sanskrit) the nectar of immortality. It is also "beauty, the characteristic by which divine forms are known ... purity of self, i.e., naturalness, which is to say reality. *Amrta* is an image as inclusive as the Greek idea of *Kosmos*." (Jamila Ismail, "News of the Universe.")
²La²mun ³mi: goddesses.
²Ndaw ⁱbpö: Sacrifice to Earth.
²Mùan ¹bpö: Sacrifice to Heaven (see glossary to CIV, 730)—these ceremonies are performed to produce the state called Amrta.
Li Chiang: the old capital of the Na-khi.
Hsiang Shan: (C) Elephant Mountain.
Lung Wang: (C) the dragon king.

 The characters correspond to "Jade stream."

785: **Artemisia:** see glossary to CX (778). "Nine bundles of artemisia purified ²Ndu (the Na-khi equivalent of the Chinese *Yang* principle) and thus the plant is especially important in ²Mùan ¹bpö rites" (J. Ismail, *op. cit.*).
Arundinaria: canebrake bamboo which is used for making winnowing sieves. The winnowing tray is also an emblem of Dionysus (see Frazer, *The Golden Bough*, "Spirits of the Corn and the Wild," Vol. I, page 5).

CXIII

786: **Θρῆνος:** *Threnos*, lament, dirge.
Agassiz: see glossary to XCIII (625).
Linnaeus: Karl von Linné (1707-1778), Swedish naturalist and botanist. His system of plant classification is used to this day.
Paré (Ambroise): see glossary to CIV (741).
Twedell: Dr. Francis (1863-19??), author of medical works on fighting tuberculosis. **Donnelly:** Dr. Leo G. (*d.* 1958), a friend of Pound's who served as an orthopaedic surgeon in France in World War I. He later founded the Social Credit Party in Detroit.
Pumpelly: Raphael (1837-1923), American geologist, who crossed the Gobi desert.
I'd eat his liver, ... done it: In *Across America and Asia*, Pumpelly writes about an acquaintance called Parkyn "who had spent two years in the wild life of the first rush to the gold fields of Australia.... Parkyn stayed one night at a wayside house in the 'bush'. He was eating when a man entered and handed the cook something wrapped in paper, telling him to cook it. Then he sat down opposite Parkyn. When the

man had emptied his dish, he leaned back and said: "There! I told the damned.... I'd eat his damned liver, and I've done it!" Only Pound could have put this story into a *Paradiso!*

787: **Hesperides:** In Greek mythology, the Daughters of Evening. They live far in the West, near the Atlas mountains, guarding a tree that produces golden apples.

Sir Ian: see glossary to CIV (740).

788: **Kalenda Maja:** "The feast of Venus Genetrix, which survived as May Day" (*Spirit of Romance*, page 18). "It is equally discernable upon study that some non-Christian and inextinguishable source of beauty persisted throughout the Middle Ages maintaining song in Provence, maintaining the grace of Kalenda Maya" (*Selected Prose*, page 58).

Li Sao: (C) encountering sorrow. (See glossary to LVIII, 322.)

Schwungeld: (G) inflationary decrease in the value of money—a technical term from Silvio Gesell.

789: **Sac Cairoli:** Catholic priest who wrote *Il Giusto Prezzo Medioevale: Studio Economica Politica* (Merate, 1913).

790: **scala altrui:** (I) another's stair. Cacciaguida predicts more bad luck for Dante, including exile: "You will prove how salt is the taste of another's bread, how hard the way up and down another man's stair" (*Paradiso*, XVII, 58–60.)

Syrian onyx: Syrian unguents, preserved in an onyx container and used for embalming a dead body. The line comes from *Homage to Sextus Propertius* (*Collected Shorter Poems*, page 236; *Personae*, page 219).

Ixion: in Greek mythology he was punished by being bound to a wheel of fire. Compare, "but I am bound/Upon a wheele of fire, that mine owne teares/Do scald like molten Lead" (*Lear*, IV, vi).

CXIV

791: **Fréron:** Elie (1718-1776). He fought in France against the Encyclopedists, attacking in particular Voltaire, and supported the Church and the Monarchy.

Mr. Law: see glossary to C (714).

Tom Pick: Timothy Pickering (1745-1829)—an enemy of John Adams. "When we come to be cool in the future World I think we cannot choose but smile at the gambols of Ambition Avarice Pleasure ... here below. How could any rational Being even dream that Man was a rational creature? After all, I hope to meet my Wife and Friends, Ancestors and Posterity, Sages ancient and modern. I believe I could get over all my Objections to meeting Alec Hamilton and Tim Pick, if I could perceive a Symptom of sincere Penitence in either." (Adams to Jefferson, May 29, 1818.)

o di diversa natura: (I) or of diverse nature. Giordano Bruno (1548-1600), the Italian philosopher, believed the heavens contain a multiplicity of populated planets. He was burned as a heretic. (See *I Dialoghi del Bruno*, page 64.)

162

Or that Ari...Alex: Alexander the Great (356-323 B.C.) used to send his teacher, Aristotle, samples of plants and animals from his campaigns.

bianco c(h)ade: (I) falls white (Cavalcanti, *Donna mi priegha*).

792: **Macleod:** Joseph Gordon, Scottish poet. Pound wrote to him in 1936, "*Use* or own. Damn it, I don't want to *buy* or *own* every hotel I stop in. Ownership is often a damn nuisance, and anchor. It was my parents' owning a house that put me wise and I struggled for years to own nothing that I can't pack in a suitcase." (*Selected Letters*, page 279)— "Ownership? Use? there is a difference" (XCVII, 678).

木 **m$^{4-5}$ Governed by wood...Fu Hi, etcetera:** see the early rulers of China, LIII (264). It is appropriate that the last Chinese character to appear in the *Cantos* should be that for 'wood,' a clear pictogram of a tree. (Compare 'root': XCIV, 640 etc.) (J.C.)

792-3: **This is not vanity...Old Joel's "Locke" found in Texas:** These lines concern Pound's forebears: **Sarah:** his grandmother on his father's side. **niente:** (I) nothing; **tribu:** (I) stem (of family tree); **Al:** Albert Pound, great uncle of the poet; **Joel:** Pound's great-great uncle.

793: **Tanagra mia:** Town in Boeotia. "Tanagra! think I not forget/Thy beautiful storied streets" (Landor).

τετραδάκτυλος: *tetradaktylos*, four-toed.

ubi amor, ibi oculus: see glossary to XC (606).

Quelque toile...: (F) on some canvas, "In the Louvre on some canvas." "Ah! Je trouverai bien deux yeux aussi sans clés/Au Louvre, en quelque toile"—Ah! I'll easily find two eyes without hooks/In the Louvre, on some canvas (Laforgue, "Complainte des Consolations").

To live a thousand years in a wink: based on Dante, *Purgatorio*, XI, 106–108.

bisogna esser portato: (I) it's necessary to be inspired.

William: W.B. Yeats; **Tigullio:** the gulf where Rapallo is situated.

from CXV

794: **Wyndham Lewis...mind stop:** (1884-1957) English writer and painter. He went blind *c.* 1951 and refused an operation, which, though it might have restored his sight could have damaged his brain.

garofani: (I) clove carnation.

Linnaeus: see glossary to CXIII (786).

Sulmona: the birthplace of Ovid.

And of men seeking good,/doing evil: "In *Faust* we meet 'the spirit which wills the evil and does the good.' There is, throughout life, its counterpart: namely the spirit which wills the good and does the evil." (Wyndham Lewis, *The Hitler Cult and How It Will End*, page 49.)

In meiner Heimat: (G) in my homeland. Pound told Cyril Connolly it was "roughly Rapallo."

CXVI

795: **Muss...error:** probably the error of allying himself with Hitler.
palimpsest: manuscript on which the original writing has been effaced to make room for a second writing.
cuniculi: see glossary to CI, "Del Pelo Pardi..." (724).
Litterae nihil sanantes: (L) Literature curing nothing. The phrase first occurs XXXIII (161).
The vision of the Madonna...portal: see glossary to CX, "Thy quiet house" (777).
I have...the great ball of crystal: see glossary to LXXVI (459).
Can you enter the great acorn of light?: see glossary to CVI (755).

796: **"plus j'aime le chien":** Mme Roland said, "The more I know men, the more I love dogs."
Ariadne: daughter of Minos. She helped Theseus to kill the Minotaur by giving him a thread by which he was able to find his way into the labyrinth and return. Compare, "to enter the presence at sunrise/up out of hell, from the labyrinth/the path wide as a hair" (XCIII, 632).
Spire: André (1868-1966), French poet. **In proposito:** (I) in invention (?).
chi crescera i nosti—: (I) who will increase our loves (*Paradiso*, V, 105).
terzo: Dante's heaven of Venus (*Paradiso*, VIII-IX).
to "see again": compare *a riveder le stelle*, to see again the stars (Dante, *Inferno*, last line).

797: **al poco giorno...d'ombre:** (I) to the short day and the great ring of shadow (Dante, *Rime*, 78)—the line first occurs V (20).

Notes for CXVII et Seq.

801: **Rupe Tarpeia:** see glossary to LXXIV (443).
Zagreus: Dionysus—see commentary on II.
Semele: see glossary to XCII (621).
like the double arch of a window: echoes the suicide of Marguerite, wife of Raymond of Château Roussillon, "And she went toward the window,/the slim white stone bar/Making a double arch" (IV, 13—see commentary on this canto).

802: **La faillite:** (F) the bankruptcy, failure; **François Bernouard:** a Paris printer, who went bust printing the classics—he was a friend of Rémy de Gourmont and revived "the art of steel colour engraving." (See Pound's "Paris Letter," *Dial*, November, 1920.)
Allègre: Haute-Loire, near Puy, France.
"es laissa cader"..."de joi sas alas": (Pr) and lets himself fall...for joy of his wings (from the Lark Song of Bernart de Ventadour which Pound translates in *The Spirit of Romance*, pages 41-42). Echoes LXXIV (431), LXXX (500), XCI (610) and CVII (760).
farfalla: (I) butterfly. The "gasping" sound made by a butterfly was

heard by Pound and Marcella Spann during a walk in the Tyrolese mountains.

That the kings meet...arcanum: see glossary to XLVII (237)—"the king-wings in migration" (CVI, 754), have here reached their destination.

To be men not destroyers: Pound told Olga Rudge that he intended this to be the last line of the *Cantos*.

Fragments of Cantos

Addendum for C (798-99) and the lines beginning "Now sun rises in Ram sign" (800) are confusingly placed, an error perhaps of Pound's publishers, as they are unrelated to *Drafts & Fragments*, and also have no connection with each other, apart from the fact that they were both written *c.* 1941. It is to be hoped that when a revised edition of the *Cantos* is published, both passages will be relegated to an appendix as at present they break up the sequence of *Drafts & Fragments* itself.

798: **neschek:** (H) usury—first used LII (267).

Τόκος: *Tokos*, poison.

hic mali medium est: (I) Here is the centre of evil.

Fafnir: an evil dragon in Nordic mythology.

Tò καλόν: *To kalon*, the beautiful.

Grove of Paphos: the temple of Aphrodite in Cyprus.

799: **A thousand are dead...basket:** echoes LI (252).

Χαῖρη! Ω Διώνη, Χαῖρη: *Chaire! O Dione, Chaire,* Hail! O Dione, Hail. Dione, mother of Venus; here as elsewhere in the *Cantos* probably used for Venus herself.

Sero: (I) late—first used XXV (118).

"with the silver...and turned...": quoted from XX (93).

800: **Now sun rises in Ram sign:** compare Chaucer, "Hath in the Ram his halve cours yronne" (Prologue to *Canterbury Tales*, line 8).

Jannequin: Clément, sixteenth century composer who wrote *Chant des Oiseaux*, which Pound incorporates in LXXV (450-1).

"e mobile": is capricious (Verdi).

"un' e due...mobile": one and two...that woman is capricious.

videt et urbes: (L) he [Odysseus] saw [many men] and cities—the words come from a Renaissance Latin version of the *Odyssey* (1502). See *Literary Essays*, pages 255 and 265.

Appendix A

Chronology and Select Bibliography
of Pound's Writings

1885: Born, 30 October, in Hailey, Idaho.

1887: Family moves to New York.

1889: Pound's father, Homer, appointed assistant assayer at the U.S. Mint in Philadelphia.

1898: Travels to England, Germany, Italy and North Africa with his Aunt Frank.

1901: University of Pennsylvania, Philadelphia.

1903: Hamilton College, Clinton, New York.

1905-6: Returns to University of Pennsylvania.

1907: June, receives Master's degree. Goes to Spain as Harrison Fellow to study Lope de Vega. Autumn, Professor of Spanish and French, Wabash College, Crawfordsville, Indiana.

1908: February, sails for Gibraltar, "so that leaving America I brought with me $80" (LXXX, 500). Makes his way to Venice—*A Lume Spento* published there in June. September, arrives in London. December, *A Quinzaine for this Yule*.

1909: Lectures on "The Development of Literature in Southern Europe" at Regent Street Polytechnic. April, *Personae*. Meets Dorothy Shakespear, Ford Madox Ford, W. B. Yeats, T. E. Hulme, Frederick Manning. Autumn, *Exultations*.

1910: *The Spirit of Romance*. Lectures continue. Summer, returns to America. November, *Provença*, the first collection of his poems to appear in the U.S.A.

1911: February, returns to London. *Canzoni*. Meets A. R. Orage and starts to write regularly for *The New Age*.

1912: *Ripostes*. First announcement of Imagism in the foreword to the poems of T. E. Hulme appended to that volume. *Sonnets and Ballate of Guido Cavalcanti*. October, becomes foreign correspondent of *Poetry* (Chicago).

1913: "A Few Don'ts by an Imagist" appears in *Poetry*. Meets Gaudier-Brzeska. In Paris, meets Jules Romains, Charles Vildrac and other

French poets. Articles on French poetry (*The Approach to Paris*) begin to appear in *The New Age*. Appointed literary executor of the American oriental scholar Ernest Fenollosa. Begins study of Chinese and Japanese. *Patria Mia* finished but not published in book form until 1950.

1914: Anthology *Des Imagistes*. April, married to Dorothy Shakespear. Contributes to Wyndham Lewis's *BLAST*. Part of the Vorticist movement, which Pound himself had named. September, meets T. S. Eliot.

1915: April, *Cathay*. Second (and final) number of *BLAST*. Starts work on the *Cantos*. December, *Catholic Anthology*, where Eliot's poetry appeared for the first time.

1916: *"Noh" or Accomplishment. Gaudier-Brzeska: a Memoir. Lustra.*

1917: Foreign editor of *The Little Review*. June, July and August, first three cantos appear in *Poetry*. Pound later scrapped these early drafts. *Dialogues de Fontenelle. Homage to Sextus Propertius* begun.

1918: *Pavannes and Divagations*. Meets C. H. Douglas, the founder of Social Credit. Studies of economics, money and history begin.

1919: *Homage to Sextus Propertius. Quia Pauper Amavi. Canto IV.*

1920: *Hugh Selwyn Mauberley. Instigations. Umbra.* Leaves England and is settled in Paris by Christmas.

1921: *Poems 1918-21* published in America.

1922: Helps Eliot to get *The Waste Land* into its final form. Leaves Paris to spend some months in Rapallo.

1923: Gathers material at the library of Cesena for the Malatesta cantos (VIII-XI). July, two of these appear in the *Criterion. Indiscretions.* Composes the music of his opera *Villon.*

1924: *Antheil and the Treatise on Harmony*. Leaves Paris and settles in Rapallo. *XVI Cantos.*

1926: *Personae* (Collected Shorter Poems) appears in America. June, first performance of *Villon.*

1927: Translation of Confucius's *Ta Hsio* (*The Great Digest*). Pound later rewrote this at Pisa. Launches magazine *Exile.*

1928: *How to Read*. Researches on Guido Cavalcanti approach completion. *A Draft of Cantos 17-27. Selected Poems*, edited, with an Introduction, by T. S. Eliot.

1930: *A Draft of XXX Cantos. Imaginary Letters.*

1931: *How to Read. Guido Cavalcanti Rime.*

1933: *A. B. C. of Economics. Active Anthology. Jefferson and/or Mussolini* (written, but not published until 1935).

1934: *A. B. C. of Reading. Make it New. Eleven New Cantos* (XXXI-XLI).

1935: *Social Credit: An Impact.* Alfred Venison's Poems.

1936: *The Chinese Written Character as a Medium for Poetry* by Ernest Fenollosa, edited by Pound.

1937: *Polite Essays. The Fifth Decad of Cantos* (XLII-LI). "The Jefferson-Adams Letters as a Shrine and a Monument" (*Selected Prose*, pages 117–128; *147–158*).

1938: *Guide to Kulchur.* "Mang Tsze" (*Selected Prose*, pages 95–111; *81–97*).

1939: "What is Money For?" (*Selected Prose*, pages 260–72; *290–302*). September, *Cantos LII-LXXI* completed.

1940:	*Cantos LII-LXXI* published.
1941:	Begins to broadcast from Rome Radio. Translates Enrico Pea's novel *Moscardino*.
1942:	After America's entry into the war, stops broadcasting and tries to return to America, but is prevented. 29 January, resumes broadcasting, with a proviso, which was repeated by an announcer before each broadcast: "Rome Radio, acting in accordance with the Fascist policy of intellectual freedom and free expression of opinion by those who are qualified to hold it, has offered Dr. Ezra Pound the use of the microphone twice a week. It is understood that he will not be asked to say anything whatsoever that goes against his conscience, or anything incompatible with his duties as a citizen of the United States of America." December, "Carta da Visita" (*Selected Prose*, pages 276–305; *306–335*).
1943:	July, broadcasts cease. 26 July, indicted for treason by Federal Grand Jury in U. S. District Court, District of Columbia.
1944:	Writes Cantos LXXII and LXXIII in Italian. "L'America, Roosevelt e la Cause della Guerra Presente." "Oro e Lavoro" (*Selected Prose*, pages 306–21; *336–51*). "Introduzione alla Natura Economica degli S. U. A." (*Selected Prose*, pages 137–55; *167–85*). *Orientamenti. Jefferson e Mussolini* (a rewriting, in Italian, of the book originally written in 1933).
1945:	*Ciung Iung: L'Asse che non Vacilla:* a translation into Italian of Confucius's *Ta Hsio* (*Great Digest*) and *Chung Yung* (*Unwobbling Pivot*). 24 May, held as a military prisoner at the U. S. Army Disciplinary Training Centre, Pisa, where he writes *The Pisan Cantos* and translates Confucius's *Ta Hsio* and *Chung Yung*. 17 November, flown to America to face treason charges.
1946:	13 February, declared mentally unfit to stand trial, and transferred to St. Elizabeth's Hospital, Washington, D. C.
1947:	*Confucius: The Unwobbling Pivot and The Great Digest* published in U. S. A.
1948:	*"If this be Treason . . .",* a selection by Olga Rudge of his radio speeches, published in England and America (second printing by Tipo-Litografia Armena, Venice, 1983). *The Pisan Cantos* appear in England and U. S. A.
1950:	Spring, *The Analects of Confucius* published in *The Hudson Review*.
1951:	*Selected Letters*, edited by D. D. Paige.
1954:	*Literary Essays*, edited by T. S. Eliot. *The Classic Anthology Defined by Confucius* (*The Confucian Odes*).
1955:	*Section: Rock-Drill* (Cantos LXXXV-XCV).
1956:	Sophokles: *Women of Trachis.*
1958:	18 April, the treason indictment dismissed. 7 May, officially discharged from St. Elizabeth's Hospital. 30 June, sails for Italy.
1959:	*Thrones* (Cantos XCVI-CIX). Much of this book had been completed before his release.
1960:	*Impact: Essays on Ignorance and the Decline of American Civilization.*
1964:	*Confucius to Cummings: An Anthology of Poetry*, edited with Marcella Spann.

1968:   *Pound/Joyce: the Letters of Ezra Pound to James Joyce*, with Pound's essays on Joyce, edited by Forrest Read.

1970:   *Drafts and Fragments* (Cantos CX-CXVII et seq.). These had mostly been written in 1958-59.

1972:   1 November, dies in Venice.

1973:   *Selected Prose 1909-65*, edited by William Cookson.

1977:   *Collected Early Poems. Ezra Pound and Music: The Complete Music Criticism*, edited by Murray Schafer.

1979:   *"Ezra Pound Speaking": Radio Speeches of World War II.*

1980:   *Ezra Pound and the Visual Arts*, edited by Harriet Zinnes.

1982:   *Pound/Ford: The Story of a Literary Friendship: The Correspondence between Ezra Pound and Ford Madox Ford and their writings about each other*, edited by B. Lindberg-Seyersted (Faber).

1985:   *Ezra Pound and Dorothy Shakespear: Their Letters* 1909-1914, edited by Omar Pound and A. Walton Litz (Faber).

Note: All Pound's major works are published in England by Faber and Faber except *The Spirit of Romance, Guide to Kulchur, Confucius: The Great Digest and The Unwobbling Pivot, The Confucian Analects* and *Patria Mia*, which are published by Peter Owen. Pound's sole publisher in America is New Directions, except for *Impact* (Regnery), *Jefferson and/or Mussolini* (Liveright) and *"Ezra Pound Speaking"* (Greenwood).

Appendix B

*Suggestions for Further Reading and Select Bibliography
of Sources of the Cantos*

(A) **Literary**

The Epic of Gilgamesh, translated by N. K. Sandars (Penguin Classics).

Homer: the *Odyssey* and the *Iliad.* I recommend the Loeb bi-lingual edition. There is no single great translation of either poem, so it is best to try several. The earliest, Chapman's, remains the strongest as poetry, but it is too clotted and ornate. The prose version of the *Odyssey* by W. H. D. Rouse makes the story come alive at times. For a literal, modern verse translation, Richmond Lattimore's *Iliad* and *Odyssey* are occasionally successful, particularly the latter, but the language is too far from natural speech, and the metre lacks rhythmic energy. Other versions of the *Odyssey* worth sampling are those by Pope, Cooper, T. E. Lawrence and Robert Fitzgerald. A new prose translation by Walter Shewring (O.U.P.) is also recommended.

Hesiod, the Homeric Hymns and Homerica: Loeb Classical Library provides a good bi-lingual edition.

Lyra Graeca, Loeb Classical Library (3 volumes).

Sappho: A New Translation by Mary Barnard (University of California Press, 1958).

The Greek Bucolic Poets: Theocritus, Bion and Moschus. Loeb Classical Library.

Aeschylus: *Agamemnon,* translated by Louis MacNeice (Faber).
————: *Oresteia,* translated by Hugh Lloyd-Jones.

Sophokles: *Women of Trachis,* translated by Pound (Faber).

The Periplus of Hanno. For a translation, and the Greek text, see *Paideuma,* Vol. 1, No. 2.

Catullus: *The Poems,* translated by Peter Whigham (Penguin Classics).
————: *Versions of Catullus,* by Humphrey Clucas (Agenda Editions).

Horace: *Odes and Epodes*, Loeb Classical Library.

Ovid: *Metamorphoses*, translated by Arthur Golding (Collier-Macmillan, 1965).

Propertius: Loeb Classical Library.

Virgil: *Aeneid*, translated by Gavin Douglas (Scottish Text Society). This sixteenth century Scottish version is magnificent. For those who find the Scots too difficult, I recommend Dryden's version (O.U.P.).

The Earliest English Poems and *Beowulf*, both available in an excellent translation by Michael Alexander (Penguin Classics).

Li Po and Tu Fu, translated by Arthur Cooper (Penguin Classics).

Arnaut Daniel and other Provençal poets: see Pound's *Translations* and *The Spirit of Romance*.

The Poem of the Cid, with a translation by Rita Hamilton and Janet Perry (Manchester University Press, 1975).

Guido Cavalcanti: see Pound's *Translations* and D.G. Rossetti, *Poems and Translations* (O.U.P.).

The Early Italian Poets, translated by Rossetti. (Anvil Press).

Dante: *The Divine Comedy*. I recommend the Temple Classics bi-lingual edition. The finest verse translation is by Laurence Binyon (Viking/Penguin; also available as an Agenda Edition). *La Vita Nuova* in Rossetti's translation is also included in this volume.

————: *Rime;* available in England in *Dante's Lyric Poetry*, text, translation and commentary by K. Foster and P. Boyde (O.U.P., 1967).

————: *De Vulgari Eloquentia* (The Rebel Press, 1973).

Chaucer: *The Complete Works*, edited by F.N. Robinson (O.U.P.).

Langland: *Piers Ploughman*, Everyman's Library (Dent/Dutton).

Villon: *Selected Poems* (Penguin). A bi-lingual edition, with an excellent translation in the original metres by Peter Dale.

Shakespeare, particularly the history plays which Pound regarded as "the true English EPOS"; *Pericles, Hamlet, King Lear, The Tempest...*

Ben Jonson: *Poems* (O.U.P.).

Browning: *Sordello* (O.U.P.).

French poets, Corbière, Rémy de Gourmont,....

The Poems of Laforgue, translated by Peter Dale, a bi-lingual edition (Anvil Press).

(B) **Philosophy, Theology, etc.**

Heracleitos: the fragments translated in Burnett, *Early Greek Philosophy.*

Confucius: in Pound's translations.

Li Chi: The Book of Rites, translated by James Legge (Reprinted by University Books, N.Y., 1967).

Mencius, translated by T. C. Lau (Penguin Classics).

Plato: *Phaedrus*, etc. (Loeb Classical Library).

Aristotle: *Politics; Nichomachean Ethics* (both in Loeb Classical Library).

Philostratus: *Life of Apollonius of Tyana*, translated by F. C. Conybeare (Loeb Classical Library).

Plotinus: *The Enneads*, translated by Stephen MacKenna (Faber).

Iamblichus: *Life of Pythagoras*, translated by Thomas Taylor (John Watkins).

————: *On the Mysteries of the Egyptians, Chaldeans and Assyrians*, translated by Thomas Taylor (Watkins).

St. Ambrose: *De Moribus Brachmanorum* (Migne's *Patrologia Latina*, Volume XVII, Paris, 1845).

St. Anselm: *Monologion* (in *S. Anselmi Cantuariensis Archiepiscopi Opera Omnia*, Nelson & Sons, Edinburgh, 6 volumes, 1946-61).

————: *Proslogion*, a bi-lingual edition, with translation by M. J. Charlesworth (O.U.P., 1965).

Erigena, Johannes Scotus: *De Divisione Naturae* (Migne's *Patrologia Latina*).

Richard of St. Victor: *Selected Writings on Contemplation*, translated by Clare Kirchberger (Faber, 1957).

Giordano Bruno, *I Dialoghi* (Augusto Guzzo, Torino, 1932).

Lord Herbert of Cherbury: *De Veritate* (Bristol University Press, 1937).

Gists from Agassiz. Available from Omni Publications, P.O. Box 216, Hawthorne, California 90250, U.S.A.

Frazer, James: *The Golden Bough* (Macmillan).

Upward, Allen: *The Divine Mystery* (Garden City Press, 1913; reprinted 1976 by Ross-Erikson, 223 Via Sevilla, Santa Barbara, California 93109, U.S.A.).

————: *The New Word* (London, 1907).

Leo Frobenius: 1873-1973 An Anthology of his Writings, translated into English and edited by Eike Haberland (Franz Steiner Verlag GmbH, Wiesbaden, West Germany, 1973).

(C) **General, Historical and Economic**

The Works of John Adams, with a Life of the Author, notes, and illustrations, by his grandson, Charles Francis Adams (Little, Brown and Co., Boston, 1850-56, ten volumes).

The Adams-Jefferson Letters, edited by Lester J. Cappon (Chapel Hill, 1959).

Benton, Thomas Hart: *Thirty Years View, or a History of the Working of the American Government for Thirty Years 1820-1850* (New York, 1854-56).

The Diary of John Quincy Adams.

Brooks Adams: *The Law of Civilization and Decay* (Macmillan, 1896).

————: *The New Empire* (Macmillan, 1902).

Burkhardt, Jacob: *The Civilization of the Renaissance in Italy* translated by S. G. C. Middlemore (Oxford and London, 1945).

Coke, Sir Edward: *Institutes of the Laws of England* (1628-44). A new edition of the *Second Institute* (on *Magna Carta*) has recently been published by Omni (for address see Agassiz entry above). Catherine Drinker Bowen, *The Lion and the Throne* (Hamish Hamilton, 1957), provides background to the Coke cantos.

Del Mar, Alexander: *History of Monetary Systems* (Effingham Wilson, 1895; reprinted 1973 by The National Poetry Foundation, University of Maine at Orono). A part of this, *Roman and Moslem Moneys*, has been published separately by Omni.
————: *Barbara Villiers, A History of Monetary Crimes* (1899), also reprinted by Omni.

de Mailla, J.-A. M. Moyriac, *Histoire Générale de la Chine... traduites du Tong-Kien-Kang-Mou* (Paris, 13 volumes, 1777-85).

Douglas, C. H.: *Economic Democracy* (Cecil Palmer, 1920; reprinted by Omni).
————: *Credit, Power and Democracy* (Chapman & Hall).
————: *The Monopoly of Credit* (Chapman & Hall, 1931).

Gesell, Silvio: *The Natural Economic Order* (English translation published by Hugo Fack, Texas, 1934).

Hollis, Christopher: *The Two Nations* (Routledge, 1937).

The Writings of Thomas Jefferson, Memorial Edition, 20 volumes (Washington, 1903-4).

Kitson, Arthur: *The Bankers' Conspiracy! which started the World Crisis* (London, 1933; reprinted by Omni, 1967).

The Kuan Tzu: Economic Dialogues in Ancient China. Published and edited by Lewis Maverick (Far Eastern Publications, 26 Hall of Graduate Studies, Yale University, New Haven, Connecticut, U.S.A., 1954).

Le Livre du Préfet (The Eparch's Book), edited by Jules Nicole (Geneva, 1893). Greek text reprinted in *Paideuma*, Vol. 2 No. 2.

Orage, A.R.: *Political and Economic Writings* (Stanley Nott, 1936).

Rémusat, Madame de: *Mémoires,* translated by Hoey-Lillie, 3 volumes (New York, Appleton, 1880).

Rock, Joseph F.: *The Ancient Na-khi Kingdom of Southwest China*, 2 volumes (Cambridge, Massachusetts, Harvard-Yenching Institute Monograph Series, Vol. VIII).

The Sacred Edict of K'ang Hsi, translations by F. W. Baller (The China Inland Mission, Shanghai, 1924; reprinted by The National Poetry Foundation, University of Maine at Orono, Maine, 1979).

Shu Ching: Book of History, translated by James Legge (Allen and Unwin, revised edition, 1972).

Stokes, Adrian: *The Critical Writings*, 3 volumes (Thames and Hudson, 1978).

The Autobiography of Martin Van Buren. Written 1854, but remaining in mss. until its publication as Vol. II of the "Annual Report of the American Historical Association for the year 1918" (Government Printing Office, Washington, 1920).

Waddell, L. A.: *Egyptian Civilization, its Sumerian Origin* (London, 1930).

Yriarte, Charles: *Un Condottiere au XVe Siècle* (Paris, 1882)—the main source of the Malatesta cantos, VIII-XI.

Zobi, Antonio: *Storia Civile della Toscana*, 3 vols. (Firenze, Presso Luigi Molini, 1851). The main source of Canto L.

Appendix C

Select Bibliography of Books and Journals About Pound

(A) **Biographical**

Cornell, Julien: *The Trial of Ezra Pound* (Faber, 1967).

de Rachewiltz, Mary: *Discretions* (Faber, 1971).

Hutchins, Patricia: *Ezra Pound's Kensington* (Faber, 1965).

Meacham, Harry M.: *Ezra Pound at St. Elizabeth's* (Twayne, New York, 1967).

Norman, Charles: *Ezra Pound* (MacDonald, 1969).

Stock, Noel: *The Life of Ezra Pound* (Routledge, 1970; Penguin Books, 1974; North Point Press, 1982).

(B) **Critical**

Agenda, Vol. IV, No. 2 (1965), Vol. VIII, Nos. 3-4 (1970) and Vol. 17, Nos. 3-4, Vol. 18, No. 1 (1980), ed. William Cookson, London, 1959–

Alexander, Michael: *The Poetic Achievement of Ezra Pound* (Faber, 1979).

Baumann, Walter: *The Rose in the Steel Dust: An Examination of the Cantos* (University of Miami Press, 1970).

Brooke-Rose, Christine: *A ZBC of Ezra Pound* (Faber, 1971).

Brooker, Peter: *A Student's Guide to the Selected Poems of Ezra Pound* (Faber, 1979).

Bush, Ronald: *The Genesis of Ezra Pound's Cantos* (Princeton, 1976).

Davie, Donald: *Ezra Pound: Poet as Sculptor* (Routledge, 1964).
————: *Pound* (Fontana Modern Masters, 1975).

Davis, Earle: *Vision Fugitive: Ezra Pound and Economics* (Kansas University Press, 1968).

Dekker, George: *Sailing After Knowledge: The Cantos* (Routledge, 1963).

Dembo, L. S.: *The Confucian Odes* (Faber, 1963).

175

D'Epiro, Peter: *A Touch of Rhetoric: Ezra Pound's Malatesta Cantos* (UMI Research Press, Ann Arbor, Michigan/Bowker Publishing Company, Epping, Essex, England, 1984).

Edwards, J. H. and Vasse, W. W.: *The Annotated Index to the Cantos I-LXXXIV* (University of California Press, Berkeley, 1957).

Eliot, T. S.: *Ezra Pound: His Metric and Poetry* (Chicago, 1917)—reprinted in *To Criticise the Critic* (Faber, 1965).
————: Introduction to the *Selected Poems* (Faber, 1928).

Emery, Clark: *Ideas into Action: A Study of Pound's Cantos* (University of Miami Press, 1958).

Espey, J. J.: *Ezra Pound's Mauberley: A Study in Composition* (Faber, 1955).

Flory, Wendy Stallard: *Ezra Pound and the Cantos: A Record of Struggle* (Yale, 1980).

Fraser, G. S.: *Ezra Pound* (Oliver and Boyd, 1960).

Gallup, Donald: *A Bibliography of Ezra Pound* (Rupert Hart-Davis, 1963; second edition, 1969).

Eastman, Barbara: *Ezra Pound's Cantos: the Story of the Text* (National Poetry Foundation, University of Maine at Orono, 1979).

Hesse, Eva (ed.): *New Approaches to Ezra Pound* (Faber, 1969).

Henault, Marie (ed.): *Studies in the Cantos* (Charles E. Merrill Studies, Columbus, Ohio, 1971).

Homberger, Eric (ed.): *Ezra Pound: The Critical Heritage* (Routledge, 1972).

Kenner, Hugh: *The Poetry of Ezra Pound* (Faber, 1951).
————: *The Pound Era* (Faber, 1971).

Leary, Lewis (ed.): *Motive and Method in the Cantos* (New York, 1964).

Leavis, F. R.: *New Bearings in English Poetry* (Chatto and Windus, 1932; second edition, 1950).

Makin, Peter: *Provence and Pound* (University of California Press, 1978).
————: *Pound's Cantos* (Unwin Critical Library).

Paideuma: A Journal Devoted to Ezra Pound Scholarship, ed. Carroll F. Terrell, University of Maine at Orono, 1972–

Pearlman, Daniel: *The Barb of Time: On the Unity of Pound's Cantos* (O.U.P., 1969).

Quinn, Sister Bernetta, O.S.F.: *Ezra Pound: An Introduction to the Poetry* (Columbia University Press, 1972).

Rosenthal, M. L.: *A Primer of Ezra Pound* (Macmillan, New York, 1960).
————: *Sailing into the Unknown: Yeats, Pound and Eliot* (O.U.P., 1978).
———— and Sally M. Gall: *The Modern Poetic Sequence: The Genius of Modern Poetry* (O.U.P., 1983).

Russell, Peter (ed.): *Ezra Pound: A Collection of Essays* (Peter Nevill, 1950). Revised, enlarged edition, entitled *An Examination of Ezra Pound* (Gordian

Press, N.Y., 1973) available from Peter Russell, "Monna Mea," via Palagio, Piandisco 52026 Pr. Arezzo, Italy.

Ruthven, K. K.: *A Guide to Ezra Pound's Personae* (Berkeley, California, 1969).

Sanders, Frederick K.: *John Adams Speaking: Ezra Pound's Sources for the Adams Cantos* (University of Maine at Orono Press, 1978).

Sieburth, Richard: *Instigations: Ezra Pound and Rémy de Gourmont* (Harvard, 1979).

Stock, Noel: *Reading the Cantos* (Routledge, 1965).

Sullivan, J. P.: *Ezra Pound and Sextus Propertius: A Study in Creative Translation* (Faber, 1965).

———— (ed.): *Ezra Pound: A Critical Anthology* (Penguin Books, 1970).

Surette, Leon: *A Light from Eleusis: A Study of Ezra Pound's Cantos* (Oxford University Press, 1970).

Terrell, Carroll F.: *The Companion to the Cantos*, Vol. I (University of California Press, 1980).

Thomas, Ron: *The Latin Mask of Ezra Pound* (UMI Research Press, Ann Arbor, Michigan/Bowker Publishing House, Epping, Essex, England, 1984).

Wilhelm, James J.: *Dante and Pound: the Epic of Judgement* (University of Maine at Orono Press, 1974).

————: *The Later Cantos of Ezra Pound* (Walker, New York, 1977).

Witemeyer, Hugh: *The Poetry of Ezra Pound: Forms and Renewals 1908-1920* (University of California Press, Berkeley, 1969).

Yeats, W. B.: *A Packet for Ezra Pound* (Dublin, 1928; reprinted in *A Vision*, Macmillan, 1962).

Yip, Wai-lim: *Ezra Pound's Cathay* (Princeton University Press, 1960).